SOURCES, STORIES, AND SONGS

ANTHOLOGY

World

ADVENTURES IN TIME AND PLACE

- Biographies and Autobiographies
- Diaries and Journals
- Fiction and Nonfiction Selections
- Folk Tales and Fables
- Letters
- Oral Histories
- Plays
- Poems
- Songs
- Speeches
- Visual Documents

 McGraw-Hill
School Division
New York   Farmington

PROGRAM AUTHORS

Dr. James A. Banks
Professor of Education and Director of the Center for Multicultural Education
University of Washington
Seattle, Washington

Dr. Barry K. Beyer
Professor Emeritus, Graduate School of Education
George Mason University
Fairfax, Virginia

Dr. Gloria Contreras
Professor of Education
University of North Texas
Denton, Texas

Jean Craven
District Coordinator of Curriculum Development
Albuquerque Public Schools
Albuquerque, New Mexico

Dr. Gloria Ladson-Billings
Professor of Education
University of Wisconsin
Madison, Wisconsin

Dr. Mary A. McFarland
Instructional Coordinator of Social Studies, K–12, and Director of Staff Development
Parkway School District
Chesterfield, Missouri

Dr. Walter C. Parker
Professor and Program Chair for Social Studies Education
University of Washington
Seattle, Washington

NATIONAL
GEOGRAPHIC
SOCIETY

Washington, D.C.

Acknowledgments

Excerpt from SEEING EARTH FROM SPACE by Patricia Lauber. ©1990 Patricia Lauber. Orchard Books, a division of Franklin Watts, Inc., NY.

"Scenes from the Stone Age" from an article in TIME MAGAZINE 2/13/95, Vol. 145 by Robert Hughes. ©1995 Time Inc. Time Magazine.

"First Fruits of the Field," from HIDDEN STORIES IN PLANTS. Kabyle legend retold by Anne Pellowski. ©1993 Anne Pellowski. Macmillan Publishing Company, Inc., NY.

"A Father's Complaint" from HISTORY BEGINS AT SUMER by Samuel Noah Kramer. ©1959 Samuel Noah Kramer. Doubleday & Co., Inc., NY.

"Where the Mind is Without Fear" from CALLIOPE, WORLD HISTORY FOR YOUNG PEOPLE, March/April 1993 by Rabindranath Tagore. ©1993 Cobblestone Publishing, Inc., NH.

"O Magnificent and Many" from SUNFLOWER SPLENDOR: THREE THOUSAND YEARS OF CHINESE POETRY. Translated by C.H. Wang. ©1975 Wu-chi Liu and Irving Lo. Indiana University Press by arrangement with Doubleday, Inc.

"A Letter from a Han Emperor" from GEMS OF CHINESE LITERATURE. Wen Ti, translated by Herbert A. Giles. ©1884 Bernard Quaritch, Kelly & Walsh, London, Shanghai.

Excerpt from "The Birds" from ARISTOPHANES: FOUR COMEDIES. Translated by Dudley Fitts. ©1959, 1962 Dudley Fitts. Harcourt, Brace & World, Inc., NY.

"Funeral Speech for Athenian Heroes" from THUCYDIDES. Translated by B. Jowett. ©1881 Clarendon Press, Oxford.

"The Eruption of Mount Vesuvius" from PLINY, LETTERS. Printed in VOICES OF THE PAST. An original translation by James H. Hanscom. ©1967 The Macmillan Company, NY.

"Theodora's Bravery" from HISTORY OF THE WARS, VOL. 1. Procopius, translated by H.B. Dewing. ©1914 Harvard University Press, Cambridge, MA.

"A Description of Constantinople" from EARLY TRAVELS IN PALESTINE. Edited by Thomas Wright. ©1848 Henry G. Bohn, London.

"An Islamic Hospital" from A MEDICAL HISTORY OF PERSIA AND THE EASTERN CALIPHATE by Cyril Elgood. © 1951, reprint 1979 by Cambridge University Press, London, UK.

"An Honest Counsellor" from THE SUBTLE RUSE: THE BOOK OF ARABIC WISDOM AND GUILE. Translated by Rene R. Khawam. ©1980 English translation by East-West Publications (U.K.) Ltd., London.

Excerpt from INCIDENTS OF TRAVEL IN CENTRAL AMERICA, CHIAPAS AND YUCATAN by John L. Stephens. ©1969 Dover Publications, Inc., NY.

"The Emperor of Mali" from MASALIK AL ABSAR FI MAMALIK AL AMSAR by Ibn Fadh Allah al Omari; book by Basil Davidson. French version of Gaudefroy-Demombynes translated ©1927, Paris.

"Epic of Liyongo" from ANTHOLOGY OF SWAHILI POETRY by Ali A. Jahadhmy. ©1975 Ali Ahmed Jahadhmy. Heinemann Educational Books Ltd., London.

"The Hoca and the Candle" from A TREASURY OF TURKISH FOLKTALES FOR CHILDREN. Retold by Barbara K. Walker. ©1988 by Barbara K. Walker. Linnet Books, an imprint of The Shoe String Press, Inc., CT.

"2–Rabbit, 7–Wind" from 2–RABBIT, 7–WIND: POEMS FROM ANCIENT MEXICO RETOLD FROM NAHUATL TEXTS by Toni de Gerez. Copyright © 1971 Viking Press, NY.

"Backward on the Donkey" from THE ART OF THE TURKISH TALE, Vol. 1. Retold by Barbara K. Walker. Copyright ©1990. Texas Tech University Press, TX.

Excerpts from THE TRAVELS OF MARCO POLO. Edited by Manuel Komroff. ©1930 Horace Liveright, Inc. NY.

Excerpt from "Sugar Mapling" printed in NATIVE PEOPLE'S MAGAZINE, Fall 1992, Vol. 6, No. 1 issue. Copyright ©1992 by Media Concepts Group, Inc., Phoenix.

(continued on page 212)

McGraw-Hill School Division

A Division of The McGraw-Hill Companies

McGraw-Hill School Division
Two Penn Plaza
New York, New York 10121

Printed in the United States of America

ISBN 0-02-147632-2 / 6/7

3 4 5 6 7 8 9 079 02 01 00

TABLE OF *Contents*

📼 = audio cassette

iii

UNIT

6 A CENTURY OF CONFLICT   **141**

USING PRIMARY SOURCES AND LITERATURE WITH SOCIAL STUDIES

The readings in the *Adventures in Time and Place Anthology* have been carefully selected to enhance social studies concepts and to provide enjoyable and worthwhile reading experiences for students. All readers bring to the reading experience their own backgrounds and prior knowledge. Exposing students to a variety of viewpoints while encouraging them to question and ponder what they read will help them to become critical readers and thoughtful citizens.

The readings include **primary sources, secondary sources,** and **literature.** These fall into several categories, including:

- songs
- official documents
- oral histories
- posters
- diaries and journals
- photographs and graphics
- personal recollections
- political cartoons
- poems
- folktales
- letters
- autobiographies and biographies
- newspaper articles
- fiction and nonfiction
- speeches

The readings offer you a unique teaching tool. The following suggestions will help your students use the readings to build and extend their knowledge of social studies as well as to sharpen their analytical skills.

PRIMARY AND SECONDARY SOURCES

A **primary source** is something that comes from the time that is being studied. Primary sources include such things as official documents of the time, diaries and journals, letters, newspaper articles and advertisements, photographs, and oral histories. A **secondary source** is an account of the past written by someone who was not an eyewitness to those events. Remind students of the difference between primary and secondary sources. Point out that primary sources give historians valuable clues from the past because they provide firsthand information about a certain time or event. Primary sources let the reader see how people lived, felt, and thought.

However, primary sources express the view of only one person. Thus, it is important for students to understand the point of view of the writer and to find out all that they can about his or her background to decide whether the writer is credible, or believable. Secondary sources often compare and analyze different points of view and give a broader view of the event. Once again, however, it is important for students to understand the writer's point of view and analyze his or her credentials. Suggest to students that, when they read primary and secondary sources, they ask themselves these questions:

- Who created the source?
- Can the writer be believed?
- Does the writer have expert knowledge of the subject?
- Does the writer have a reason to describe the events in a certain way?
- Does the writer have a reputation for being accurate?

When you work with the primary sources in this Anthology, you may wish to encourage students to think about the following as they read some of the various sources:

Diaries and Journals Was the diary or journal originally written to be shared with the public? Was it commissioned by a government official, such as the Columbus log was?

Speeches Was the intent of the speech to persuade the audience to adopt a particular point of view or was the speech merely informative? Was the speech delivered during a criticial time in a nation's history? Did historical circumstances influence the speechmaker?

Newspaper Articles Did the newspaper in which the article appeared have a particular political stance or bias that might have influenced the writer?

Official Documents Are there any words or phrases in the document that you do not understand? If so, what other source can you consult for clarification?

LITERATURE

In social studies, literature is used to motivate and instruct. It also plays a large role in assisting students to understand their cultural heritage and the cultural heritage of others. For example, the folktales included in the *Adventures in Time and Place Anthology*, such as "Kokoom" from the Cree culture, were chosen to offer students glimpses of the wisdom various cultures deem important to impart. The songs, stories, and poetry of different cultures offer students opportunities to compare and contrast and hence understand aspects of cultural identity. Epics, such as *The Illiad*, give students opportunities to view ancient history from a classic perspective that has endured through the ages and offers teaching opportunities to integrate history with writing, drama, and art projects.

This year you will be reading about many different peoples, places, and times in your Social Studies textbook. This Anthology, or collection of documents created by different people, will make the information in your textbook come to life in a special way. It includes diaries, songs, stories, plays, posters, poems, speeches, and even ancient pictographs and hieroglyphics. As you read and study these primary sources, you will be able to see and hear what it was like to live in other times and places. The documents in this Anthology will help you to better understand the world around you and the people—famous and nonfamous—who have shaped our world.

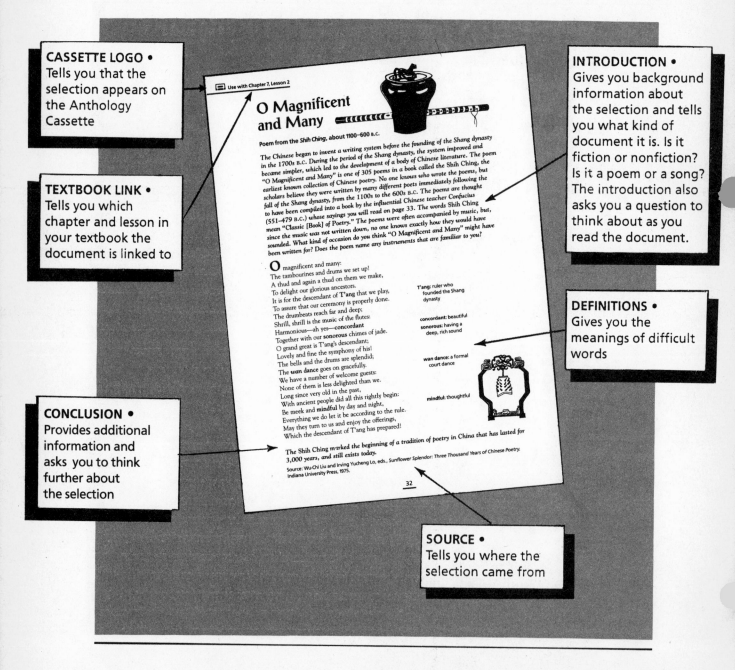

CASSETTE LOGO •
Tells you that the selection appears on the Anthology Cassette

TEXTBOOK LINK •
Tells you which chapter and lesson in your textbook the document is linked to

CONCLUSION •
Provides additional information and asks you to think further about the selection

INTRODUCTION •
Gives you background information about the selection and tells you what kind of document it is. Is it fiction or nonfiction? Is it a poem or a song? The introduction also asks you a question to think about as you read the document.

DEFINITIONS •
Gives you the meanings of difficult words

SOURCE •
Tells you where the selection came from

Within the image, the sample anthology page reads:

Use with Chapter 7, Lesson 2

O Magnificent and Many

Poem from the *Shih Ching*, about 1100–600 B.C.

The Chinese began to invent a writing system before the founding of the Shang dynasty in the 1700s B.C. During the period of the Shang dynasty, the system improved and became simpler, which led to the development of a body of Chinese literature. The poem "O Magnificent and Many" is one of 305 poems in a book called the Shih Ching, the earliest known collection of Chinese poetry. No one knows who wrote the poems, but scholars believe they were written by many different poets immediately following the fall of the Shang dynasty, from the 1100s to the 600s B.C. The poems are thought to have been compiled into a book by the influential Chinese teacher Confucius (551–479 B.C.) whose sayings you will read on page 33. The words Shih Ching mean "Classic [Book] of Poetry." The poems were often accompanied by music, but, since the music was not written down, no one knows exactly how they would have sounded. What kind of occasion do you think "O Magnificent and Many" might have been written for? Does the poem name any instruments that are familiar to you?

O magnificent and many:
The tambourines and drums we set up!
A thud and again a thud on them we make,
To delight our glorious ancestors.
It is for the descendant of **T'ang** that we play,
To assure that our ceremony is properly done.
The drumbeats reach far and deep;
Shrill, shrill is the music of the flutes:
Harmonious—ah yes—**concordant**
Together with our **sonorous** chimes of jade.
O grand great is T'ang's descendant;
Lovely and fine the symphony of his!
The bells and the drums are splendid;
The **wan dance** goes on gracefully.
We have a number of welcome guests:
None of them is less delighted than we.
Long since very old in the past,
With ancient people did all this rightly begin:
Be meek and **mindful** by day and night,
Everything we do let it be according to the rule.
May they turn to us and enjoy the offerings,
Which the descendant of T'ang has prepared!

T'ang: ruler who founded the Shang dynasty

concordant: beautiful
sonorous: having a deep, rich sound

wan dance: a formal court dance

mindful: thoughtful

The Shih Ching marked the beginning of a tradition of poetry in China that has lasted for 3,000 years, and still exists today.

Source: Wu-Chi Liu and Irving Yucheng Lo, eds., *Sunflower Splendor: Three Thousand Years of Chinese Poetry.* Indiana University Press, 1975.

32

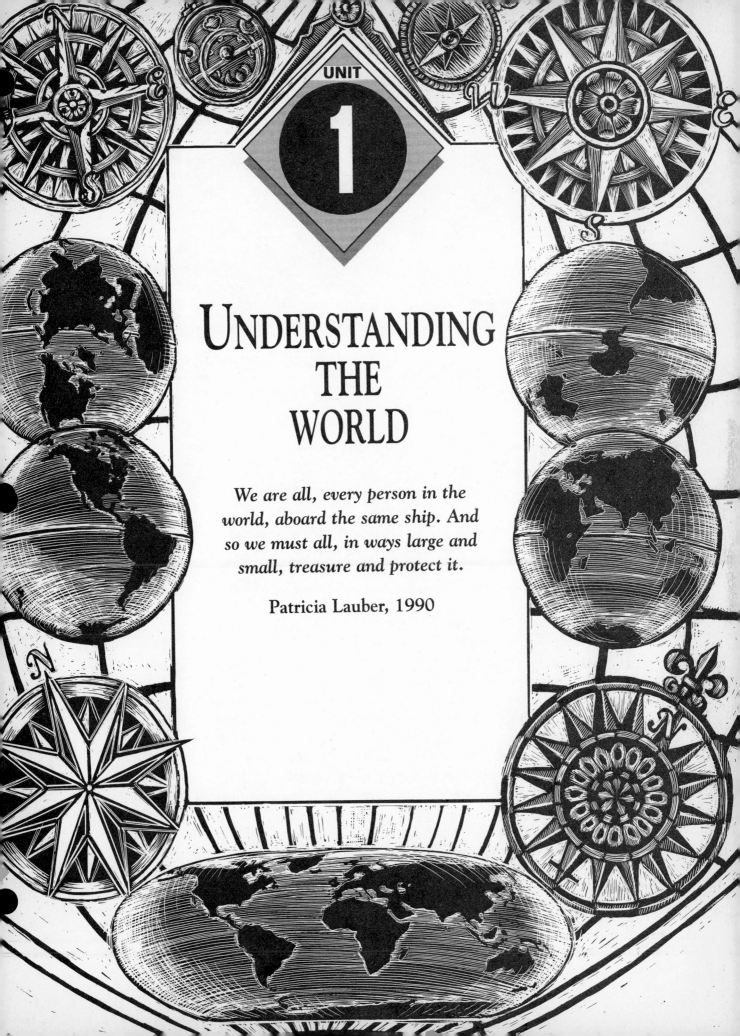

UNIT

1

UNDERSTANDING THE WORLD

We are all, every person in the world, aboard the same ship. And so we must all, in ways large and small, treasure and protect it.

Patricia Lauber, 1990

Seeing Earth from Space

by Patricia Lauber, 1990

The study of geography tells us that Earth is divided into regions. There are physical regions, climate regions, cultural regions, and political regions. When astronauts see Earth from space, however, the only borders visible are between the land, sea, and sky. As you read this excerpt from Seeing Earth from Space *by Patricia Lauber, think about the astronauts' view of Earth from space. How might this sight change a person's viewpoint about the planet? How could seeing the planet as a single island in space help different cultures work together for the good of all?*

The Apollo astronauts who landed on the moon found themselves in a strange new world. No one had walked this ground before; the only footprints were their own. Nowhere was there a trace of life other than their own, only craters, seas of hardened lava, hills, and rocks. Above them stars and planets shone with a brilliance never seen on Earth, for the moon has no atmosphere to dim their light. Yet for the astronauts the most exciting sight was Earth. It was more than home.

Seen from the surface of the airless, barren moon or from the orbiting spacecraft, Earth was an island of life in the black sea of space, the only outpost of life to be seen. All the men and women who have flown in space—Americans, Soviets, foreign guests—have been awed by the beauty of the earth. They have also been surprised by its size. To a person standing on its surface, the earth appears both large and sturdy. From space it seems small and fragile.

These men and women are often concerned by the man-made changes they see on the earth. They look down at the island of Madagascar, where tropical forests are being felled. They see that the ocean around it is red-brown, colored by soil eroding from land without trees and carried to the sea by rivers.

They look down and see the slick of an oil spill in the sea. They think about the birds and fishes and mammals and plants that will die and about beaches with tarry sands. They know that from Earth the atmosphere seems to be boundless, an ocean of air that we take for granted and breathe without thinking about it. From space they see that the atmosphere is only a thin shell surrounding the earth. Just before sunrise and just after sunset they can see it—the red layer is the air we breathe; above it is the stratosphere; the blue layer is the ionosphere. Beyond the shell is space, black and empty.

Space travelers often return with their thinking changed. On Earth we think of boundaries. The view from space is different. Rivers meander or rush from country to country without stopping, on their way to the sea. Forests reach from one country into another. Sand and dust from the Sahara spread across the Atlantic and blow toward the Americas. Smoke travels hundreds of miles on the winds. An ocean stretches from continent to continent, and the same waters wash the shores of both.

Space travelers see that the earth is one planet, small and fragile, wondrous and lovely. It is the spaceship in which we journey around the sun, and our life-support system is its air and waters and lands. We are all, every person in the world, aboard the same ship. And so we must all, in ways large and small, treasure and protect it.

Author Patricia Lauber has written many science books for young people. Included among her more than ninety books are The News About Dinosaurs, Tales Mummies Tell, *and* The Eruption and Healing of Mount St. Helens. *Lauber says, "We share the world as if we are on a spaceship. It has everthing we need—air, food, water. We all breathe the same air and drink the same water. When one person pollutes, it affects everyone. We have to see what we are doing to the planet."*

Source: Patricia Lauber, *Seeing Earth From Space.* Orchard Books, 1990.

Easter Island

by Thor Heyerdahl, 1989

Archaeologists and anthropologists often find themselves trying to solve mysteries. Anthropologists are scientists who study human history. For many years one of the world's greatest mysteries lay on a tiny Polynesian island in the Pacific Ocean. This island is more than 1,500 miles (2,400 km) from any other inhabited place. It is named Easter Island. Thousands of years ago people settled there and developed a unique culture that included a written language and remarkable buildings.

When Europeans first reached Easter Island in 1722, they were amazed by what they saw. They found hundreds of gigantic stone statues standing on cliffs and hillsides overlooking the Pacific Ocean. Some of these statues—which consisted of heads, crowns, and bodies without legs—were as tall as a four-story building! Near these statues lay wooden tablets, carved with writing symbols. Where, the Europeans wondered, did these statues come from? How were these statues—some weighing as much as 50 tons (45,000 kg)—moved into their standing positions?

In 1955 an anthropologist from Norway named Thor Heyerdahl (hī ur DAHL) visited Easter Island to try to find the answers to these mysteries. As you read his account of this trip, notice the skills and cooperation that the Easter Islanders demonstrated in order to carve a moai (MOH ih)—their word for statue. What does Heyerdahl think of the islanders' explanations of how the moai moved?

The mayor [of Easter Island] was sitting on the floor, chipping away at a [statue of a] bird-man figure, when I entered his modest village home. He was known as by far the best sculptor on the island. . . . He was an amazing character. His brain was as sharp as his face, and he was always prepared to find a solution to any problem.

Did he know how his ancestors carved and raised the big *moai*? Of course. If he knew, was he willing to show me? Yes, how big did I wish the *moai* to be? If it was to be big, he would need help from some of the [other] men. . . .When I asked him why, if he knew, he had not revealed his secret to all those who had asked the same question before me, he answered calmly, "Nobody asked *me*."

In my subsequent dealings with the Easter Islanders I was to understand that this reply was **symptomatic** of the local character. They don't give away anything precious unless you ask for it directly. And anything hidden and not known to others is a treasure. . . .

symptomatic: typical

One night all the members of the expedition were wakened in their tents by the strangest choral singing any of us had ever heard— beautifully harmonized, but almost eerie and totally unlike any music we knew. It was the mayor and his family, who had come to perform an ancient ceremony essential to the success of their enterprise the following day, when they proposed to demonstrate how the work in the quarry was done. A child danced in a paper bird-man mask. Early next morning the mayor and his closest relatives had collected a large number of the stone pickaxes that had lain strewn about the quarry ever since the day work suddenly stopped. They held the picks in their hands, and when the points wore down they sharpened them again simply by chipping off pieces with another stone axe of the same kind. The name for these tools on Easter Island was *toki*, and *toki* is also the ancient word for stone axe among the aboriginal population of North Chile.

After three days' work, the outline of a statue had begun to take shape. . . . No tools were used except the hard [stone] *toki* and water bottles made of **gourds**. The workers constantly sprayed the surface with water to soften up the rock, the interior of which was very hard. . . .

gourds: hollowed-out shells of a type of fruit

By the third day, we began to see the complete **contour** of the *moai*. We did not have enough time to see them finish the carving, but calculated that it would take about a year for a medium-sized *moai*. There had to be elbowroom between the sculptors, who stood side by side, which meant that the number of men who could work on each statue at one time was very limited. . . .

contour: shape

When I asked the successful mayor how the statues had been moved the long distance from the quarries, he answered, with natural conviction, "The *moai* walked."

These people had been giving that same answer to the same question ever since the first missionaries had asked it. I did not, of course, take the answer seriously. . . . [Perhaps the *moai* had been dragged, I said.]

"This was not the way it was done," said the islanders.

Leonardo was the name of one of those who argued that the stones had walked in an upright position. It sounded so meaningless that I would long since have forgotten the episode had I not written it down in my own book on the expedition at the time.

"But, Leonardo," I said, "how could they walk when they had only heads and bodies and no legs?"

"They wriggled along like this," said Leonardo, and gave a demonstration by edging himself along the rock with feet together and stiff knees.

Upon learning that the word toki—meaning "stone ax"—had the same meaning among both the people of Easter Island and those in northern Chile, Thor Heyerdahl was provided with an important clue. Perhaps the first settlers on Easter Island had come from South America. This theory gained further support when the statues on Easter Island were found to be similar to ancient carvings done by the inhabitants of Peru. These discoveries provided one answer to the questions surrounding the origins of the people of Easter Island. Some anthropologists reject Heyerdahl's theory. They believe that the island's original inhabitants, instead of being South American, were Polynesian sailors from the west.

By watching carefully, Heyerdahl also learned how the people of Easter Island carved the moai. *But what did the islanders mean when they said that the* moai *had walked? Like the missionaries who had come before him, Heyerdahl dismissed their explanation. Then, in the 1980s, an engineer from Czechoslovakia named Pavel Pavel believed he understood what the islanders meant. In 1986 Heyerdahl returned to Easter Island with Pavel. In the account below, Heyerdahl describes what happened.*

It was a great day with an air of suspense and nervous anticipation among the islanders when all was ready for Pavel Pavel to show us how a *moai* could walk. None of the elders doubted that their ancestors had formerly made the statues perform. . . . Old Leonardo was as sure now as he had been thirty years before: the legless stone busts had walked by wriggling forward from side to side. And again he showed us the motion, with the soles of his feet put together, before we had told him or anybody else about the experiment we were to conduct. . . .

Leonardo's sister Elodia. . . sang in a low voice a **monotonous** song in a jerky tempo that matched Leonardo's movements. While she sang an old text and tune she obviously knew by heart, her brother made a string figure like a cat's cradle, which he swung in time to the song. This was repeated during the actual experiment as a kind of magical **invocation.**

The islanders refused to help Pavel until they had observed the ancient custom of baking a pig and sweet potatoes in an **umu** earth oven. . . .

Pavel had indeed worked out the **ingenious** technique by which the statues were moved—the same technique that we use ourselves to "walk" a heavy refrigerator or a stone too big to carry unaided. . . . All that was needed were four ropes. Two were attached to the top of the statue and used to pull it to each side alternately, while the other two were fastened down at the base and alternately pulled forward. As one team pulled on the top rope to make the statue tilt to the right, the other team pulled the left-hand side of the base forward before the giant tipped back again. The teams then changed sides, causing the **colossus** to waddle along like a drunken man. The technique required great precision and intensive training, but was incredibly effective when the waddling became rhythmic. We reckoned that a well-drilled team of fifteen men could make a twenty-ton [18,000 kg] statue "walk" at least an average of [one] hundred yards [90 m] a day. . . .

monotonous: repetitive

invocation: prayer

umu: islanders' name for an oven

ingenious: clever

colossus: gigantic statue

We all felt a chill down our backs when we saw the sight that must have been so familiar to the early ancestors of the people around us. A stone colossus of an estimated ten tons [9,000 kg] "walking" like a dog on a leash. . . . After the successful performance, we all embraced a beaming Pavel Pavel. And Leonardo and Elodia willingly accepted part of the honor. We could all read from Leonardo's face that he had known the truth the whole time: it was the song he and Elodia had sung that had made the *moai* move.

The statue had indeed walked. I could find no better word for it in any European language. I suddenly had an idea. The Easter Island verb for "walk" is *haere*. But when the *moai* started to move, the old islanders used the verb *neke-neke*. I looked this up in [a] dictionary of the Easter Island language, and read: "*neke-neke*: to inch forward by moving the body, due to disabled legs or the absence thereof."

What other language in the world would have a special word for walking without legs? . . .

The technical problems behind the great stone giants were solved. The mysteries that had [long puzzled] visitors and . . . scientists . . . existed no more. The **genesis** of the blind giants dotting the slopes . . . was known, and how they walked. . . . The way each of these incredible feats had been accomplished with help from neither machinery or outer space—all these former puzzles now had their answers.

genesis: origin

One big question emerged: Why had nobody but the islanders themselves taken their ancestral traditions seriously? They would have given us all these answers. I confessed to my two friends that the value of the local oral history was, in a sense, one of the strangest discoveries we had made. A hundred years ago the Easter Islanders had answered all the questions that were put to the elders among them. We from the outside world had recorded what they told us, and saved the answers as primitive fairy-tales. . . .

Thor Heyerdahl believed that he had solved many mysteries during his stays on Easter Island in 1955 and 1986. He concluded that South Americans had traveled great distances across the Pacific Ocean long before Europeans had begun exploring the seas. Heyerdahl learned how the giant statues were made and how they "walked." But he could not solve every mystery. The carved writings on wooden tablets on Easter Island have not yet been translated.

Perhaps Heyerdahl's major discovery was understanding the importance of the stories and oral traditions handed down by people for hundreds of years. As you have learned, many types of documents can teach us about cultures and civilizations throughout the world. Newspapers, hot off the morning presses, and stone monuments thousands of years old—as well as songs, poems, tales, speeches, oral histories, and other types of documents—all provide clues about the world around you. By learning to understand these many sources of information, you can gain a better understanding of the world and prepare for the challenges of tomorrow.

Source: Thor Heyerdahl, *Easter Island: The Mystery Solved*. New York: Random House, Inc., 1980.

OLD STONE AGE CAVE PAINTINGS

about 18,000 B.C.

During the Old Stone Age, people began to develop the idea that pictures, or symbols, could stand for objects. Soon Old Stone Age artists began to draw pictures in permanent places. Archaeologists have found paintings colored with yellow or red iron oxide and other mineral pigments, mostly showing animals, in caves used by the people of the Old Stone Age. Scientists do not believe that the people of this period lived in these caves, but they are not sure what the caves were used for. How do you think the Old Stone Age people might have used these caves? What significance do you think the paintings might have had?

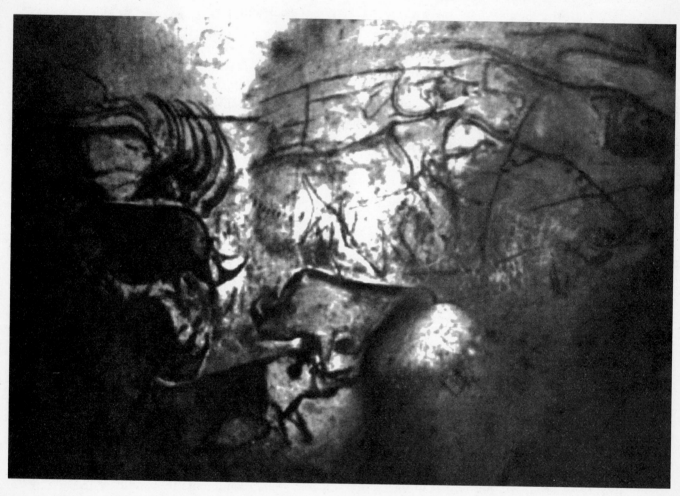

This painting is one of more than 300 discovered in early 1995 in a cave near Avignon, France. Since 1940 an average of one Old Stone Age cave has been found per year in southwestern Europe. Many more may lie under water but may never be discovered. The people of the Old Stone Age lived during the Ice Age. When Earth warmed at the end of the Ice Age, melting ice covered the land on which they lived with water.

Source: Robert Hughes, "Scenes from the Stone Age," *Time* (Vol. 145, February 13, 1995).

First Fruits of The Field

Kabyle Legend Retold by Anne Pellowski, 1990

Archaeologists know that sometime during the New Stone Age, people who once got their food only by hunting and gathering began to raise plants and animals to eat. This practice is called agriculture. Who first got the idea to grow their own food, and how did they get the idea? Nobody knows. So, people try to answer this question through stories known as legends. Many cultures pass down legends to explain events in nature and cultural traditions. Legends are often partially based on facts and are popularly believed to be true. The Kabyle people of northern Africa tell the following legend to explain how people learned to grow their own food. Why do you think the storyteller might have used an ant to teach the humans?

First Man and First Woman wandered around under the earth. One day they found a pile of wheat in a corner, and next to that a pile of barley. In other corners they found piles of seeds and grains of all kinds that are good to eat or to **season** food.

season: flavor

"What does this mean?" they wondered.

Near the wheat and barley ran an ant. First Parents saw the ant. It scratched the **hull** off a kernel of barley and then ate the grain inside.

hull: outer covering of a seed

"What are you doing?" First Parents asked the ant. "Can you tell us about these seeds and grains?"

The ant said, "Do you know of a spring or a pool or a river?"

First Parents said, "No, we do not know of such things. But we do know of a fountain."

The ant answered, "Then you do know Water. Water is there for you to drink. It is there for you to wash yourselves and your clothing. But Water is also there so that you can grow and cook your food. If you cook each of these grains, each in its own way, you will always have good food. Come with me. I want to show you."

The ant led First Parents to her passageway under the earth.

"This is my path. Come with me." The ant led First Parents up through the passageway and out onto the earth. She led them to a river and said, "Here flows much Water. You can use it to drink, and to wash yourselves and your clothing. And this is also the Water that you can use to cook your grains, after you have ground them up."

The ant led First Parents to a pair of stones and said, "We can use these stones to grind kernels into flour."

The ant helped First Man and First Woman grind some grains into flour. Then the ant showed them how to mix the flour with water, how to make a fire, and how to bake flat loaves of bread.

When they had eaten the bread until they were full, First Man said to First Woman, "Come, let us visit the earth." They took grains of wheat and barley and many other seeds. They wandered here and there. Often, they dropped a few kernels of grain or seeds. Rain fell on them and the kernels and seeds grew into plants.

When First Man and First Woman passed by on their return, they saw the plants, heavy with grain or seed pods. They dug into the earth and saw that each plant had grown from one grain or seed.

"In the future, we will eat half of the grain and plant the remaining half. We will wait until after the first rain falls."

This they did, and that is how the grains and seeds of plants were spread wider and wider, until they could be found growing over much of the earth.

The development of agriculture was a giant step in history. People no longer had to move from place to place in order to follow their food supply. They began to settle in one place and build communities. As people's farming techniques improved, not everyone had to be involved in the growing of food. New, specialized occupations developed. Some people continued to farm, while others ground grain into flour, and still others baked the bread. The development of agriculture changed civilization forever.

Source: Anne Pellowski, *Hidden Stories in Plants*. New York: Macmillan Publishing Co., 1990.

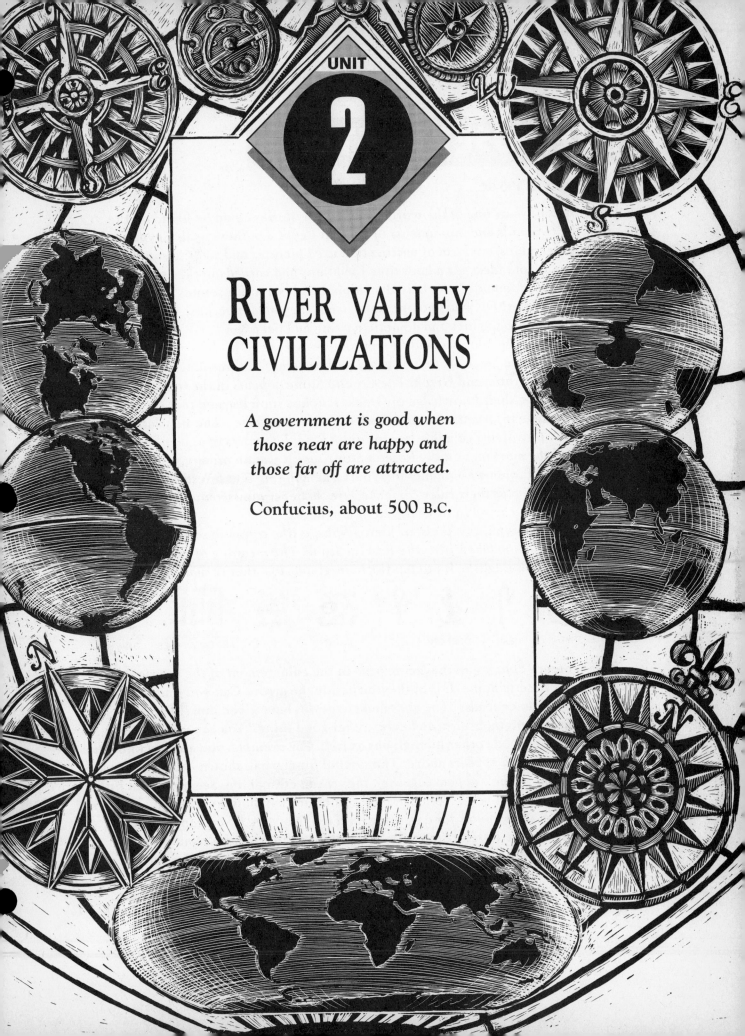

RIVER VALLEY CIVILIZATIONS

A government is good when those near are happy and those far off are attracted.

Confucius, about 500 B.C.

THE ROSETTA STONE

Egyptian Decree, 196 B.C.

For hundreds of years one of the world's greatest mysteries could be found on the walls of the pyramids and monuments of ancient Egypt. On these walls Egyptians had carved hieroglyphics, a system of writing that used pictures and signs to stand for objects, sounds, and ideas. At a later time Egyptians had carved another system of writing known as demotic, which used an alphabet to stand for sounds. What did these symbols mean? For years no one knew what they meant because the knowledge of how to read hieroglyphics and demotic writing had been lost.

But in 1799 archaeologists made a remarkable discovery. In the Egyptian town of Rosetta they found a piece of stone marked with carvings in three languages: hieroglyphics, demotic, and Greek. The Rosetta Stone appears in the inset on the facing page. Using their knowledge of Greek, scholars soon learned that the stone recorded the same information in the three different languages. The translation of the Rosetta Stone provided a valuable key for unlocking the secrets of ancient Egypt.

What did the markings on the Rosetta Stone say? It was an order given by a pharaoh named Ptolemy Epiphanes in 196 B.C., demanding that priests in Egypt honor him and accept him as their ruler. To make sure that everyone would obey this order, the pharaoh had it carved in three different languages.

Reading hieroglyphic symbols, or hieroglyphs, is like trying to solve a puzzle. Look at the sentence below taken from the Rosetta Stone. The meaning of each hieroglyph is given below it in English. Try to put the hieroglyphs together to make a sentence.

GOOD   EVERYTHING   HEALTH   STRENGTH   LIFE   MIGHT   VICTORY   THE GODS AND GODDESSES   GAVE HIM

This sentence appears on the facing page in the enlargement of the top right section of the Rosetta Stone. It is in the line beside the arrow. Can you find it? In English, this sentence reads: "The gods and goddesses have given him [Pharaoh] victory, might, strength, health, and every other good thing." You can use some of these symbols to decode other hieroglyphs as well. For example, you already know the symbol for life, which appears above. The symbol for eternal, shown below, is a snake. When these two symbols appear together, they mean eternal life. See if you can find this phrase on the next page. Notice that by combining symbols you can make longer phrases. Look at the symbols for day, seven, and ten. Now see if you can find the phrase 17 days on the Rosetta Stone. Try to locate the other symbols and phrases explained below. What do you suppose that the other hieroglyphs on the Rosetta Stone might mean?

ETERNAL   GOD   HOUSE   HOUSE OF GOD OR TEMPLE   DAY   SEVEN   TEN   PRIEST

Thanks to the Rosetta Stone, people can now read hieroglyphic writing to learn about life in ancient Egypt. To find out about one of the most important Egyptian leaders in history, read the next document on page 14.

A Queen's Promise

by Hatshepsut, 1500 B.C.

One of ancient Egypt's best-known pharaohs was Queen Hatshepsut (hat SHEP soot) (1520–1482 B.C.). She was one of Egypt's few female rulers. During her reign, from about 1503 to 1482 B.C., Egypt enjoyed peace and prosperity and expanded its trade w East Africa and Asia. Like other Egyptian rulers, Hatshepsut ordered the building of gigantic monuments and temples. One of them was a huge stone obelisk, a tall four-side pillar. Hatshepsut's obelisk is made of a single piece of red granite and still stands today Like most Egyptian monuments, it is carved with hieroglyphics. Thanks in part to the Rosetta Stone, which you can read about on pages 12–13, historians have been able to translate Hatshepsut's obelisk. As you read part of the obelisk below, notice that Hatshepsut connects herself to the gods. In what ways does she claim to be a powerful ruler?

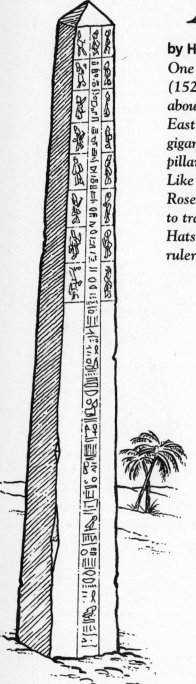

Now my heart turns **to and fro,**
In thinking what will the people say,
They who shall see my monument in after years,
And shall speak of what I have done. . . .
In order that my name may endure in this temple,
For eternity and everlastingness,
They are each of one block of hard granite,
Without seam, without joining together! . . .
Lo, the god knows me well,
Amun, Lord of **Thrones-of-the-Two-Lands;**
He made me rule **Black Land** and **Red Land** as reward,
No one rebels against me in all lands.
All foreign lands are my subjects,
He placed my border at the limits of heaven,
What **Aten** encircles labors for me.
He gave it to him who came from him,
Knowing I would rule it for him.
I am his daughter in very truth,
Who serves him, who knows what he **ordains.**
My reward from my father is **life-stability-rule** . . .
　　　eternally like **Re.**

to and fro: back and forth

Thrones-of-the-Two-Lands: Upper and Lower Egypt
Black Land: the Nile Valley
Red Land: the desert
Aten: the sun

ordains: orders
life-stability-rule: rule for life
Re: the sun god

After Hatshepsut's death her stepson, Thutmose III, became ruler of Egypt. Because he had long been her rival for power, he tried to destroy everything Hatshepsut had built. However, because she had built so many temples and monuments, many survived. You can read more about Hatshepsut in the next selection on pages 15–21.

Source: Joanna Bankier and Deirdre Lashgari, eds., *Women Poets of the World.* New York: Macmillan Publishing Co., Inc., 1983.

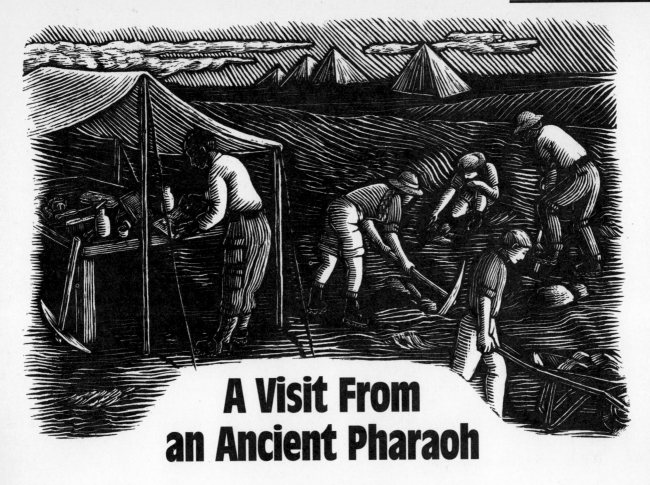

A Visit From an Ancient Pharaoh

by Carolyn Clark, 1996

Hatshepsut (hat SHEP soot) was the best known and most powerful female Pharaoh of Egypt. She came to the throne in 1503 B.C. when her husband, Thutmose II, died. Her stepson, Thutmose III, was too young to accept the responsibilities of being Pharaoh, so Hatshepsut and Thutmose III ruled together in name. However, the power of the throne belonged to Hatshepsut. Before Hatshepsut became ruler, Egypt often conquered other nations in order to gain wealth and power. How was Hatshepsut's reign different?

CAST OF CHARACTERS

The Archaeologist
Archaeology Assistants: Andrea, John, Karen, Roberto
Hatshepsut
Senemut (SEN uh mut)
Royal Guard (up to 4 students)

Play begins with The Archaeologist in the front as if lecturing before an audience, assistants in background, sitting still in "digging" positions. Hatshepsut and other ancient Egyptian characters are offstage.

15

The Archaeologist: Good afternoon, ladies and gentlemen. Thank you for asking me here today to share my recent archaeological findings from ancient Egypt. As you will see, my team and I found much more than we expected. Our adventure began as we were digging for artifacts from around 1500 B.C....

(The Archaeologist joins assistants.)

Andrea: How long have we been here?

The Archaeologist: Three months, two weeks, and one day.

John: Seems like since the time of the pharaohs!

Karen: And all we've found is...

All Assistants Together: SAND!!

Roberto: Sand in my shoes!

Andrea: Sand in my hair!

John: Sand in my sandwich!

Karen: Sand in my...

The Archaeologist: *(interrupting and pointing at a pottery jar)* Wait! I think I've found something here!

Andrea: It's about time!

Roberto: What is it?

The Archaeologist: It looks like pottery. A jar, maybe, but let's leave it right where it is, for now.

John: I'll get the camera so that we can take a photograph of the object in the spot where we found it.

Karen: Here's the whisk brush. I'll help you clean it.

Andrea: I can check the exact ground level.

Karen brushes off the jar. John photographs the jar. Andrea studies a chart on a clipboard.

The Archaeologist: This looks like it could be from the pharaoh Hatshepsut's era, but we'll have to use carbon-14 dating on it when we get back to the lab to be sure. That will tell us the level of radioactive carbon within the pottery and help us determine its age.

Roberto: *(carefully picking up the jar)* Look! It *is* a jar.

Karen: *(sniffing)* Aah, I smell something really sweet.

Andrea: Yes, like perfume, or incense.

John: It's coming from inside the jar. It smells wonderful!

The Archaeologist: What you are smelling is myrrh, which comes from the sticky resin of a tree. It was used as incense in ancient times.

John: Well, whatever it is, I feel like something important is about to happen.

Hatshepsut enters and very slowly crosses the stage holding onto Senemut's arm. They are surrounded by a royal guard.

Karen: Me too. Am I dreaming, or is there some lady dressed in gold coming toward us right now?

Roberto: If you're dreaming, then so am I, and it's a strange dream. She looks like an ancient Egyptian!

Andrea: And look at all those people around her. They look pretty ancient, too.

John: Maybe it's a costume party.

Andrea: In the middle of the desert?

Karen: Look around, Andrea. This is really weird, but we're not in the desert anymore. We're on the banks of a river, and I think it's the Nile.

The Archaeologist: *(slowly, through clenched teeth)* I am a scientist. These things don't happen to scientists.

Roberto: Calm down, Professor. Here they come.

Royal Guard member I: Can we arrest them, please, your Majesty?

Royal Guard member II: Oh, come on, we haven't arrested anybody in almost 3,500 years.

Royal Guard member III: They look dangerous to me!

Hatshepsut: (*smiles at archaeology crew, then turns back to the soldiers*) Royal Guard! We will not arrest these people unless they threaten us. I know you are frustrated because I have never sent you into battle, but I will not allow any violence from you, except in self-defense! Besides, these are people of good will. I've been watching them for months.

John: You've been watching us? Excuse me, but who are you?

Hatshepsut: I am Hatshepsut, pharaoh of Egypt. This (*indicates the person beside her*) is Senemut, my trusted advisor, and these are members of my royal guard.

The Archaeologist: Your majesty, I would like to know how you managed to appear here today. I would also like to know why we started out our day in the desert and ended up standing on the banks of the Nile River. But I won't ask because I am a scientist, and as a scientist, I am sure I must be imagining the whole thing.

Hatshepsut: (*smiles mysteriously and shrugs*) As you wish.

Andrea: Well, I think she's real, and I have a question. You're a woman. How did you become pharaoh of Egypt?

Hatshepsut: Is that really so strange to you? My father was pharaoh. My husband was pharaoh. I am of royal blood and trained to be a leader. My culture has goddesses, why not a female pharaoh?

Karen: Then why are you the only woman pharaoh I've ever heard of?

Hatshepsut: It is true that men were favored as leaders. But when my husband died, the only other choice for pharaoh was my stepson, Thutmose. He was only a child—certainly not ready to be ruler of Egypt. I agreed to let him share the title of pharaoh with me. But the power was mine.

Karen: Didn't the men object?

Hatshepsut: No ruler is popular with everyone. I did what I could to prove that a good leader is a good leader, male or female. That's why, when you see statues of me, sometimes I am shown as a woman and sometimes as a sphinx, with my head on the body of a lion. At other times I am shown as a man—with a big, heavy beard! (*Hatshepsut strokes her chin and shakes her head.*)

John: Please tell us why you are here.

Hatshepsut: When I first noticed you digging in the sand, I didn't know what you were doing. I thought you might be treasure hunters or grave robbers. Then when you found my jar of myrrh, I saw how carefully you treated it. The jar isn't valuable, so I realized you were looking for knowledge, not gold. And I knew you could see my beloved Egypt much more clearly with my help.

Roberto: *(pointing into the distance)* Look! Over there at the river! Ships! *(Everyone looks toward imaginary river.)*

Hatshepsut: Yes, those are my ships. Five beautifully crafted, wooden sailing ships returning from the land of Punt. They were gone for two years. Instead of sending out military expeditions, I sent out trade expeditions. We took goods that we had in surplus—like papyrus, jewelry, and bronze weapons—and exchanged them for things we had too little of. We traded a certain amount of our goods for an equal value of their goods. That way we all got what we needed, as well as things for pleasure, too!

John: Can we see what they brought?

Hatshepsut: Of course! *(speaking to one of the royal guard members)* Royal guard member! Go and get some of the jewels from Punt!

Royal Guard member: Yes, your majesty.

Royal Guard member exits.

Andrea: Why are all those soldiers getting off the ships? I thought you said this wasn't a military expedition.

Hatshepsut: My soldiers helped with the trade expeditions. They enjoyed it, and it kept them occupied in peaceful activities.

Karen: Look! There's an artist, drawing a picture of the whole scene. Who are those other people—the ones who are writing?

Hatshepsut: Those are scribes. Some wrote down the events of the day, while others kept account of the goods that came from the ships.

Roberto: They're starting to unload the cargo. I see boxes of gold, and elephant tusks.

John: And leopard skins, and is that ... *(pointing)* ... is that a family of chimpanzees?

The Archaeologist: Those look like very important people getting off the ship right now, but they aren't dressed like Egyptians. Who are they?

Hatshepsut: They are important representatives from the land of Punt. I'm glad they returned with the expedition. Their customs were different from ours, but we respected each other's differences. I enjoyed meeting with them.

Karen: There's that marvelous perfume smell again. Mmmmmmm.

Hatshepsut: Myrrh and frankincense. Those are the best fragrances in the world. Oh, they are unloading my myrrh trees! I asked for eighty-one myrrh trees to plant around my temple at Deir al-Bahri (DER el BAHR ee).

Senemut: I designed the temple. I wanted her majesty to have a beautiful monument to be remembered by. Unfortunately, young Thutmose destroyed much of the evidence of her majesty's existence. I was never able to finish the temple.

Hatshepsut: Yes, Thutmose. I hate to say too much—he was my stepson. But Thutmose certainly did long for power, and he sometimes used it in destructive ways. However, the most important monument to me is not made from stone. It is a message made from the lessons of history and passed on through each generation.

Andrea: *(softly)* What is the message, your majesty?

Hatshepsut: The message I wish to hear echoing through history is this: The wealth of my empire did not depend on conquering other nations. It depended on cooperation with other nations. We traded the things we had plenty of and got what we needed in return. Our lives were made richer. Other nations were made richer, and we could live alongside each other in peace. Leaving this knowledge to the world will stand as my monument. Will you help me? Will you be my messengers?

Archaeologist and Assistants: Yes, your majesty.

Royal Guard member returns carrying jewels.

Hatshepsut: Thank you. *(Taking jewels from the royal guard member and handing them to The Archaeologist)* Please take these jewels as a token of my appreciation. We believe they will bring you luck.

The Archaeologist: Pharaoh, we are grateful to you. We will try to make your voice from the past become a voice of the future.

Hatshepsut and Senemut: Goodbye!

Archaeologist and Crew: Goodbye!

Everyone but The Archaeologist exits—ancient Egyptians to one side, archaeology crew to the other. The Archaeologist comes back to center and faces audience.

The Archaeologist: Did we really see Hatshepsut? My scientific training tells me it is impossible, and no scientific journal would ever accept my story. But we have her jewels, and more importantly, we have her message: Nations *can* live together in peace.

THE END

After Hatshepsut's death in 1483 B.C., Thutmose III became the sole Pharaoh. He attempted to remove all traces of Hatshepsut's life and influence. Unlike Hatshepsut, whose reign was mostly peaceful, Thutmose III became known as one of the world's first great generals. He returned to the idea of gaining wealth and power through force. He led many military campaigns and extended Egypt's rule to the Euphrates River. Thutmose died in 1450 B.C.

The Epic of Gilgamesh

Sumerian Epic, 3000–2000 B.C.

One of the oldest stories in the world is The Epic of Gilgamesh, *an ancient Sumerian tale that was written between 4,000 and 5,000 years ago. The story comes from Mesopotamia—in what is today the Middle East—and was originally carved on clay tablets. Gilgamesh was said to have been the king of Uruk, an ancient city in Mesopotamia, around 2700 B.C. In the epic Gilgamesh goes on a long journey in search of eternal youth and encounters monsters, gods, and the mighty forces of nature. In the excerpt below, a god tells Gilgamesh about a great flood that once swept the land. How does the god manage to survive the flood?*

For six days and six nights the winds blew, torrent and **tempest** and flood overwhelmed the world, tempest and flood raged together like warring hosts. When the seventh day dawned the storm from the south **subsided**, the sea grew calm, the flood was stilled; I looked at the face of the world and there was silence, all mankind was turned to clay. The surface of the sea stretched as flat as a roof-top; I opened a hatch and the light fell on my face. Then I bowed low, I sat down and I wept, the tears streamed down my face, for on every side was the waste of water. I looked for land in vain, but fourteen leagues distant there appeared a mountain, and there the boat grounded; on the mountain of Nisir the boat held fast, she held fast and did not budge. One day she held, and a second day on the mountain of Nisir she held fast and did not budge. A third day, and a fourth day she held fast on the mountain and did not budge; a fifth day and a sixth day she held fast on the mountain. When the seventh day dawned I loosed a dove and let her go. She flew away, but finding no resting-place she returned. Then I loosed a swallow, and she flew away but finding no resting-place she returned. I loosed a raven, she saw that the waters had retreated, she ate, she flew around, she **cawed**, and she did not come back. Then I threw everything open to the four winds, I made a sacrifice and poured out a **libation** on the mountain top.

tempest: storm

subsided: died down

cawed: squawked

libation: liquid offering

After telling this story, the god presents Gilgamesh with a plant that will give him eternal life. A serpent tricks him, however, causing Gilgamesh to lose the plant and the promise of eternal life. The Epic of Gilgamesh *is the oldest epic known to human history. Like* The Iliad *and the* Aeneid, *which you can read excerpts from on pages 36–38 and 49–50, it is considered one of the world's greatest works of literature.*

Source: N. K. Sandars, ed., *The Epic of Gilgamesh*. London: Penguin Group, 1960.

A Father's Complaint

by a Sumerian scribe, about 1700 B.C.

Parents from every culture want the best for their children. However, sometimes parents and children disagree about what is best. The excerpt below was written by a father from Sumer, in southern Mesopotamia, 3,700 years ago. This father was a scribe whose son chose not to follow in his footsteps. What did this father think about his son's path in life?

I, never in all my life did I make you carry reeds to the **canebrake**....I never sent you to work as a laborer. "Go, work, and support me," I never in my life said to you.

Others like you support their parents by working. If you spoke to your kin, and appreciated them, you would **emulate** them. . . . You certainly don't labor like them—they are the sons of fathers who make their sons labor, but me—I didn't make you work like them.

. . . Among all [humankind's] craftsmen who dwell in the land, as many as **Enki** [brought into existence], no work as difficult as the scribal art did he [bring into existence]. For if not for **song**—like the banks of the sea, the banks of the distant canals, is the heart of song distant—you wouldn't be listening to my counsel, and I wouldn't be repeating to you the wisdom of my father. It is in **accordance** with the fate decreed by **Enlil** for man that a son follows the work of his father.

I, night and day, am I tortured because of you. Night and day you **waste** in pleasures. You have accumulated much wealth, have expanded far and wide, have become fat, big, broad, powerful, and puffed. But your kin waits expectantly for your misfortune, and will rejoice at it because you looked not to your humanity.

canebrake: thicket of reeds

emulate: try to equal

Enki: the god of water, arts, and crafts

song: poetry

accordance: agreement

Enlil: god of the atmosphere

waste: spend

Being a scribe was a highly honored profession because few people could write. Scribes studied hard and did accounting, writing, and record keeping for everyone, including the king. In fact, the reason this father's words of disappointment have survived through the centuries is because of his profession! This letter would have originally been written in cuneiform, one of the earliest known written languages. Cuneiform symbols communicate through pictures instead of sounds. The pictures were scratched onto a moist clay tablet with sharpened reeds, then baked until the tablet hardened.

Source: Hanscom, Hellerman and Posner, eds., *Voices of the Past: Readings in Ancient History.* The Macmillan Company, 1967.

Praying at the Western Wall

by Brent Ashabranner, 1984

Judaism is one of the world's oldest religions, its traditions dating back thousands of years. Around 960 B.C., Solomon became king of the Jewish people, and built a magnificent building—known as the First Temple—in Jerusalem. The First Temple became the center of the Jewish religion. Four hundred years later the First Temple was destroyed and a new temple was built. This new temple, called the Second Temple, was remodeled by King Herod around 30 B.C. But 100 years later, in A.D. 70, Roman soldiers attacked Jerusalem and destroyed the Second Temple. All that remained of it was one giant wall. Today this wall is known as the Western Wall, or Kotel, and is the most sacred monument of Judaism. Many Jews travel to the Western Wall to pray. Among them is a 12-year-old boy named Gavriel, who lives in Jerusalem. In the following excerpt from a book describing his life, Gavriel attends morning prayer at the Western Wall with his father and four brothers. What are some of the rituals that Gavriel performs with his father? How do these rituals relate to Gavriel's religious beliefs?

When Abe and his sons go to morning prayer, the sun is just turning the eastern sky a rosy pink. Gavriel has learned from his father that morning prayer cannot be said until the light is just right. "Just enough to tell a light blue thread from a white one," Abe says. Gavriel rubs the sleep from his eyes as they walk to the Kotel, the Western Wall, but he does not wish that he were back in bed.

He has a special feeling for the Jewish quarter at this time of day, before the noise and bustle have really begun, before the narrow streets are crowded. He likes going to prayer with his father. He carries a blue velvet pouch which holds his father's prayer shawl and *tefillin*, which are small leather boxes containing Biblical verses.

They pass the rebuilt ruins of a **Crusader** lodging place and then walk down several flights of stone stairs—140 steps in all—to reach the Kotel. Morning is Gavriel's favorite time to come to the Western Wall. Some people are always there when they arrive but not so many as there will be later in the day. The sounds of prayer rise clearly in the cool, clean air. Swallows swoop overhead making little cries. It is a peaceful place to be.

Abe puts on his prayer shawl and the *tefillin*, which are provided with long leather straps. He places one of the *tefillin* on his left arm facing his heart and winds the leather strap around his left forearm seven times. The other *tefillin* he places in the center of his forehead, looping the leather strap around his head to keep the *tefillin* in place.

Crusader: name for Christian soldiers who fought from the 11th to 13th centuries to recapture Jerusalem from the Muslims

Gavriel knows the *tefillin* signify that the **covenant** with God is a matter of serious concern every day of the week. He remembers the passage from **Deuteronomy**: "And these words which I command thee this day shall be upon thine heart... And thou shalt bind them for thine hand, and they shall be for **frontlets** between thine eyes."

When the *tefillin* are properly attached, Abe begins to pray, and his sons join him. He has taught them the proper way of prayer just as he learned it from his father. They pray aloud, and Gavriel concentrates intently, not just saying words but thinking very hard about what they mean. This concentration, this thinking about what the prayer means, is called *kavvanah*, and it is of great importance. As with his father and other men in prayer at the Wall, the intensity of his concentration causes Gavriel's eyes to close and his body to sway.

"... O purify our hearts to serve Thee in truth, for Thou art God in truth, and Thy word is truth, and endureth forever...."

On many nights Abe helps Gavriel in his study of the **Talmud**. In just a few months Gavriel will become *bar mitzvah*, a son of the commandment. This will happen on the day he is thirteen years old. Then, in a religious sense, he will be a man and able to understand the commandments of the Torah and observe them on his own responsibility. Now it is Abe's responsibility to see that Gavriel really has that understanding.

Gavriel takes his religion seriously. Whenever he leaves the apartment or returns to it, he touches a piece of the **Torah**, called *mezuzah*, which has been nailed to the doorframe. He does the same with a piece of the Sacred Book that has been fastened to his classroom door at school.

And at family gatherings around the dinner table on the holy day of **Shabbat** or at **Passover**, when songs of praise and thanksgiving are sung, Gavriel's clear voice is loudest, after that of his father.

covenant: agreement

Deuteronomy: holy book of Jewish scripture

frontlets: decorated headbands

Talmud: Jewish law based on interpretations of sacred texts

Torah: Jewish scripture

Shabbat: Jewish sabbath from sundown Friday to sundown Saturday

Passover: Jewish holiday celebrating Exodus from Egypt

Today over 17 million people—or about 1 in 330 people in the world—are Jews. Judaism emerged in western Asia almost 4,000 years ago in what is today the nation of Israel. About 2,000 years ago another major religion—called Christianity—developed in the same region. To learn more about Christianity, read the document on pages 52–53.

Source: Brent Ashabranner, *Gavriel and Jemal: Two Boys of Jerusalem*. New York: Dodd, Mead & Company, 1984.

Life of a Hindu Priest

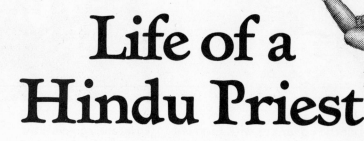

NATARAJ

by Hardwari Lal, 1984

About 4,000 years ago, the religion of Hinduism begin to develop on the subcontinent of India. Hinduism developed from ancient beliefs and stories. Hindus believe in many different gods. Some of these gods are pictured in the illustrations accompanying this selection. Hindus also believe that all parts of nature are holy. Hardwari Lal is a 55-year-old Hindu pandit, or priest, who works at a temple in Bhatinda, a town in northern India near the Pakistani border. As you read Hardwari Lal's description of his duties in a selection from an oral history, think about how the rituals he and other Hindus perform relate to their religious beliefs.

My day at the temple begins at half-past four in the morning and ends at eight o'clock every night. It's a long day, but I don't mind one bit, as I devote all the time to the service of God.

Which God, you ask? Well, we Hindus have 330 million **deities**. We believe that the God Brahma is the Creator of the World. Vishnu is the God who preserves the world and the God Shiva is the destroyer of the world.

deities: gods

Among the more popular gods and goddesses are Radha and Krishna, Ram and Sita, Hanuman the monkey god, Ganesha the elephant-headed god, and the Goddess Durga, who rides a tiger. We have lots of **idols** of these gods and goddesses in our temple. You'll find lots of temples in India, at least one every mile or so, for religion is very important here.

idols: statues

It's part of my duty as a priest to offer prayer to the idols, to bathe them with milk and honey, and to dress them. Then, every day, other temple priests and I have to organize the distribution of free food. Our temple feeds about thirty or forty poor people every day. The temple gets its money from donations.

Only a **Brahman** can become a priest in a temple. He must be learned in the ancient Sanskrit texts known as *Vedas*. He must also know how to conduct weddings, birth and death ceremonies, and so on.

Brahman: member of the Hindu priest class

Most marriages are finally arranged after comparing the horoscopes of the boy and girl. If the astrologer feels that they will get along, he fixes an **auspicious** day and hour for the wedding. Last year, for almost eight months, practically no weddings took place, as the stars weren't in the right position.

Anyhow, on the chosen day, the bridegroom dresses in style with a shining crown on his head and **garlands** of flowers and **rupees** round his neck. He then sits on a white horse—though some people prefer automobiles nowadays. Escorted by a band of drummers and trumpeters and a whole lot of relatives and friends, the groom goes through the streets to the bride's home. The bride has to wear lots of jewelry and dress in red or pink.

The priests light the sacred fire of sandalwood and incense and begin reciting **mantras** from the *Vedas*. Then we take a pink cloth and tie one end to the bridegroom and the other end to the bride. The bride and bridegroom have to walk around the sacred fire seven times to become husband and wife. For tens of centuries, Hindu weddings have been performed in the same way.

As for funerals, we Hindus usually burn our dead, though we bury infants.

There are so many holy cities and places. They're usually on the banks of rivers or up on the snowy mountains. Cities like Hardwar, Rishikesh and Varanasi are on the riverside. Pilgrimage centers like Badrinath, Kedarnath and Amarnath are high up in the mountains. Half the year the pilgrims can't get to them because of the snow.

But I must tell you about the Kumbh *Mela*, which is held every twelve years and is the world's greatest religious fair. At Kumbh, millions and millions of Hindus gather from all over India to take a bath in the holy Ganges [River].

With so much going on, life remains busy and full for me. I can't tell you how happy and fortunate I feel serving God and the people.

SHIVA   **PARVATI**   **KRISHNA**   **RAMA**   **SITA**

Today nearly 800 million people—or about one in seven people in the world—are Hindus. Most Hindus live in India and Southeast Asia. Around 2,500 years ago a Hindu prince founded another major religion of the world. To learn about this religion, read the document on pages 30–31.

Source: Veenu Sandal, *We Live in India*. New York: The Bookwright Press, 1984.

Mahabharata

Ancient Hindu Epic, about 400 B.C.

About 2,500 years ago—no one knows exactly when—a great Hindu poem was written in India. This ancient epic, called the Mahabharata (muh HAH bah ruh tuh), consists of 100,000 stanzas and tells the heroic story of two families who fought to control a kingdom in northern India. Combined with the story are legends, tales, and religious discussions. These religious discussions deal with many basic Hindu ideas. Below are two precepts, or principles, from the Mahabharata. What are some of the lessons that these precepts teach Hindus about life?

Enjoy the pleasure
bestowed on you,

and bear the pain
bestowed on you,

wait patiently for
what time brings,

as does the farmer
with the fruit.

Let us overcome
the angry man
   with gentleness,

the evil man
   with goodness,

the miser
   with generosity,

the liar
   with truth.

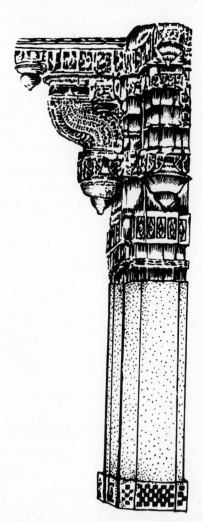

The Mahabharata is one of two great Hindu epics. Its deeply religious poems continue to be read by people all over the world.

Source: Daisy Aldan, *Poems from India*. New York: Thomas Y. Crowell Company, 1969.

WHERE THE MIND IS WITHOUT FEAR

by Rabindranath Tagore, 1910

The cultural traditions of India, such as dance, music, and poetry, have always been greatly influenced by Hindu teachings. Through much of India's history, poets, such as the writers of the epic the Mahabharata, on page 28, have written many works from the Hindu perspective. The poem below is by a Hindu named Rabindranath Tagore (ruh BEEN druh naht tuh GAWR) (1861–1941). Tagore was the most famous writer from India in the early twentieth century. His poetry won the 1913 Nobel prize in literature. Tagore often wrote about Indian politics and social concerns, but he also worked to increase understanding between the many different cultures and religious groups of the world. His strong Hindu beliefs made peace and hope central ideas in many of his writings. As you read "Where the Mind Is Without Fear," think about what Tagore's hope is for his country.

Where the mind is without fear and the head is held high;
Where knowledge is free;
Where the world has not been broken up into **fragments** by
    narrow **domestic** walls;
Where words come out from the depths of truth;
Where tireless **striving** stretches its arms towards perfection;
Where the clear stream of reason has not lost its way into the
    dreary desert sand of dead habit;
Where the mind is led forward by **thee** into everwidening thought
    and action—
Into that heaven of freedom, my **Father**, let my country awake.

fragments: pieces
domestic: national
striving: struggling
thee: you
Father: God

Rabindranath Tagore was a patriot who believed in peaceful solutions. In the early twentieth century, most Indian people wanted independence from Great Britain, which had ruled them for many years. Mohandas Gandhi, whose letter you will read on page 173, was another famous leader who believed in nonviolent methods to achieve independence for India. Although much of the groundwork was laid before his death, Tagore did not live long enough to see Indian independence. India finally became self-governing in 1947.

Source: *Calliope World History Magazine for Young People* (Vol. 3, No. 4, Mar/Apr 1993). Peterborough, NH: Cobblestone Publishing Inc., 1993.

Becoming a Buddhist Master

by Sek Bao Shi, 1985

Around 563 B.C. a Hindu prince named Siddhartha Gautama was born in the foothills of the Himalaya Mountains in what is today Nepal. After trying for years to understand suffering and find widsom, Siddhartha decided that suffering was caused by desires. By freeing himself of desires, Siddhartha said he reached peace and was free of pain and suffering. When he told his followers what he had learned, they began to call him the Buddha, a title meaning "the Awakened One." From Siddhartha's teachings a new religion called Buddhism developed and spread throughout Southeast Asia. Sek Bao Shi was a 41-year-old resident of Singapore who was working toward becoming a Buddhist master. As you read this account of her life from an oral history, notice the different rituals and practices that she follows. How do her Buddhist beliefs shape her life?

*I*t's 4:30 A.M. The sky is dark and it's rather cold, but I'm up and so are the other five members of our Buddhist Order. Only women live in our temple. By 5:00 A.M. we're chanting Buddhist **sutras** at our first service of the day.

sutras: teachings, scriptures

At 7:00 A.M. we make our first offering of biscuits or bread and a cup of tea to Lord Buddha. A short service accompanies the offering.

Then we have our breakfast of bread or oatmeal and a hot drink. We are **vegetarians**, because we don't believe in harming any living creature.

vegetarians: people who do not eat meat

After breakfast, there are chores to do. These include cleaning, washing and preparing lunch. At 11:00 A.M., after the rice is cooked, we make a second offering to Lord Buddha. We have our lunch soon after and this is the final meal of the day.

To become a member of the Buddhist Order, it's customary to follow a Master or *Shi Fu* of one's choice for five years. When I decided to leave home, give up my job, rid myself of my worldly possessions, shave my head and devote myself to practicing Lord Buddha's teachings, I asked to be her **disciple**. I was very happy to be accepted. I have been my *Shi Fu's* disciple for three years now.

disciple: follower

My decision to join the Buddhist Order was not made overnight. I had been thinking about it since I was 9. As a child, I often accompanied my mother, a devout Buddhist, to the Kuan Yin Temple to make offerings to Kuan Yin, the Goddess of Mercy.

After completing my secondary schooling, I entered the civil service. Still deeply interested in the teachings of Lord Buddha, I became a vegetarian. As a lay devotee I went to the Buddhist Union Shrine to help out in religious and administrative activities. I also resolved to abstain from harming others, from stealing, from telling lies, from being unchaste and from all forms of intoxicating drinks and drugs. I spent seventeen years in this way until finally deciding to join the Buddhist Order at the age of 38.

Since then, I have been staying at the Leng Jin Temple to study the Buddhist scriptures with my *Shi Fu*. In addition, she teaches me how to **meditate**, conduct Buddhist services and beat the drum and cymbals during special ceremonies. I also have more than 500 rules to observe now.

meditate: focus one's thoughts

I've found peace and happiness in the teachings of our Lord Buddha who said, "The gift of Truth excels all other gifts." I want to seek this Truth through the study of the Buddhist scriptures. I know it can be found within ourselves.

I am glad for the opportunity to practice what I believe in. There's complete freedom of worship in Singapore and wherever you go you will see temples, mosques, churches and other places of worship near to each other.

As a Buddhist, I'm very happy to see our people understanding and accepting one another's customs and religion. It makes for a much happier world.

Today more than 330 million people—or about 1 in 17 people in the world—are Buddhists. Buddhism, along with Judaism, Christianity, Islam, and Hinduism, all began in Asia. Over the course of hundreds of years, these five religions have spread to every part of the world. They have had an enormous impact on both world civilization and history.

Source: Jessie Wee, *We Live in Malaysia & Singapore*. New York: The Bookwright Press, 1985.

O Magnificent and Many

Poem from the *Shih Ching*, about 1100–600 B.C.

The Chinese began to invent a writing system before the founding of the Shang dynasty in the 1700s B.C. During the period of the Shang dynasty, the system improved and became simpler, which led to the development of a body of Chinese literature. The poem "O Magnificent and Many" is one of 305 poems in a book called the Shih Ching, the earliest known collection of Chinese poetry. No one knows who wrote the poems, but scholars believe they were written by many different poets immediately following the fall of the Shang dynasty, from the 1100s to the 600s B.C. The poems are thought to have been compiled into a book by the influential Chinese teacher Confucius (551–479 B.C.) whose sayings you will read on page 33. The words Shih Ching mean "Classic [Book] of Poetry." The poems were often accompanied by music, but, since the music was not written down, no one knows exactly how they would have sounded. What kind of occasion do you think "O Magnificent and Many" might have been written for? Does the poem name any instruments that are familiar to you?

O magnificent and many:
The tambourines and drums we set up!
A thud and again a thud on them we make,
To delight our glorious ancestors.
It is for the descendant of **T'ang** that we play,
To assure that our ceremony is properly done.
The drumbeats reach far and deep;
Shrill, shrill is the music of the flutes:
Harmonious—ah yes—**concordant**
Together with our **sonorous** chimes of jade.
O grand great is T'ang's descendant;
Lovely and fine the symphony of his!
The bells and the drums are splendid;
The **wan dance** goes on gracefully.
We have a number of welcome guests:
None of them is less delighted than we.
Long since very old in the past,
With ancient people did all this rightly begin:
Be meek and **mindful** by day and night,
Everything we do let it be according to the rule.
May they turn to us and enjoy the offerings,
Which the descendant of T'ang has prepared!

T'ang: ruler who founded the Shang dynasty

concordant: beautiful

sonorous: having a deep, rich sound

wan dance: a formal court dance

mindful: thoughtful

The Shih Ching *marked the beginning of a tradition of poetry in China that has lasted for 3,000 years, and still exists today.*

Source: Wu-Chi Liu and Irving Yucheng Lo, eds., *Sunflower Splendor: Three Thousand Years of Chinese Poetry.* Bloomington: Indiana University Press, 1975.

The Sayings of Confucius

by Confucius, about 500 B.C.

For thousands of years China has been shaped by the values of family loyalty and hard work. A major influence on Chinese civilization has been Confucius (kun FYOO shus), a philosopher and teacher born in 551 B.C. In the hope of preventing wars, Confucius taught that kindness and respect in the family form the foundation of a peaceful society. Confucius stressed that rulers are also obligated to be honest and just. The passages below are some of Confucius's teachings that his students later wrote down. How do the teachings of Confucius still relate to life today?

Having only **coarse** food to eat, plain water to drink, and a bent arm for a pillow, one can still find happiness therein. Riches and honor acquired by **unrighteous** means are to me as drifting clouds.

coarse: simple

unrighteous: unjust

Those who know the truth are not up to those who love it; those who love the truth are not up to those who delight in it.

By nature men are pretty much alike; it is learning and practice that set them apart.

Shall I teach you what knowledge is? When you know a thing, say that you know it; when you do not know a thing, admit that you do not know it. That is knowledge.

Tzu Kung asked: "Is there any one word that can serve as a principle for the conduct of life?" Confucius said: "Perhaps the word '**reciprocity**': Do not do to others what you would not want others to do to you."

The gentleman first practices what he preaches and then preaches what he practices.

The gentleman understands what is right; the inferior man understands what is **profitable**.

The gentleman makes demands on himself; the inferior man makes demands on others.

reciprocity: mutual sharing

A government is good when those near are happy and those far off are attracted.

profitable: money-making

After Confucius died in 479 B.C., his teachings were handed down by others. His ideas about respect and honesty became part of the fabric of Chinese society and spread across Southeast Asia. His teachings remain a major influence throughout much of Asia and the world.

Source: Wm. Theodore de Bary, ed., *Sources of Chinese Tradition*, New York and London: Columbia University Press, 1960.

A Letter from a Han Emperor

by Emperor Wen Ti, about 160 B.C.

Around 200 B.C. China's emperor, Shihuangdi (SHEE hwahng dee), ordered the connection and strengthening of the walls along the northern border of the empire. These walls, like the Great Wall built many centuries later, served as a division from and protection against the people of the northern steppes. In spite of these walls, however, the Chinese sometimes had conflicts with their northern neighbors. The following excerpt is from a letter written by the Han emperor Wen Ti, who ruled China from 179–157 B.C. The letter was sent to the Captain, the leader of the Hsiung-nu (SYUNG NOO) people of the northern steppes. What cultural differences does Wen Ti mention in his letter? Do Wen Ti and the leader of the Hsiung-nu seek a peaceful resolution to their conflict?

We respectfully trust that the great Captain is well. We have respectfully received the two horses which the great Captain forwarded to Us.

The first Emperor of this dynasty adopted the following policy:— All to the north of the Long Wall, comprising the nations of the bow and arrow, to be **subject to** the great Captain: all within the Long Wall—namely, the **families of the hat and girdle**, to be subject to the House of Han. Thus, these peoples would each pursue their own **avocations**,—Ours, agriculture and manufacture of cloth; yours, archery and hunting,—in the acquisition of food and **raiment**. Father and son would not suffer separation; **suzerain** and **vassal** would rest in peace; and neither side would do violence to the other.

But of late We hear that certain worthless persons have been **incited** by the hope of gain to shake off their natural allegiance. **Breaches of** moral obligation and of treaty have occurred. There has been forgetfulness of family ties; and the tranquility of suzerain and vassal is at an end. This, however, belongs to the past. Your letter says, "The two States had become friendly; their rulers friends. The tramp of armies had been stilled for more peaceful occupations, and great joy had come upon successive generations at the new order of things." We truly rejoice over these words. Let us then **tread** together this path of wisdom in due compassion for the peoples committed to our charge. Let us make a fresh start. Let us secure quiet to the aged; and to the young, opportunity to grow up, and, without risk of harm, to **complete their allotted span**.

subject to: ruled by

families of the hat and girdle: people of the Han empire

avocations: occupations

raiment: clothing

suzerain: high-ranking, wealthy noble

vassal: lesser noble

incited: moved to action

Breaches of: breaks in

tread: walk

complete their allotted span: live out their lives

Like many other world leaders, both past and present, Emperor Wen Ti and the Captain worked together to achieve peace, despite their peoples' differences.

Source: Hanscom, Hellerman and Posner, eds., *Voices of the Past: Readings in Ancient History.* The Macmillan Company, 1967.

NEW IDEAS AND NEW EMPIRES

There are mighty monuments of our power which will make us the wonder of this and of succeeding ages.

Pericles, 431 B.C.

The Iliad

by Homer, about the 700s B.C.

More than 3,000 years ago, a rich civilization flourished in ancient Greece. Theater and poetry played an important role in Greek life. The Greeks often gathered at festivals to watch plays and to hear epics, or long poems, that celebrated their history and their many gods and goddesses. The earliest of the Greek poets whose works still survive is Homer, who probably lived between the 9th and 7th centuries B.C. One of Homer's greatest epics, The Iliad, tells about the Trojan War, which Greece fought against Troy in the 12th century B.C. In the excerpt below, the Greek hero Achilles has just learned that his best friend Patroklos has died in battle. What role do Greek gods and goddesses play in The Iliad?

Achilles' goddess-mother heard the sound of his grief as she sat within the depths of the Ocean. She came to him as he was still moaning terribly. She took his hand and clasped it and said, "My child, **why weep'st thou?**" Achilles ceased his moaning and answered, "Patroklos, my dear friend, has been **slain**. Now I shall have no joy in my life save the joy of **slaying** Hector who slew my friend."

Thetis, his goddess-mother, wept when she heard such speech from Achilles. "Shortlived you will be, my son," she said, "for it is **appointed** by the gods that after the death of Hector your death will come."

"**Straightway** then let me die," said Achilles, "since I let my friend die without giving him help. . . . Here I stayed, a useless **burthen** on the earth, while my comrades and my own dear friend fought for their country—here I stayed, I who am the best of all the Greeks. But now let me go into the battle and let the Trojans know that Achilles has come back, although he **tarried** long."

why weep'st thou: why do you cry?

slain: killed

slaying: killing

appointed: decided

straightway: immediately

burthen: burden

tarried: waited

"But **thine** armor, my son," said Thetis. "Thou hast no armor now to protect thee in the battle. Go not into it until thou seest me again. In the morning I shall return and I shall bring thee armor that **Hephaistos**, the **smith** of the gods, shall make for thee."

So she spoke, and she turned from her son, and she went to Olympus where the gods have their **dwellings**. . . .

Now Thetis, the mother of Achilles, went to Olympus where the gods have their dwellings and to the house of Hephaistos, the smith of the gods. That house shone above all the houses on Olympus because Hephaistos himself had made it of shining bronze. . . .

Hephaistos was lame and crooked of foot and went limping. He and Thetis were friends from of old time, for, when his mother would have **forsaken** him because of his crooked foot, Thetis and her sister **reared** him within one of the Ocean's caves and it was while he was with them that he began to work in metals. So the lame god was pleased to see Thetis in his dwelling and he welcomed her and clasped her hand and asked of her what she would have him do for her.

Then Thetis, weeping, told him of her son Achilles, how he had lost his dear friend and how he was moved to go into the battle to fight with Hector, and how he was without armor to protect his life, seeing that the armor that the gods had once given his father was now in the hands of his foe. And Thetis **besought** Hephaistos to make new armor for her son that he might go into the battle.

She no sooner finished speaking than Hephaistos went to his workbench. . . .

For the armor of Achilles he made first a shield and then a **corselet** that gleamed like fire. And he made a strong helmet to go on the head and shining **greaves** to wear on the ankles. The shield was made with five folds, one fold of metal upon the other, so that it was so strong and thick that no spear or arrow could pierce it. And upon this shield he hammered out images that were a wonder to men. . . .

Not long was he in making the shield and the other wonderful pieces of armor. As soon as the armor was ready Thetis put her hands upon it, and flying down from Olympus like a hawk, brought it to the feet of Achilles, her son. . . .

Then Achilles put his shining armor upon him and it fitted him as though it were wings; he put the wonderful shield before him and he took in his hands the great spear that Cheiron the **Centaur** had given to Peleus his father—that spear that no one else but Achilles could wield. He bade his **charioteer** harness the **immortal** horses Xanthos and Balios. Then as he mounted his chariot Achilles spoke to the horses. "Xanthos and Balios," he said, "this time bring the hero that goes with you back safely to the ships, and do not leave him dead on the plain as **ye** left the hero Patroklos."

Then Xanthos the immortal **steed** spoke, answering for himself and his comrade. "Achilles," he said, with his head bowed and his mane touching the ground, "Achilles, for this time we will bring thee safely

thine: your

Hephaistos: Greek god of fire
smith: one who makes metal objects
dwellings: homes

forsaken: abandoned
reared: raised

besought: begged

corselet: armor for the upper body
greaves: armor for the leg below the knee

centaur: creature that is half-human, half-horse
charioteer: driver of a chariot, or carriage
immortal: godlike

ye: you
steed: horse

37

back from the battle. But a day will come when we shall not bring thee back, when thou too shalt lie with the dead before the walls of Troy."

Then was Achilles troubled and he said, "Xanthos, my steed, why dost thou remind me by thy **prophecies** of what I know already—that my death too is appointed, and that I am to **perish** here, far from my father and my mother and my own land."

prophecies: predictions

perish: die

Then he drove his immortal horses into the battle. The Trojans were **affrighted** when they saw Achilles himself in the fight, blazing in the armor that Hephaistos had made for him. They went backward before his **onset**. And Achilles shouted to the captains of the Greeks, "No longer stand apart from the men of Troy, but go with me into the battle and let each man throw his whole soul into the fight."

affrighted: frightened

onset: attack

And on the Trojan side Hector cried to his captains and said, "Do not let Achilles drive you before him. Even though his hands are as irresistible as fire and his fierceness as terrible as flashing steel, I shall go against him and face him with my spear." . . .

And when Achilles saw Hector before him he cried out, "Here is the man who most deeply wounded my soul, who slew my dear friend Patroklos. Now shall we two fight each other and Patroklos shall be **avenged** by me." And he shouted to Hector, "Now Hector, the day of thy triumph and the day of thy life is at its end."

avenged: revenged

But Hector answered him without fear, "Not with words, Achilles, can you affright me. Yet I know that thou art a man of might and a stronger man than I. But the fight between us depends upon the will of the gods. I shall do my best against thee, and my spear before this has been found to have a dangerous edge."

He spoke and lifted up his spear and flung it at Achilles. Then the breath of a god turned Hector's spear aside, for it was not appointed that either he or Achilles should be then slain. Achilles darted at Hector to slay him with his spear. But a god hid Hector from Achilles in a thick mist. . . .

Then on toward the City, [Achilles] went like a fire raging through a **glen** that had been **parched** with heat. Now on a tower of the walls of Troy, Priam the old King stood, and he saw the Trojans coming in a **rout** toward the City, and he saw Achilles in his armor blazing like a star—like that star that is seen at harvest time and is called Orion's Dog; the star that is the brightest of all stars, but yet is a sign of evil. And the old man Priam sorrowed greatly as he stood upon the tower and watched Achilles, because he knew in his heart whom this man would slay—Hector, his son, the protector of his City.

glen: valley
parched: burned dry
rout: retreat

In a later battle Achilles killed the Trojan leader Hector. But, just as the gods had predicted, Achilles was also killed in battle, the result of a wound from a Trojan arrow. After many long years of warfare, the Greeks finally defeated the Trojans. For hundreds of years, the Greeks retold the story of the battles, gods, and heroes described in The Iliad. *Today this epic poem remains one of the greatest works of literature ever written.*

Source: Padraic Colum, *The Children's Homer.* New York: Macmillan Publishing Company, 1982.

HOW THE CITY OF ATHENS GOT ITS NAME

by Navidad O'Neill, 1996

Cultures create myths or traditional stories that express a belief, often about the world around them. Like most myths, ancient Greek myths centered around gods and goddesses. The Greeks believed their gods and goddesses lived on Mount Olympus, watching over the humans below. We know that the city of Athens was named for Athena, the goddess of wisdom, who was also known as a protector of cities. The following play is a myth that tells how the city of Athens might have gotten its name. Can you think of other ways the city could have chosen a name?

CAST OF CHARACTERS

Clio: the storyteller of history
Alpha: one Greek chorus (4–8 students)
Omega: another Greek chorus (4–8 students)
Athena: goddess of wisdom
Poseidon: god of the sea
Athenians: the Alpha and Omega choruses together

Clio: Once, many, many years ago—about two thousand five hundred years ago—there lived a people we now call the ancient Greeks. The ancient Greeks lived a sea away from ancient Africa and a mountain and a sea away from ancient Persia. And over 5,000 miles away from

39

North America. Now the ancient Greeks loved two things above all: cities and stories. So I, Clio, an ancient Greek storyteller known as a muse, will a-*muse* you with a story about the people of a city by the sea—with a little help from my friends…

Enter Alpha and Omega choruses, squabbling with one another. (Chorus parts are spoken.)

Clio: Or what we now call, a Greek Chorus.

Chorus members clear their throats in dismay.

Clio: I mean, two Greek Choruses.

Alpha Chorus: We are divided.

Omega Chorus: We can't agree.

Alpha: We live in a city.

Omega: We live by the sea.

Alpha: The still and blue Aegean Sea.

Omega: The gigantic, great, gray, stormy sea.

Alpha: But we don't have a name for our city by the sea.

Omega: We are citizens of the rocks, of the sand, of the sea.

Alpha: We could call our city Alpha, after the first letter in the alphabet.

Omega: We could call it Omega, after the last letter in the alphabet.

Alpha: But that's rather dull. You must admit.

Omega: If we were smart, we would name our city after one of the Olympian gods or goddesses and receive special protection.

Alpha: We're smart.

Clio: The Olympians were the most important gods and goddesses worshiped by the ancient Greeks, including the people of the city by the sea. The Greeks believed that the Olympians lived on Mount Olympus.

Now these Olympians each ruled over a different aspect of Greek life. For instance, Apollo was the god of music and light; Artemis was the goddess of the hunt. If you wanted to protect your home, you might give praise to Hestia, the goddess of the hearth. If you were a warrior, you might ask for the protection of the god of war—Ares. If you wanted help finding a boyfriend or girlfriend, you might seek the help of Aphrodite, the goddess of love.

Clio: But our story today is about two of the greatest Olympians: Athena and Poseidon.

Enter Athena.

Clio: Athena was goddess of wisdom. At her side she carried an owl, as a symbol of wisdom.

Enter Poseidon.

Clio: Poseidon was the god of the sea. He carried a trident, or three-pointed spear. Both were very powerful—and both wanted to be the protector of the new city on the rocky coast of Greece.

Alpha: We want Athena. Wisdom is the most important of all virtues. If we are a wise city, we will be an important city.

Omega: We want Poseidon. From the sea we get our food and our means of travel. He will make us a strong city.

Alpha: Athena!

Omega: Poseidon!

Alpha: Athena!

Omega: Poseidon!

Clio: What if you stage a contest?

Alpha and Omega: A contest?

Clio: A contest to determine who would make the better protector of the city.

Alpha and Omega: What would the contest be?

Clio: What if you ask Athena and Poseidon each for a gift? Then decide who shall be the protector by who gives the city the better gift.

Alpha and Omega: Presents! That will help us make a decision—and we get presents!!!

Alpha: *(simultaneously with Omega)* Although we still think Athena will be the better protector.

Omega: (*simultaneously with Alpha*) Although we still think Poseidon will be the better protector.

Exit Alpha and Omega choruses.

Clio: And so a contest was held.

Athena and Poseidon arm wrestle. They struggle through the following lines, while they are at a stalemate, with neither side winning.

Athena: These people need wisdom.

Poseidon: These people need the gifts of the sea.

Athena: Without wisdom, they could not learn how to fish.

Poseidon: Without fish to eat, they would not have the energy to think and be wise.

Clio: This isn't the kind of contest the people of the city by the sea had in mind. Do you remember the gift they asked from each of you?

Athena and Poseidon: Ah, yes, the gift!

Clio: So Athena and Poseidon went away to think.

Poseidon: To fish. I do my best thinking when I fish.

Clio: So Athena and Poseidon went away to think and fish.

Exit Athena and Poseidon.

Enter Alpha and Omega choruses.

Alpha: What will they bring us?

Omega: What do we need?

Alpha: Something gold, perhaps. Hurry, Athena!

Omega: Something gigantic, I hope. Hurry, Poseidon!

Alpha and Omega: Let us go to the Acropolis and wait.

Clio: The Acropolis was a huge rock to the north of the city, where the people of the city by the sea would gather. The people went to the Acropolis and waited. Poseidon arrived first.

Enter Poseidon.

Poseidon: I have prepared my gift.

Clio: And then Poseidon banged his trident three times on the rock of the Acropolis and a spring of water poured forth.

Alpha: AHHHHH! This is truly wonderful! Water is the most important resource of any city.

Omega: All praise Poseidon, god of our fair city! We shall call ourselves Poseidonians in your honor.

The smallest member of the Alpha Chorus: But this water is salty! We cannot drink it.

Alpha: It is. It is salty.

Omega: What can we do with a spring of salt water? We cannot even sail upon it.

Alpha: Look, here comes Athena, goddess of wisdom!

Enter Athena.

Clio: Athena knelt down and made mysterious motions with her hands. Suddenly, out from between the rocks sprang forth an olive tree.

Alpha: It is small, this tree, but look at its fruit.

Athena: The fruits are called "olives."

Omega: We could press the olives and make oil. With the oil we could cook. With the oil we could light our lamps.

Alpha: And we could sell the oil to others to light their lamps and cook their food.

The smallest member of the Alpha Chorus: It would be very tasty in salad, too, don't you think?

Alpha: Athena! You shall be our protector.

Omega: We shall name our great city after you.

Alpha: It will be called Athens.

Omega: A place where democracy and art, poetry and drama, philosophy and mathematics, medicine and history will all flourish.

Alpha: And we will call ourselves, who live here, Athenians.

The Alpha and Omega choruses become one chorus of Athenians.

The smallest member of the Alpha Chorus: Athenians is a much better description than "people of the city by the sea."

Clio: And the Athenians built a great temple to Athena right on the very rocks of the Acropolis. This temple is called the Parthenon.

Athena: And I shall do my part by guarding over your city. However, you must learn to be a patient people, for this tree takes several years to bear fruit. But if you do have faith, you will be rewarded, for this tree will not grow in rich farmland but only in the poor rocky soil where you make your home.

Athenians: And we shall be known as a great civilization for many, many years to come.

Athena: And whenever people tell stories of your history, they will mention the olive tree. For besides giving you food and light, its branch held aloft shall be a universal sign of peace. And by the olive branch, Athens shall be known.

Athena begins to exit, waving.

Athenians: Peace to you, Athena.

Athena: And peace to you, old man of the sea.

Poseidon: Peace to you, Athena, and your Athenians.

Athena and Poseidon exit waving, while the Athenians stay and wave at the audience.

THE END

The name "Athens" has served the city well through the years. Athens was the center of the ancient Greek civilization, and it still stands today as the capital of modern Greece.

The Birds

by Aristophanes, 414 B.C.

The ancient Greeks often held celebrations, or festivals. Plays, both funny and serious, were an important part of these festivals. Aristophanes (ar uh STOF uh neez) (about 450–388 B.C.) was an Athenian writer famous for his comedies. He was an expert in a special kind of comedy, called satire, that uses humor to criticize people and their actions. Those who attended a performance of The Birds in Aristophanes' day would have recognized the bird characters as people, sometimes important government leaders of Athens. Why might Aristophanes have disguised his characters as birds? In The Birds, Aristophanes was protesting Athens's war with Sicily. A peace seeker, Pisthetairos (pihs tay TĪ rohs), persuades the birds (who stand for ideal Athenians) to build a perfect walled city in the sky between Heaven and Earth. The birds (Athenians) could get over the wall, but humans (Sicilians) could not. What images come to mind as you read this excerpt describing how the wall was built?

SCENE

[*Reenter* PISTHETAIROS *with his attendants*]

PISTHETAIROS: The **omens** are favorable, I'm glad to say. Strange that we've had no news about the wall.—But here comes a messenger now, puffing like an Olympic sprinter.

[*Enter* FIRST MESSENGER, *wildly*]

MESSENGER: Where is he? Where is he? Where is he?

PISTHETAIROS: Where is who?

MESSENGER: The Chief. Pisthetairos.

PISTHETAIROS: Here.

MESSENGER: Great news! Great news! Your Wall is finished!

PISTHETAIROS: That *is* great news.

MESSENGER: Oh how shall I describe the splendor of that Wall, the [incredible] hugeness? Take two chariots, hitch four fat Wooden Horses to each one, let [two drivers] meet head-on—, they'd pass each other without a scratch. It's that big.

omens: signs from the gods and goddesses

PISTHETAIROS: Holy **Heraklês**!

MESSENGER: And tall? Look, I measured it myself: it stands six hundred feet!

PISTHETAIROS: Merciful **Poseidon**! What workmen could build a wall as high as that?

MESSENGER: Birds, only birds. Not a single Egyptian **hodcarrier** or stonemason or carpenter in the gang; birds did it all, and my eyes are popping yet. Imagine thirty thousand Cranes from **Libya**, each one with a belly full of stones for the **Rails** to shape up with their beaks; ten thousand Storks, at least, all of them making bricks with clay and water flown up by **Curlews** from the earth below.

PISTHETAIROS: **Mortar**?

PISTHETAIROS: **Herons** with **hods**.

PISTHETAIROS: How did they manage it?

MESSENGER: *That* was a triumph of technology! The Geese shoveled it up with their big feet.

PISTHETAIROS: Ah feet, to what use can **ye** not be put!

MESSENGER: Why, good Lord! There were Ducks to set the bricks, and flights of little apprentice Swallows with **trowel** tails for the mortar in their bills.

PISTHETAIROS: Who wants hired labor after this?—But the **joists** and beams?

MESSENGER: All handled by birds. When the Woodpeckers went to work on those **portals** it sounded like a shipyard!—So there's your Wall, complete with gates and locks, watchfires burning, patrols circling, the guard changed every hour. But I must wash off this long trek of mine. You'll know what to do next.

[*Exit* FIRST MESSENGER]

KORYPHAIOS (kor IHF ī ohs): Surprises you, hey? That quick job on your Wall?

PISTHETAIROS: Surprises me? Why, it's a lie come true!

The wall blocks the people of Sicily from communicating with their gods and makes them surrender. The play ends with a victory for the Athenians. Aristophanes wrote 55 plays altogether. Eleven of them have survived and are still performed today. One of them, The Clouds, makes fun of the philosopher Socrates.

Source: Dudley Fitts, translator, *Aristophanes*. Harcourt, Brace & World, Inc., 1959 and 1962.

Heraklês: Hercules, a very powerful Greek god

Poseidon: Greek god of the sea

hodcarrier: stone carrier

Libya: country in northern Africa

Rails: small marsh birds

Curlews: long-legged birds

Mortar: material containing cement, used in building walls

Herons: long-necked wading birds

hods: trays for carrying stones or mortar

ye: you

trowel: tool for spreading mortar

joists: beams used to support a floor or ceiling

portals: gates or other entrances

Funeral Speech for Athenian Heroes

by Pericles, 431 B.C.

The Greek leader Pericles (PER ih kleez) (about 495–429 B.C.) helped to make the government of Athens open to all citizens. Although only free men were considered citizens, Pericles worked to ensure that both rich and poor alike could participate and share in the responsibilities of leadership. This form of government developed into what we call a democracy. Leaders were chosen for their talents and skills, not because of their wealth. This selection is from a speech given by Pericles at a public funeral for the Athenian men who died in a war against Sparta in 431 B.C. It was written down by the historian Thucydides (thoo SIHD ih deez) who lived about the same time as Pericles. What does Pericles think about his government and his city? Why is this funeral an appropriate time for him to speak about the government and way of life in Athens?

Our form of government does not enter into rivalry with the institutions of others. We do not copy our neighbors, but are an example to them. It is true that we are called a democracy, for the **administration** is in the hands of the many and not of the few. But while the law secures equal justice to all alike in their private **disputes**, the claim of excellence is also recognized. When a citizen is in any way **distinguished**, he is preferred to the public service, not as a matter of privilege, but as the reward of merit. Even poverty is not a **bar**, but a

administration: government

disputes: disagreements

distinguished: famous for significant achievements

bar: block

man may benefit his country whatever be **the obscurity of his condition**....

And we have not forgotten to provide for our weary spirits many relaxations from **toil**. We have regular games and sacrifices throughout the year. At home the style of our life is refined; and the delight which we daily feel in all these things helps to banish **melancholy**. Because of the greatness of our city the fruits of the whole earth flow in upon us; so that we enjoy the goods of other countries as freely as of our own.

Then, again, our military training is in many respects superior to that of our **adversaries**. Our city is thrown open to the world, and we never **expel** a foreigner or prevent him from seeing or learning anything of which the secret if **revealed** to an enemy might profit him. We rely, not upon management or trickery, but upon our own hearts and hands. And in the matter of education, whereas **they** from early youth are always undergoing laborious exercises which are to make them brave, we live at ease, and yet are equally ready to face the **perils** which they face....

...An Athenian citizen does not neglect the state because he takes care of his own household; and even those of us who are engaged in business have a very fair idea of politics. We alone regard a man who takes no interest in public affairs, not as a harmless but as a useless character. If few of us are **originators**, we are all sound judges, of a policy. The great **impediment** to action is, in our opinion, not discussion, but the **want** of that knowledge which is gained by discussion preparatory to action.... To sum up: I say that Athens is the school of **Hellas**, and that the individual Athenian in his own person seems to have the power of adapting himself to the most varied forms of action with the **utmost versatility** and grace.... And we shall **assuredly** not be without witnesses; there are mighty monuments of our power which will make us the wonder of this and of succeeding ages.... Such is the city for whose sake these men nobly fought and died. They could not bear the thought that she might be taken from them; and every one of us who survive should gladly toil on her behalf.

the obscurity of his condition: his family origins

toil: hard work

melancholy: sadness

adversaries: enemies
expel: force out
revealed: shown

they: Spartans

perils: dangers

originators: lawmakers
impediment: block
want: lack

Hellas: Greece

utmost versatility: great ease
assuredly: definitely

Pericles concluded the speech with his belief that it was worthwhile for the citizens of Athens to work, fight, and give their lives, if necessary, for their city. Pericles took great pride in his city, its people, and its democracy. You may have heard United States government leaders make similar remarks about our country.

Source: Hanscom, Hellerman and Posner, eds., *Voices of the Past: Readings in Ancient History*. The Macmillan Company, 1967.

THE AENEID

by Virgil, 19 B.C.

The Roman empire left many great monuments, such as the Colosseum, giant aqueducts, and stone roads. But one of Rome's greatest monuments is not a building at all. It is an exciting epic called the Aeneid (ih NEE ihd). This epic, written by the poet Virgil around 19 B.C., is a grand adventure story about the history of Rome. The Aeneid is based on a mythical Trojan character called Aeneas who is half-god and half-man. After the Trojan War, which Homer described in The Iliad on pages 36–38, Aeneas sees a star in the sky and begins a long journey at sea, in hopes of founding a new kingdom. In the excerpt below, Aeneas arrives in Sicily, an island located in the Mediterranean Sea in southern Italy. What do the sporting events that Aeneas orders upon his arrival reveal about some of the values held by people in ancient Rome?

So they shifted their course, and let their ships run before the wind, and came in a very short time to the island of Sicily. Now Acestes, the king of the country, was the son of a Trojan woman. He had before entertained Aeneas and his people very kindly, and now, when he saw their ships coming toward the land, for he happened to be standing on the top of a hill, he was very glad, and he **made haste** to meet them. He came to the shore, having a lion's skin about his shoulders, and carrying a spear in his hand. He greeted them with many words of kindness, and sent a supply of food and drink to the ships.

made haste: hurried

The next day, early in the morning, Aeneas called all the Trojans to an assembly, and said to them: "My friends, it is a full year since we buried my dear father in this land of Sicily; yes, if I remember right, this is the very day. Let us keep it holy therefore. . . . And if the ninth day from this be fair, then we will have great games in honor of my dear father. There shall be a contest of ships, and running in a race, and games of throwing the **javelin**, and of shooting with the bow, and of boxing. . . ."

javelin: spear

And now the ninth day came, and the weather was fine. There came great crowds of people to see the games. . . . Many came to see the Trojans, and many for the sake of the games, desiring to win the prizes if they might. First the prizes were put **in the midst** for all to see. There were crowns of palm, and swords, and spears, and purple garments, and **talents** of gold and silver. . . .

in the midst: in plain view

talents: coins

For [the foot race] there came many, both Trojans and men of Sicily. . . . Aeneas said: "I will give gifts to all who run; none shall go away empty. To the first three I will give crowns of olive. The first also shall have a horse with its **trappings**; the second a **quiver** full of arrows, and a belt with which to fasten it; the third must be content with a Greek helmet."

trappings: saddle and harness

quiver: case for holding arrows

Then all the men stood in a line, and when the signal was given they started. For a short time they were all close together. Then Nisus outran the rest. Next to him came Salius, but there was a long space between them; and next to Salius was Euryalus. The fourth was one of the king's **courtiers**, Helymus by name, and close behind him the Trojan Diores. When they had nearly come to the end of the course, by bad luck Nisus slipped in the blood of an ox which had been **slain** in the place, and fell. But as he lay on the ground he did not forget his friend Euryalus, for he lifted himself from the ground just as Salius came running in, and tripped him up. So Euryalus had the first place, Helymus was second, and Diores third. But Salius loudly complained that he had been cheated. "I had won the first prize," he cried, "had not this Nisus tripped me up." But the people favored Euryalus, for he was a **comely lad**; Diores also was on the same side, for otherwise he had not won the third prize. "Then," said Aeneas, "I will not change the order; let them take the prizes as they come—Euryalus the first, Helymus the second, and Diores the third. Nevertheless I will have pity on the man who suffered not from his own fault." And he gave to Salius a lion's skin, of which the **mane** and the claws were covered with gold. . . .

courtiers: attendants

slain: killed

comely lad: handsome boy

mane: long hair on the neck

Next to this came the trial of shooting with the bow. Aeneas set up the mast of a ship, and to the top of the mast he tied a dove by a cord. This was the mark at which all were to shoot. The first hit the mast, and shook it, and all could see how the bird fluttered his wings. Then the second shot. He did not touch the bird, but he cut the string by which it was fastened to the mast, and the bird flew away. Then the third, a man of Lycia, aimed at the bird itself, and struck it as it flew, and the dove fell dead to the earth with the arrow through it. Last of all King Acestes shot his arrow. And he, having nothing at which to aim, shot it high into the air, to show how strong a bow he had and how he could draw it. Then there happened a strange thing to see. The arrow, as it went higher and higher in the air, was seen to catch fire, and leave a line of flame behind it, till it was burned up. When Aeneas saw this, he said to himself: "This is a sign of good to come," for he thought how the fire had burned on the head of his son Ascanius, and how a star had shot through the air when he was about to fly from Troy. And as this had been a sign of good at the beginning of his wanderings, so was this a sign of good at the end.

After many more adventures, Aeneas helps to unite the people of Italy and Troy. This union, according to the Aeneid, gave birth to the civilization of Rome. Many people consider the Aeneid to be the greatest work of Roman literature.

Source: Alfred J. Church, *The Aeneid for Boys and Girls*. New York: The Macmillan Company, 1962.

The Eruption of Mount Vesuvius

by Pliny the Younger, A.D. 79

In A.D. 79 Mount Vesuvius, located about seven miles from Naples, Italy, erupted, burying the smaller cities of Pompeii (pahm PAY) and Herculaneum under many feet of mud and volcanic ash. In Pompeii alone, about 2,000 people were killed. A writer named Pliny (PLIHN ee) the Younger (about A.D. 61–113) survived the eruption and wrote letters to the historian Tacitus (TA sih tus) telling about it. As you read this excerpt from one of Pliny's letters, think about the factors that made escape difficult. How are we better prepared to cope with natural disasters today?

For several days before the eruption there had been earth **tremors**, which had not caused much alarm, since they often happen in the Naples area. But that night they were so strong that they not **merely** shook but overturned everything. My mother came running to my bedroom just as I was going to go to awaken her....

tremors: shaking

merely: only

It was now six o'clock in the morning, the daylight still faint and doubtful. The buildings around us were ready to collapse, and so the narrow space where we were was very dangerous. We therefore decided that we must get out of the town. We were followed by a panic-stricken mob of poor people, who pushed us forward by pressing behind us....A black and horrible cloud belching streamers of fiery snakelike **vapors** split apart every so often to reveal great flaming forms, like lightning but much larger....

vapors: gases

Soon the cloud began to descend upon the earth and cover the sea....My mother began to beg me to escape as best I could. She said that a young man could do it, while she, slowed by age and weight, would die happily if only she knew that she had not caused my death by her delaying me. I replied that I would not be saved without her and, taking her by the hand, urged her forward. Ashes now fell upon us, thick darkness came rolling over the land like a flood. "Let us leave the road," I said, "while we can still see, so as not to be knocked down and trampled to death in the dark by the crowd behind us."...You could hear the screams of women, the cries of children, the shouts of men....Many raised their hands to **appeal** to the gods, but more believed that the gods, too, had **perished**, and that the end of the world had come....

appeal: make an earnest request

perished: died

Pliny and his mother were among the lucky ones who escaped. Mount Vesuvius is still an active volcano, last erupting in 1944. Scientists record the temperature at the mouth of Mount Vesuvius every day, since rising temperatures often give warning of an upcoming eruption. Modern archeologists are gradually uncovering Pompeii and Herculaneum. Large portions of the cities are still intact and give us a clear idea of everyday life there.

Source: Hanscom, Hellerman and Posner, eds., *Voices of the Past: Readings in Ancient History.* The Macmillan Company, 1967.

A Craftsman in Bethlehem

by Avram Hissan, 1981

Almost 2,000 years ago a Jewish woman named Mary gave birth to a son in Bethlehem, a town that still exists in Israel today. Mary's son was named Jesus. According to the New Testament of the Bible, Jesus grew up in the town of Nazareth and practiced the religion of Judaism. When he was about 30 years old, Jesus started preaching. As he traveled from village to village, he stressed that love for God required showing love for other people. Jesus won many followers, who called him the Messiah, a term for a special leader sent by God to guide the Jewish people and set up God's rule on Earth. These followers of Jesus began a new religion called Christianity. Avram Hissan is a Christian who lives in Bethlehem. In the excerpt below, Hissan expresses his love for his town and his job. How does Christianity shape his life?

This is a magic city. It's a quiet and friendly town—not so quiet at Christmas, Easter and festivals, when thousands of pilgrims from all over the world pour into our city. Its link with the Jewish people began nearly 4,000 years ago when Jacob, passing through the town, lost his young wife Rachel in childbirth. Bethlehem today has a population of 32,000—mainly Christian Arabs with professions. Many of them are gold smiths, skilled in carving. Every visitor is attracted to the Church of the Nativity, traditionally the birthplace of Jesus, where Mary gave birth and laid the child in the manger because there was no room for him in the inn. The Church of the Nativity is one of the holiest shrines **in Christendom.**

in Christendom: among Christian worshipers

For many generations now we've sold articles carved in olive wood and also goods made of mother-of-pearl. They are the most sought-after goods in Bethlehem, extremely popular with the tourists. The olive-wood industry is famous here. We have our own factory beneath our store where we make all kinds of figures and nativity sets. The majority of the olive-wood goods sold in the store are made on the premises.

We call olive wood the holy wood. We carve very large pieces too—large manager sets are bought and taken all over the world, especially at Christmas time.

Thank God, without religion we cannot live. I pray in St. Mary's Church in Bethlehem. Our services are held in the **Aramaic** language in our churches all over the world. This was the language of the Lord Our Saviour, and of our **Prophets**, Abraham, Isaac and Jacob.

I work in the store every day from 8 o'clock [in the morning] until 7 or 8 o'clock in the evening. On Sundays I go to church in the morning and then go to work. I like to take vacations, but only a day at a time. I usually go with my brother George. I like to go in and around Bethlehem, sometimes to King Solomon's Pools. This is one of our main beauty spots; it's fertile and the pool is spring-fed. . . . It was erected some 500 years ago, and is now ringed by a well-grown pine forest. These great open reservoirs form a green and beautiful park, an ideal picnic spot.

I also like to go to Jericho and to the Dead Sea where the climate is much warmer and drier than here. I'm very much a family man and I enjoy staying at home in the evenings with my family; so many friends come in to visit us and, of course, business people, mainly from the United States.

Christians and Moslems live together in Bethlehem. We have very good relations with the Jews; we have lived together now for fourteen years. We are happy and we hope for peace in the future.

Christianity spread rapidly throughout the Roman empire and much of Europe. It also spread into Africa and Asia. Europeans later introduced Christianity to other parts of the world. Today nearly 2 billion people—or almost one in three people in the world—are Christians. To learn about another important religion that emerged in western Asia, read the document on pages 56–57.

Source: Gemma Levine, *We Live in Israel*. New York: The Bookwright Press, 1983.

Aramaic: ancient language used widely in the Middle East from 600 B.C. to A.D. 800

prophets: persons who deliver messages believed to be from God

Theodora's Bravery

by Procopius, about A.D. 550

After the decline of the western Roman empire in the A.D. 400s, the Eastern Roman or Byzantine empire lived on for another 1,000 years. Justinian (483–565) became the most famous emperor of the Byzantine empire. He is best known for organizing the Roman laws under one code, called the Body of Civil Law. Also known as the Justinian Code, his work provided the basis for the legal systems of France, Germany, Italy, Russia, and Serbia until the 1800s. Justinian's wife, Theodora, was a famous actress who ruled along with him from the time he rose to the throne in 527 until her death in 548. The following selection, recorded by the historian Procopius, describes a scene that took place in Justinian's court in Constantinople in 532. Two rival groups of soldiers, called the Greens and the Blues, had banded together and were threatening to overthrow Justinian's rule. As you read, consider how a single decision, such as the one written about in this selection, may affect many thousands of people. Can you think of other women in history who have had important, decision-making roles?

At this time an **insurrection** broke out unexpectedly in **Byzantium** among the **populace**, and, contrary to expectation, it proved to be a very serious affair....

Now the emperor and his court were **deliberating** as to whether it would be better for them if they remained or if they took to flight in ships. And many opinions were expressed favoring either course. And the Empress Theodora also spoke to the following effect: "As to the belief that a woman ought not to be daring among men or to **assert** herself boldly among those who are holding back from fear, I consider that the present crisis most certainly does not permit us to discuss whether the matter should be regarded in this or some other way.... My opinion then is that the present time... is **inopportune** for flight.... For while it is impossible for a man who has seen the light not also to die, for one who has been an emperor it is unendurable to be a **fugitive**. May I never be separated from this **purple**.... If, now, it is your wish to save yourself, O Emperor, there is no difficulty. For we have much money, and there is the sea, here the boats.... As for myself, I approve a certain ancient saying that the royal purple is a good **burial-shroud**." When the queen had spoken thus, all were filled with boldness, and, turning their thoughts towards resistance, they began to consider how they might be able to defend themselves....

insurrection: rebellion

Byzantium: Constantinople

populace: people

deliberating: carefully deciding

assert: express

inopportune: not the right time

fugitive: person who flees from danger

purple: color symbolizing royalty

burial-shroud: cloth used to wrap a dead body

The emperor and his court took Theodora's advice. Justinian's forces were victorious, crushing the rebellion at Constantinople.

Source: Hanscom, Hellerman and Posner, eds., *Voices of the Past: Readings in Ancient History.* The Macmillan Company, 1967.

A Description of Constantinople

by Benjamin of Tudela, about 1165

Emperor Constantine, who ruled the Roman empire from A.D. 306 to 337, decided to move his capital from Rome to the city of Byzantium. He spent a great deal of money enlarging and improving Byzantium, and in 330 the city was renamed "New Rome." Most people, however, called it Constantinople, "the city of Constantine." A later emperor, Justinian, whom you read about on page 54, loved architecture and filled the city of Constantinople with beautiful palaces, churches, and public arenas. Of the many churches, St. Sophia, completed in 537 was known as the most beautiful. Another impressive building was the Hippodrome, a stadium that seated 40,000 people. Besides Christmas celebrations, there were circuses and sports, including chariot races, for people to watch. Read this excerpt from the writings of a traveler from Spain. In what ways might life in Constantinople be different from life in a smaller, less wealthy city?

The **circumference of** the city of Constantinople is eighteen miles....Great stir and bustle **prevails** at Constantinople in consequence of the **conflux** of many merchants, who resort **thither**, both by land and by sea, from all parts of the world for purposes of trade....In this respect the city is equalled only by Baghdad, the **metropolis** of the **Muhammadans**. At Constantinople is the place of worship called St. Sophia, and the metropolitan seat of the pope of the Greeks, who are **at variance** with the pope of Rome. It contains as many altars as there are days of the year, and possesses **innumerable** riches, which are **augmented** every year by the contributions of the two islands and of the **adjacent** towns and villages. All the other places of worship in the whole world do not equal St. Sophia in riches. It is ornamented with pillars of gold and silver, and with innumerable lamps of the same precious materials. The Hippodrome is a public place near the wall of the palace, set aside for the king's sports. Every year the birthday of Jesus **the Nazarene** is celebrated there with public rejoicings. On these occasions you may see there **representations** of all the nations who inhabit the different parts of the world....

The **tribute** which is brought to Constantinople every year from all parts of Greece, consisting of silks, and purple cloths, and gold, fills many towers. These riches and buildings are equalled nowhere in the world.

circumference of: distance around

prevails: is most common

conflux: coming together

thither: there

metropolis: city

Muhammadans: Muslims

at variance: in disagreement

innumerable: countless

augmented: increased

adjacent: nearby

the Nazarene: of Nazareth

representations: representatives

tribute: tax

Constantinople was conquered in 1453 by the Ottomans, who followed the Islamic faith. The church of St. Sophia still stands today, as an Islamic museum. After World War I the name of the city was changed to Istanbul.

Source: Hanscom, Hellerman and Posner, eds., *Voices of the Past: Readings in Medieval and Early Modern History.* The Macmillan Company, 1967.

Pilgrimage to Mecca
by Samaan bin Jabir Al Nasaib, 1987

During the seventh century a major religion called Islam emerged in the Middle East. According to Islamic faith, around A.D. 610 an Arab merchant named Muhammad heard a voice tell him that there is only one God—for which the Arabic word is Allah—and that he, Muhammad, was Allah's messenger. Followers of Muhammad's teachings became known as Muslims, or "followers of Islam." After Muhammad's death these teachings were gathered into a book called the Quran (Kaw RAN). The Quran is believed by Muslims to be the teachings of God. The Quran teaches that Muhammad is the last in the line of prophets, or people who deliver a message believed to be from God. Muslims believe that earlier prophets were Abraham, Moses, and Jesus. One of the duties that all Muslims try to fulfill at least once in their lives is to make a journey to the city of Mecca, the birthplace of Muhammad. What is this journey like? In the following selection from an oral history, a Muslim from Saudi Arabia named Samaan bin Jabir Al Nasaib describes his recent pilgrimage to Mecca. What are some of the rituals that Jabir Al Nasaib performs during his pilgrimage? How do these rituals relate to his religious beliefs?

My family traces its **descent** from the oldest of the tribes of this part of the world. Some say that we can trace our heritage back to Adam. Whether or not this is so, we have been landowners and **sheikhs** in the **Wadi Najran** for as long as anybody can remember. We grow corn, wheat and citrus fruit here.

I suppose the high spot of my life was performing the Hajj [hahj] in the company of my son Maana. The Hajj is the name we give to the pilgrimage that Muslims make to Mecca, to the Holy Kaaba [KAH buh], Abraham's "House of God." This pilgrimage is one of the "five pillars of Islam," the other four being the belief in one God, prayer five times a day, the giving of **alms** and fasting during the holy month of Ramadan. What a proud and spiritually rewarding moment it was for me to make my seven rounds of the Kaaba with my son beside me!

The Hajj requires great physical stamina as well as religious **zeal**. The Hajjis, as pilgrims are called, must all wear a special garment consisting of two white lengths of cotton, without seams, emphasizing the equality of all men in the sight of God. We put the garment on at the start of our journey, after ritual washing and prayer.

On arrival in Mecca, after further washing and prayer, the pilgrims go directly to the Kaaba and circle it seven times in an anti-clockwise

descent: origins

sheikhs: Arab leaders
Wadi Najran: region in southwest Saudi Arabia

alms: aid to the poor

zeal: enthusiasm

direction. On passing the Black Stone, they should try either to kiss it or at least touch it. This stone is a meteorite and is traditionally held to be a link between the Prophet **Mohammed**, Abraham and Adam.

Mohammed: Muhammad

After the duties of the Kaaba, pilgrims are required to run between two hills, Al Safa and Al Marwah, which both have links with Abraham's wife, Hagar. While doing this they are praying all the while. Pilgrims may then drink from the spring of Zam Zam, which is referred to in the Old Testament [of the Bible]. Male pilgrims then have their heads shaved, or more commonly today, their hair cut.

Now follows a visit to Mount Arafat, where Mohammed gave his farewell sermon. A whole afternoon is spent in the open air, on the Plain of Arafat, standing bareheaded, glorifying God and reading the **Koran**.

Koran: Quran

Crowds of pilgrims spend the night under the stars at Musdalifah, and each collects seventy small pebbles. Then they make their way to Mina, the end of the journey, where there are three stone pillars. Seven of the pebbles are then cast at the pillars, an act symbolic of mankind casting out the evil from within. Then animals are sacrificed and the meat given to the poor. Before returning home, the pilgrims throw the remaining pebbles at the pillars.

The pilgrimage ends after a final symbolic cutting of hair. Some pilgrims take this opportunity of going on to Medina, where they can visit the Tomb of Mohammed, and the Prophet's **Mosque**.

mosque: Islamic house of worship

Back on my farm in the Wadi Najran, I often remember those privileged days I spent in Mecca.

Today over 1 billion people—or about one in six people in the world—are Muslims. Judaism, Christianity, and Islam all emerged in western Asia. Thousands of miles to the east, two other major religions also developed long ago. To learn more about these other two religions, read the documents on pages 26–27 and 30–31.

Source: Abdul Latif Al Hoad, *We Live in Saudi Arabia.* New York: The Bookwright Press, 1987.

An Islamic Hospital

by Abdul-Wáhid al-Marrakhshí, about 1200

Between the late 700s and the 1200s, Islamic culture became very powerful and influential. The Muslim caliphate, centered in Baghdad, ruled many lands in parts of western Asia, northern Africa, and southern Europe. The people of the Islamic civilization were known for outstanding achievements in many areas including medical care. Ibn Sina (IHB un SEE nuh) (980–1037), a Muslim doctor, wrote medical textbooks with ideas that were far ahead of their time. His contributions to medical knowledge are still recognized as valuable. The following selection by Abdul-Wáhid al-Marrakhshí (ab dul WAY ihd al ma rak SHEE) describes one of the most famous Islamic hospitals, at Marrakesh, Morocco, in North Africa. As you read, consider how this hospital might differ from a modern hospital.

Here was constructed a hospital, which I think is unequalled in the world. First there was selected a large open space in the most level part of the town. Orders were given to architects to construct a hospital as well as possible. So the workmen **embellished** it with a beauty of sculpture and ornamentation even beyond what was demanded of them. All sorts of suitable trees and fruit trees were planted there. Water there was **in abundance**, flowing through all the rooms. . . .

embellished: decorated

in abundance: plentiful

A daily allowance of thirty **dinars** was assigned for the daily ration of food, exclusive of the drugs and chemicals which were on hand for the preparation of **draughts, unguents, and collyria**. For the use of the patients there were provided day-dresses and night-dresses, thick for winter, thin for summer.

dinars: gold coins

draughts, unguents, and collyria: medicines

After he was cured, a poor patient received on leaving the hospital a sum of money **sufficient** to keep him for a time. Rich patients received back their money and clothes. In short, the Founder did not **confine** the use of the hospital to the poor or to the rich. **On the contrary**, every stranger who fell ill at Marrakesh was carried there and treated until he either recovered or died. Every Friday the Prince after the mid-day prayer mounted his horse to go and visit the patients and to learn about each of them. He used to ask how they were and how they were being treated. This was his use until the day of his death.

sufficient: enough

confine: restrict

On the contrary: instead

The Islamic government also had "moving hospitals" that took beds and medical supplies by camel to places where patients could not get to a hospital.

Source: Cyril Elgood, *A Medical History of Persia and the Eastern Caliphate*. London: Cambridge University Press Associated, 1951. Reprint 1979.

The Ringdove

by Bidpai, about A.D. 300
Translated by Abdallah Ibn al-Muqaffa,
about A.D. 750

The Ringdove is a fable from an ancient book that has been one of the most popular tales in the Middle East for centuries. According to legend, around the year A.D. 300, an Indian king asked a teacher and philosopher named Bidpai to write a book that would guide him toward being a better ruler. Bidpai hid himself away for a year and wrote the Kalila wa Dimna, a collection of fables in which animals are the main characters. Bidpai based the Kalila wa Dimna on stories that had been told in India for hundreds of years. About 450 years later, a writer named Abdallah Ibn al-Muqaffa translated the Kalila wa Dimna into Arabic. Ibn al-Muqaffa's version is the oldest translation that still exists. In 1354, an Arab artist created a set of beautiful drawings to accompany Ibn al-Muqaffa's version of the Kalila wa Dimna. The pictures on these pages, which combine drawings and Arabic writing, are from this version. As you read The Ringdove, notice how the animals— both in pictures and in words—demonstrate human qualities. What does this fable say about friendship and cooperation? What might a king who lived hundreds of years ago have learned about ruling by reading this fable?

The king said to the philosopher that now that he had heard the story of the envious and **deceitful** man who brought **corruption** among friends, he would like to know how a man is received into brotherhood among his fellows and how strangers of **alien** races can come to love and trust one another.

The philosopher answered that nothing is equal in value to brotherhood because brothers can help in times of trouble, rescue one another from hidden **snares**, and protect their **kin** from enemies, like the crow, the mouse, the tortoise, and the gazelle.

There was a fertile region with abundant grass and trees frequented by **fowlers** and hunters. An old and wise crow lived in a tree that was particularly large and rich in **foliage**. One day the crow saw a hunter

deceitful: dishonest
corruption: bad habits
alien: different

snares: traps
kin: relatives

fowlers: people who catch birds
foliage: leaves

spreading a net below the tree and covering it with safflower seeds. Soon a flock of doves flew in. Their leader, a ringdove, spotted the seeds but did not notice the net. When the doves landed on the ground to feast on the seeds, the snare was drawn and they were caught in the net.

The ringdove suggested that the group unite and fly away together before they were caught by the hunter. The birds followed his advice, flapped their wings **in unison**, and took off with the net just as the hunter was approaching.

in unison: together

The crow decided to follow them. The doves flew over hills and houses with the hunter in hot pursuit. They eventually lost the man and landed near a burrow where a mouse lived. The ringdove called her friend, Zirak, the mouse, who came out of his burrow and saw the birds entangled in the net. He began to gnaw the ropes and finally cut through the snare. The doves rejoiced at being freed; they congratulated each other and thanked the mouse before flying off. Zirak returned to his home.

The crow, impressed by the friendship between the ringdove and the mouse, decided to stay on. He called out to Zirak and told the mouse that he would like them to be friends. Zirak, knowing well that crows are the natural enemies of mice, was slightly **apprehensive** at first but became convinced of the crow's sincerity and accepted his offer of brotherhood. A strong bond soon developed between the two, and they came to rely on one another.

apprehensive: fearful

The crow, noticing that their homes were too close to men, suggested that they move to another area. He knew of a **secluded** region full of vegetation and water where his friend, the tortoise, lived.

secluded: isolated
ample: enough
befallen: happened to

The mouse agreed and the crow took him by the tail and flew to the pond of the tortoise. The three friends enjoyed each other's company and passed their days in peace and happiness.

One day a gazelle came running into their neighborhood and frightened them. The tortoise dove into the water, the mouse scurried into his burrow, and the crow took flight and hid in a tree. When they saw that no one was pursuing the gazelle and that the animal was merely thirsty, they came out of hiding. The gazelle told them that he was running away from hunters. The friends asked him to join them and live in their peaceful place. The gazelle moved in, enjoyed good company and **ample** food and drink.

It became the custom of the four friends to meet every day, talk about their lives and experiences, and share their meal together. One day the gazelle failed to show up and the crow, the mouse, and the tortoise were worried that some misfortune had **befallen** him. The crow took to the air, searched for

the gazelle, and saw that he was caught in a hunter's net. He reported what he had seen to the mouse and the tortoise, who then set out to rescue their friend. When they reached the gazelle, the mouse began to gnaw the net and eventually freed him. The gazelle turned to the tortoise and said that if the hunter came back, he could run away, the crow could fly, and the mouse could hide; but, the slow and defenseless tortoise would probably be caught. As they were talking, the hunter arrived; the gazelle, the crow, and the mouse ran away and hid, but the tortoise, who could not move fast enough, was captured by the man. The hunter bound him and took him away, slung over his shoulders.

The friends, distressed by the loss of their brother, devised a plan to free him. They decided that if the gazelle pretended to be wounded and lay down with the crow who would appear to lick his wound, they might deceive the hunter. The gazelle followed their plan and lay down in the path of the hunter with the crow over him; the mouse hid nearby and they waited for the man. When the hunter arrived and saw them, he let go of the tortoise and went after the gazelle. The crow took flight and the gazelle jumped up and ran, luring the hunter away from the tortoise. The mouse quickly went to the tortoise and severed the ropes binding him.

By the time the hunter returned, the friends were safely far away. The man was disappointed and ashamed of himself for having lost his catch. He had become quite **leery** of this region and moved onto another area.

leery: suspicious

The crow, the mouse, the tortoise, and the gazelle rejoiced; they embraced and kissed each other, greatly relieved that now they could live in complete peace and happiness.

The tales of the **Kalila wa Dimna** *have been translated into dozens of languages. Why do you think such stories survive for centuries and remain popular worldwide? If you wrote a fable, what would your story be about, and what qualities would you give to different animals? What would your fable teach?*

Source: Esin Atil, *Kalila wa Dimna: Fables from a Fourteenth-Century Arabic Manuscript*. Washington, DC: Smithsonian Institution Press, 1981.

An Honest Counsellor

Anonymous, about 1300

A parable is a story that teaches a lesson. "An Honest Counsellor" is a parable from the Islamic culture. Instead of simply saying, "Honesty will be rewarded," the storyteller gives an example to illustrate this point. The caliph, al-Radi bi'l-Lah (al RAH dee bihl LAH), plays a good-natured trick on his friend to test his true feelings. As you read, consider whether the caliph's friend ends up using a little trickery of his own. Do you think this parable teaches its lesson effectively?

Al-Radi bi'l-Lah played a trick on a companion to whom he confided his secrets before becoming Caliph and who served him well by attending to his interests and giving him good advice. When he became Caliph, that man appeared before him one day.

- We have a friend, said al-Radi, and we want to do something for him, so we are **bestowing** a portion of the **frivolous goods** of this world upon him. I have given orders for him to be given a hundred thousand pieces of silver. Do you think we should do something for his children too?

bestowing: giving
frivolous goods: riches

- Oh Master, replied the companion, this would be a waste and misuse of funds from the Public Treasury. The **Emir of the Faithful** has large outlays on behalf of the State. If he really has to give a present, ten thousand pieces of silver would be a fine **windfall**, with the tax revenues from Kis.

Emir of the Faithful: Caliph

windfall: unexpected gain

Al-Radi kept insisting that it was too small a gift, so his companion thought it would be quite in order to increase it to thirty thousand pieces of silver. When al-Radi did not manage to raise the proposed figure any higher, he ordered the sum to be handed to him immediately, saying:

- I meant that as a gift for you.
- Emir of the Faithful, replied his companion, I suggest that the money should be **confiscated** to punish me for not coming to court before this.

confiscated: taken away

- Come more often, replied the Caliph, as long as I live. The finest way a man can behave is to do good to others.

He then gave instructions for a hundred thousand gold pieces to be paid out to him.

"An Honest Counsellor" comes from a collection of parables called The Subtle Ruse: The Book of Arabic Wisdom and Guile. *"Subtle ruse" means skillfull trickery. No one knows who wrote the stories in this book, but the author left clues that he lived around 1300. Can you think of other books that contain parables?*

Source: René R. Khawam, translator, *The Subtle Ruse: The Book of Arabic Wisdom and Guile.* Great Britain: East-West Publications Ltd., 1980.

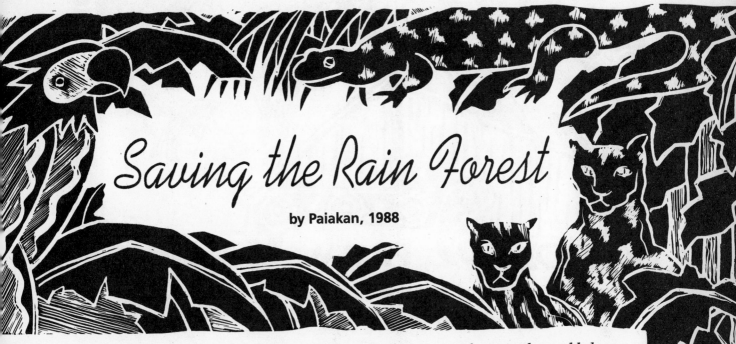

Saving the Rain Forest

by Paiakan, 1988

The Amazon region of South America contains the largest rain forest in the world, home to thousands of different kinds of plants and animals. In recent years new settlers have moved in and destroyed large portions of the forest. Careless development also threatens the way of life of Indians who have lived in the rain forest for many hundreds of years. A Kayapó (kah yuh POH) Indian leader named Paiakan (pī uh KAHN) has met with world leaders and urged them to listen to the people who have long made the rain forest their home. In the following excerpt from a speech given in 1988, Paiakan describes how all forms of life in the rain forest depend upon one another. What is the main point that the author is trying to make? What reasons and evidence does he give to support his claims?

The forest is one big thing: it has people, animals, and plants. There is no point saving the forest if the people and animals who live in it are killed or driven away. The groups trying to save the race of animals cannot win if the people trying to save the forest lose; the people trying to save the Indians cannot win if either of the others lose; the Indians cannot win without the support of these groups; but the groups cannot win without the help of the Indians, who know the forest and the animals and can tell what is happening to them. No one of us is strong enough to win alone; together, we can be strong enough to win.

In 1988 the Brazilian government filed criminal charges against Paiakan, saying that his work trying to save the rain forest interfered with the government. Many groups protested, and a court dismissed the charges. Like Paiakan, many people are presently working to preserve the people, the plant life, and the animals of the rain forest.

Source: Susanna Hecht and Alexander Cockburn, *The Fate of the Forest: Developers, Destroyers, and Defenders of the Amazon*. London and New York: Verso, 1989.

FROM
MOUSE TO BAT

Maya Fable Retold by Victor Montejo, 1991

Between A.D. 250 and A.D. 900, the ancient Maya had a rich civilization in what are today the countries of Mexico, Guatemala, Honduras, and El Salvador. They left many written records of their civilization in the form of books and temples carved with glyphs and other pictures. They also left oral records such as fables, stories, and tales that have been passed down from one generation to the next. This practice of using fables to teach a lesson has continued to the present day. Victor Montejo (mahn TAY hoh), a Maya born in 1952, recently collected some of the fables and stories that he heard while growing up in Guatemala. As you read this Maya fable, try to determine the moral of the story.

When the Creator and Shaper made all the animals, each **species** was eager to know where they would live, and he assigned their **habitats** to them.

The happiest were the birds who flew singing to the trees to build their nests. Only *Tx'ow* [tshoh], the mouse, didn't move. He stood there open-mouthed **contemplating** the marvelous flight of the birds.

"Go on," the Creator told him. "Go eat the kernels of corn, seeds, and all the forgotten pieces of food."

But *Tx'ow* wouldn't move. His body shook with resentment.

The Creator, very angry, picked him up by the tail and threw him in the bush. *Tx'ow* still could not say a word. He only stared at the flight of the singing birds with his eyes popping out. Then he looked at himself and became very sad. He could make little jumps, but fly? No, he could never achieve that.

species: category of animals
habitats: places to live

contemplating: thinking about

Now is the time to act, he said to himself. He decided to call together all the members of his species. There weren't many in those times. Well, he thought, they must be as discontented as I am.

Tx'ow easily convinced his brothers and sisters that they deserved more. One afternoon the **delegation** of mice came before the god, as he rested from the work of creation.

delegation: group

"What do you want? Speak up," he ordered them.

The delegation tried to speak but it could not. All they could say was, *witz'itz'i, witz'itz'i* [weets eets EE].

The wise god understood what they had come for and he said to them, "You want to fly like the birds?"

The delegation broke out in a big racket of *witz'itz'i, witz'itz'i* nodding their heads yes.

"Very good," the Creator said, "Tomorrow you should appear at *tx'eqwob'al* [tshay kwoh BAHL], the place for jumping, and I will give you your opportunity."

The mice went away satisfied, believing that a favorable **resolution** was at hand. To celebrate, there was a great rejoicing among the [tree] roots that night.

resolution: outcome

When the sun came up, the Creator was waiting at the place he had chosen to meet the unhappy mice. "Ready for the test?" he asked. "Those who can jump over this **ravine** will instantly receive wings and go flying away. And those who do not succeed will remain as they are."

ravine: steep valley

The discontented mice filed up one by one and launched out on the grand adventure. Those whose efforts carried them to the other side received wings and went flying off to the caverns, looking still like mice except for their wings. Those who did not succeed resigned themselves to their fate.

When the great test was over, the Creator warned them, "I don't want you returning to bother me anymore. You who are mice will continue eating grain and seeds. If you want, you can climb the trees and make your nests there. On the other hand those who now have wings will from now on be called *Sotz'* [sohtz], the bats. For them day will be night. They will feed on mosquitoes and blood, and sleep hanging upside down from the walls of *nhach'en* [nah CHAYN], the caverns, today and forever."

So it was that *Tx'ow*, the mouse, learned to accept himself and understood that his relatives, the bats, had not found happiness in their new condition either. They lost their tails and their toes grew long in order to cling to the rocks.

Today about 4 million Maya live in Mexico and the countries of Central America. The oral tradition—the passing down of stories, beliefs, and history—remains a central part of Maya culture.

Source: Victor Montejo, *The Bird Who Cleans the World and Other Mayan Fables*. Willimantic, CT: Curbstone Press, 1991.

INCIDENTS OF TRAVEL

by John Lloyd Stephens, 1841

The Maya culture flourished in Middle America from about A.D. 250 to 900. The Maya people lived in large cities with big temples, pyramids, and other buildings made from stone. They also used stone to carve tall, impressive monuments covered with picture writing, called hieroglyphics. John Lloyd Stephens (1805–1852) was an American explorer and travel writer who visited Middle America in 1839 and 1841. Very few people knew that the Maya civilization had existed until he wrote best-selling books about his adventures. Read this excerpt from one of Stephens's books. What was Stephens's reaction as he uncovered these Maya ruins near the city of Copán in what is now Honduras?

It is impossible to describe the interest with which I explored these ruins. The ground was entirely new; there were no guide-books or guides; the whole was [an unknown] soil. We could not see ten yards before us, and never knew what we should stumble upon next. At one time we stopped to cut away branches and vines which **concealed** the face of a monument, and then to dig around and bring to light a **fragment**, a sculptured corner of which **protruded** from the earth. I leaned over with breathless anxiety while the Indians worked, and an eye, an ear, a foot, or a hand was **disentombed**...The beauty of the sculpture, the **solemn** stillness of the woods, disturbed only by the scrambling of monkeys and the chattering of parrots, the **desolation** of the city, and the mystery that hung over it, all created an interest higher, if possible, than I had ever felt among the ruins of the Old World....

concealed: hid
fragment: piece
protruded: stuck up
disentombed: uncovered
solemn: majestic
desolation: loneliness

Of the **moral** effect of the monuments themselves, standing as they do in the depths of a tropical forest, silent and solemn, strange in design, excellent in sculpture, rich in ornament, different from the works of any other people, their uses and purposes, their whole history so entirely unknown, with hieroglyphics explaining all, but **perfectly unintelligible**, I shall not pretend to convey any idea. Often the imagination was pained in gazing at them.

moral: emotional

perfectly unintelligible: impossible to read

Since Stephens's discovery archaeologists have spent much time studying the Maya civilization. However, no one has ever found out exactly why the Maya people abandoned many of their cities in the 900s. Descendants of the Maya still live in the southern part of Middle America and carry on many ancient traditions.

Source: John Lloyd Stephens, *Incidents of Travel in Central America, Chiapas and Yucatan.* Dover Publications, 1969.

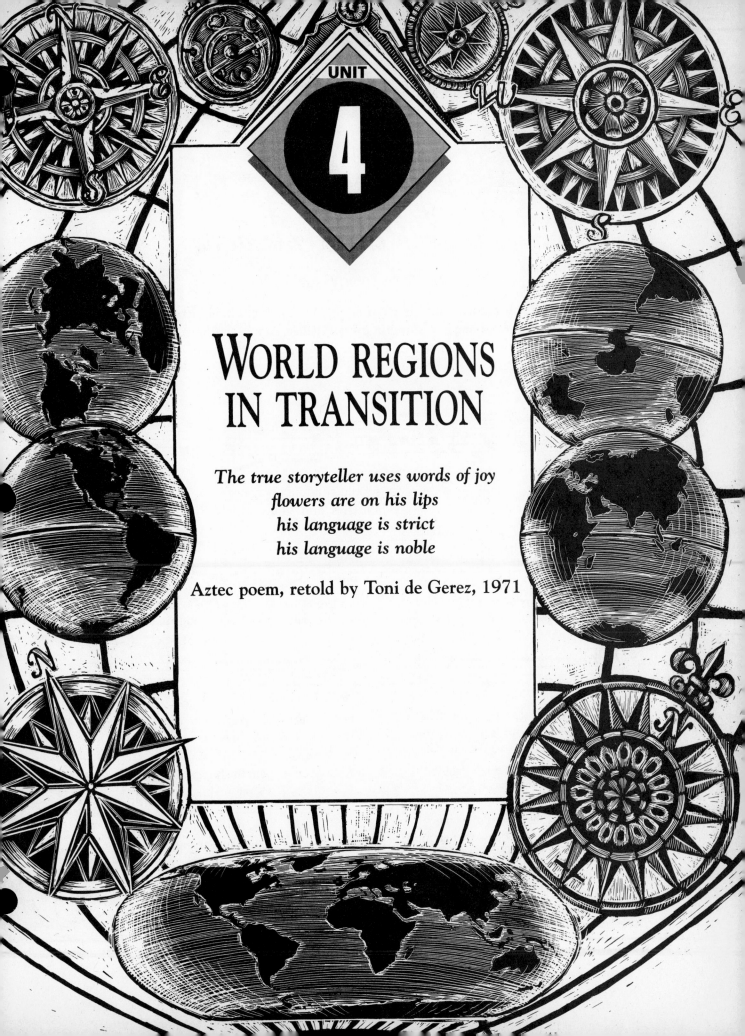

WORLD REGIONS IN TRANSITION

The true storyteller uses words of joy
flowers are on his lips
his language is strict
his language is noble

Aztec poem, retold by Toni de Gerez, 1971

Sur le Pont d'Avignon

Traditional French Song, 1200s

Festivals in France are always a time for singing and dancing. One of France's best-loved folk songs describes merry making in an old walled city in southern France called Avignon. How does this song show many different people from the same community enjoying themselves?

Traditional French Song

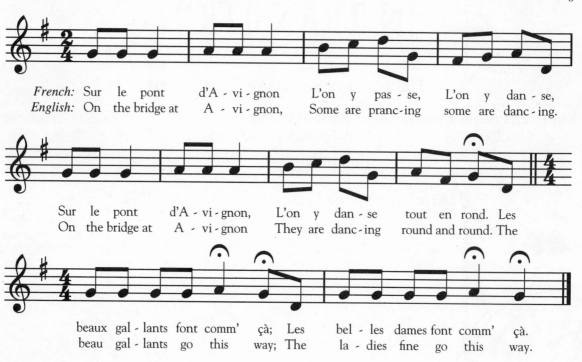

French: Sur le pont d'A - vi - gnon L'on y pas - se, L'on y dan - se,
English: On the bridge at A - vi - gnon, Some are pranc - ing some are danc - ing.

Sur le pont d'A - vi - gnon, L'on y dan - se tout en rond. Les
On the bridge at A - vi - gnon They are danc - ing round and round. The

beaux gal - lants font comm' çà; Les bel - les dames font comm' çà.
beau gal - lants go this way; The la - dies fine go this way.

Sur le pont d'Avignon
L'on y passe,
L'on y danse,
Sur le pont d'Avignon,
L'on y danse tout en rond.
Les Abbés font comm' çà,
Les soldats font comm' çà.

On the bridge at Avignon,
Some are prancing
Some are dancing.
On the bridge at Avignon
They are dancing round and round.
The Abbés grave go this way,
The soldiers brave go this way.

Source: Dorothy Gordon, *Around the World in Song.* New York: E.P. Dutton & Co., Inc., 1932.

Tale of King Arthur

Retold by James Knowles, 1923

One of the best-known tales of the Middle Ages, a period in Europe from about A.D. 500 to 1500, involves a king of England named Arthur. According to legend, King Arthur lived in the A.D. 400s. The tale of King Arthur, which has been told over and over again for hundreds of years, concerns heroic deeds, tragic love stories, and magical powers. In the excerpt below, a wizard named Merlin has cast a magic spell and taken young Arthur away from his father, King Uther. A knight named Sir Ector has then raised Arthur as his own son. As you read this excerpt, notice the amazing feat that Arthur performs to become king. According to the storyteller, what were the qualities that made a great leader in the Middle Ages?

Now Arthur the prince had all this time been nourished in Sir Ector's house as his own son, and was fair and tall and **comely**, being of the age of fifteen years, great in strength, gentle in manner, and accomplished in all exercises proper for the training of a knight.

> **comely:** attractive

But as yet he knew not of his father; for Merlin [the magician] had so dealt, that none save Uther and himself knew **aught** about [Arthur]. Wherefore it **befell**, that many of the knights and barons who heard King Uther speak before his death, and call his son Arthur his successor, were in great amazement; and some doubted, and others were displeased.

> **aught:** anything
> **befell:** happened

Anon the chief lords and princes set forth each to his own land, and, raising armed men and **multitudes** of followers, determined every one to gain the crown for himself; for they said in their hearts, "If there be any such a son at all as he of whom this wizard forced the king to speak, who are we that a beardless boy should have rule over us?"

> **anon:** soon
> **multitudes:** crowds

So the land stood long in great peril, for every lord and baron sought but his own advantage; and the **Saxons**, growing ever more adventurous, wasted and overran the towns and villages in every part.

> **Saxons:** Germanic tribe that conquered parts of England in the fifth century

Then Merlin went to Brice, the **Archbishop of Canterbury**, and advised him to require all the earls and barons of the **realm** and all knights and gentlemen-at-arms to come to him at London, before Christmas, that they might learn the will of Heaven who should be king. This, therefore, the archbishop did, and upon Christmas Eve were met together in London all the greatest princes, lords, and barons; and . . . the archbishop **besought** Heaven for a sign who should be lawful king of all the realm.

And as they prayed, there was seen in the churchyard, set straight before the doorways of the church, a huge square stone having a naked sword stuck in the midst of it. And on the sword was written in letters of gold, "Whoso pulleth out the sword from this stone is born the rightful King of Britain."

At this all the people wondered greatly; and, when [the religious service] was over, the nobles, knights, and princes ran out eagerly from the church to see the stone and sword; and a law was **forthwith** made that whoso should pull out the sword should be **acknowledged straightway** King of Britain.

Then many knights and barons pulled at the sword with all their might, and some of them tried many times, but none could stir or move it.

When all had tried in vain, the archbishop declared the man whom Heaven had chosen was not yet here. "But God," said he, "will doubtless make him known **ere** many days."

So ten knights were chosen, being men of **high renown**, to watch and keep the sword; and there was proclamation made through all the land that whosoever would, had leave and liberty to try and pull it from the stone. But though great multitudes of people came, both gentle and simple, for many days, no man could ever move the sword a hair's **breadth** from its place.

Now, at the New Year's Eve a great tournament was to be held in London. . . .To which tournament there came, with many other knights, Sir Ector, Arthur's foster-father, who had great possessions near to London; and with him came his son, Sir Key, but recently made knight, to take his part in the **jousting**, and young Arthur also to witness all the sports and fighting.

But as they rode towards the jousts, Sir Key found suddenly he had no sword, for he had left it at his father's house; and turning to young Arthur, he prayed him to ride back and fetch it for him. "I will with a good will," said Arthur; and rode fast back after the sword.

But when he came to the house he found it locked and empty, for all were gone forth to see the tournament. Whereat, being angry and impatient, he said within himself, "I will ride to the churchyard and take with me the sword that sticketh in the stone, for my brother shall not go without a sword this day."

So he rode and came to the churchyard, and **alighting** from his horse he tied him to the gate, and went to the **pavilion**, which was

archbishop of Canterbury: important leader of the Church of England

realm: kingdom

besought: begged

forthwith: immediately

acknowledged: recognized

straightway: right away

ere: before

high renown: great fame

breadth: width

jousting: competition in which knights carrying spears charge at each other on horseback

alighting: getting off

pavilion: large tent

pitched near the stone, wherein **abode** the ten knights who watched and kept it; but he found no knights there, for all were gone to see the jousting.

abode: stayed

Then he took the sword by its handle, and lightly and fiercely he pulled it out of the stone, and took his horse and rode until he came to Sir Key and delivered him the sword. But as soon as Sir Key saw it he knew well it was the sword of the stone, and riding swiftly to his father, he cried out, "Lo! here, sir, is the sword of the stone, wherefore it is I who must be king of all this land."

When Sir Ector saw the sword, he turned back straight with Arthur and Sir Key and came to the churchyard, and there alighting, they went all three into the church, and Sir Key was sworn to tell truly how he came by the sword. Then he confessed it was his brother Arthur who had brought it to him.

Whereat Sir Ector, turning to young Arthur, asked him—"How gottest thou the sword?"

"Sir," said he, "I will tell you. When I went home to fetch my brother's sword, I found nobody to deliver it to me, for all were **abroad** to the jousts. Yet was I **loth** to leave my brother swordless, and **bethinking me** of this one, I came **hither** eagerly to fetch it for him, and pulled it out of the stone without any pain."

Then said Sir Ector, much amazed and looking **steadfastly** on Arthur, "If this indeed be thus, 'tis thou who shalt be king of all this

abroad: gone
loth: reluctant
bethinking me: thinking
hither: to this place
steadfastly: firmly

71

land—and God will have it so—for none but he who should be rightful Lord of Britain might ever draw this sword forth from that stone. But let me now with mine own eyes see thee put back the sword into its place and draw it forth again."

"That is no mystery," said Arthur; and straightway set it in the stone. And then Sir Ector pulled at it himself, and after him Sir Key, with all his might, but both of them in vain: then Arthur reaching forth his hand and grasping at the **pommel**, pulled it out easily, and at once.

pommel: knob on the handle

Then fell Sir Ector down upon his knees upon the ground before young Arthur, and Sir Key also with him, and straightway did him **homage** as their **sovereign** lord.

homage: honor
sovereign: supreme

But Arthur cried aloud, "Alas! mine own dear father and my brother, why kneel ye thus to me?"

"Nay, my Lord Arthur," answered then Sir Ector, "we are of no blood-kinship with thee, and little though I thought how high thy kin might be, yet wast thou never more than foster-child of mine." And then he told him all he knew about his infancy, and how a stranger had delivered him, with a great sum of gold, into his hands to be brought up and nourished as his own born child, and then had disappeared.

But when young Arthur heard of it, he fell upon Sir Ector's neck, and wept, and made great **lamentation**, "For now," said he, "I have in one day lost my father and my mother and my brother."

lamentation: wailing

"Sir," said Sir Ector presently, "when thou shalt be made king be good and gracious unto me and mine."

"If not," said Arthur, "I were no true man's son at all, for thou art he in all the world to whom I owe the most; and my good lady and mother, thy wife, hath ever kept and fostered me as though I were her own; so if it be God's will that I be king hereafter as thou sayest, [ask] of me whatever thing thou wilt and I will do it; and God forbid that I should fail thee in it."

"I will but pray," replied Sir Ector, "that thou wilt make my son Sir Key, thy foster-brother, **seneschal** of all the lands."

seneschal: agent in charge

"That shall he be," said Arthur, "and never shall another hold that office, save thy son, while he and I do live."

Anon they left the church and went to the archbishop to tell him that the sword had been achieved. And when he saw the sword in Arthur's hand he set a day and **summoned** all the princes, knights, and barons to meet again at St. Paul's Church and see the will of Heaven **signified**. So when they came together, the sword was put back in the stone, and all tried, from the greatest to the least, to move it; but there before them all not one could take it out **save** Arthur only.

summoned: sent for

signified: fulfilled

save: except

Throughout the centuries, the legend of King Arthur has been retold in novels, poetry, plays, operas, and films. Other versions of the tale of King Arthur focus on great battles, epic quests, or searches, and the legendary Knights of the Round Table.

Source: Sir James Knowles, compiler, *King Arthur and His Knights*. New York: Blue Ribbon Books, 1923.

CONTRACT BETWEEN A VASSAL AND LORD Agreement from the 600s

During the Middle Ages, many Europeans lived in fear of attack from invaders and from each other. To protect themselves, Europeans developed a system known as feudalism. Under feudalism people provided certain services to each other in exchange for protection. Kings granted large estates to nobles, or lords, who promised to defend the king's territory. In turn the lords made contracts with less powerful nobles called vassals. When a vassal and lord exchanged vows, they often marked the occasion with a grand ceremony. Below is a standard contract between vassal and lord dating from the 7th century. As you read this contract, notice what vassal and lord promise each other. What do you think are some of the benefits and drawbacks of taking such an oath for both lord and vassal?

VASSAL:

I _____ , Since it is known familiarly to all how little I have **whence** to feed and clothe myself, I have therefore **petitioned** your **Piety**, and your good will has permitted me to hand myself over or commend myself to your **guardianship**, which I have thereupon done; that is to say, in this way, that you should aid and **succor** me as well with food as with clothing, according as I shall be able to serve you and deserve it.

And so long as I shall live I ought to provide service and honor to you, suitably to my free condition; and I . . . must remain during the days of my life under your power or defense.

whence: with which
petitioned: sought help from
Piety: Lordship
guardianship: care
succor: help

LORD:

It is right that those who offer to us unbroken **fidelity** should be protected by our aid. And since _____ , a faithful one of ours, by the favor of God, coming here in our palace with his arms, has seen fit to swear trust and fidelity to us in our hand, therefore we herewith **decree** and command that for the future _____ , above mentioned, be **reckoned** among the number of the **antrustions**.

fidelity: loyalty

decree: order
reckoned: counted
antrustions: followers

Life in Europe during the Middle Ages was often harsh and brutal, especially for serfs—the least powerful members of feudal society—who lived and worked on the land belonging to the nobles. Unlike the lords and vassals, serfs were not protected by any written contracts. Serfs had to follow the rules of the nobles.

Source: James Harvey Robinson, *Readings in European History*, Volume 1. Boston: Athenaeum, 1904.

Notebooks from the Renaissance

by Leonardo da Vinci, about 1482–1519

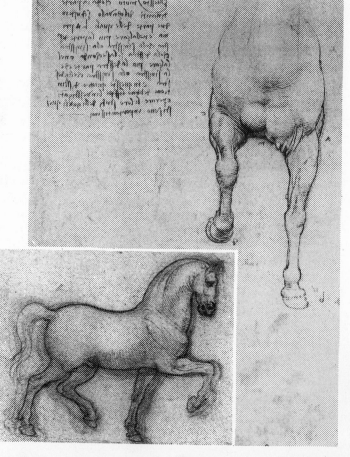

From about 1350 to 1600, Europe witnessed a rebirth of art, learning, and culture known as the Renaissance. No one embodied the spirit of the Renaissance more than Leonardo da Vinci (1452–1519). An Italian artist, scientist, and inventor, Leonardo studied every part of nature to better understand the world around him. Throughout his life da Vinci kept notebooks in which he sketched drawings and jotted down ideas. Da Vinci, who was left-handed, wrote backward from right to left so that his handwriting can only be read by holding it up to a mirror. As you read the selections and look at the drawings from da Vinci's notebooks, think about how his drawing and ideas capture the spirit of the Renaissance. In what ways was da Vinci a person far ahead of his time?

A Man when running throws less weight on his legs than when standing still. And in the same way a horse which is running feels less the weight of the man he carries. Hence many persons think it wonderful that in running, the horse can rest on one single foot.

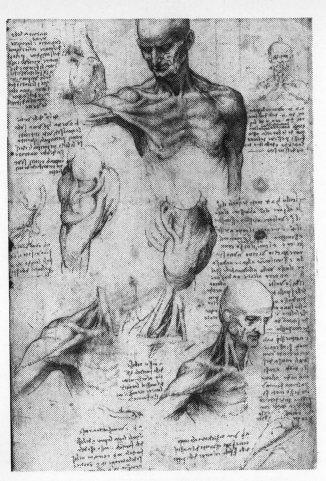

Give the measurement of each muscle, and give the reasons of all their functions, and in which they work and what makes them work. . . . First draw the spine of the back; then clothe it by degrees, one after the other, with each of its muscles and put in the nerves and arteries and veins to each muscle by itself; and besides these note the vertebrae to which they are attached; which of the intestines come in contact with them; and which bones and other organs. . . .

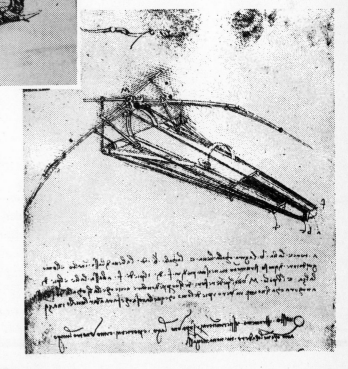

A Bird is an instrument working according to mathematical law, which instrument it is in the capacity of man to reproduce. . . . A man with wings large enough and [properly] attached might learn to overcome the resistance of the air . . . and raise himself upon it. Remember that your bird must imitate no other than the bat, because its membranes serve as . . . the frame of the wings. . . . [Take apart] the bat and on this model arrange the machine. . . .

Nature is [taken in] through the senses, mainly through the sense of sight. The art of painting is [part of] the process of seeing. . . . . The painter must analyze this experience in order to reproduce the visual image appearing in the eye on his picture place. His painting should give the impression of a window through which we look out into a section of the visible world. . . . The mind of a painter should be like a mirror, which always takes the color of the object it reflects and is filled by the images of as many objects as are in front of it. Therefore you must know that you cannot be a good painter unless you . . . represent by your art every kind of form produced by nature.

Leonardo da Vinci is remembered today for some of his great paintings, such as the Mona Lisa and The Last Supper. He is also remembered for his great sketches and ideas for inventions. Many of these inventions—such as the airplane—were so advanced that they could not actually be built for hundreds of years after da Vinci's death.

To learn about another person who also captured the spirit of the Renaissance, read the next document on page 77.

Source: Irma A. Richter, ed., *Selections from the Notebooks of Leonardo de Vinci*. London: Oxford University Press, 1952.

This Scepter'd Isle

from *Richard II* by William Shakespeare, 1597

The Renaissance that began in Italy in the 1300s gradually spread to the rest of Europe. By the late 1500s the Renaissance was flourishing in England, especially in the theater. Some of the world's greatest plays were written in this period by a London actor named William Shakespeare (1564-1616). Born in the town of Stratford-on-Avon, Shakespeare wrote tragedies, comedies, and histories. The excerpt below is from a speech at the beginning of Richard II, a historical play that takes place in the late 1300s. In this speech, a duke named John of Gaunt describes England to his nephew, King Richard II. How does Shakespeare's language help express John of Gaunt's feelings about England?

This royal throne of kings, this **scepter'd** isle,   **scepter'd:** royal
This earth of majesty, this seat of **Mars**,   **Mars:** the Roman god
This other Eden, **demi**-paradise,   of war
This fortress built by Nature for herself   **demi:** half
Against **infection** and the hand of war,
This happy breed of men, this little world,   **infection:** injury;
This precious stone set in the silver sea,   invasion
Which serves it in the office of a wall
Or as a moat defensive to a house,
Against the envy of less happier lands,
This blessed plot, this earth, this **realm**,   **realm:** kingdom
this England. . . .

In this speech John of Gaunt presents a positive view of his nation in the late 1300s. But the play, Richard II, traces a dark period in England's history when war tore the nation apart. Richard II is one of more than 35 plays written by Shakespeare. The beautiful language, complex characters, and great depth of feeling found in all his plays have made Shakespeare one of the finest English-language playwrights who ever lived.

Fall Rain Fall Rain **by Ladysmith Black Mambazo, 1987**

What is the most important thing that falls from the sky? To most people throughout the world the most important thing is rain. Without rain most crops cannot grow and animals cannot live. In the following song the South African band Ladysmith Black Mambazo combines rock and Zulu rhythms to create a chant that celebrates rain. What other parts of nature does this song describe?

Oh rain, oh rain
Oh rain, oh rain, beautiful rain
Don't disturb me, beautiful rain
Oh come, never come, oh come, never come
Oh come to me beautiful rain
Rain
Rain, rain, rain, rain
Beautiful rain
Rain, rain, rain, rain
Beautiful rain
Oh come, never come, oh come, never come
Oh come to me beautiful rain
When the sun says good night to the mountain
I am dreaming of the sun
Say good night
When the sun says good night to the mountain
I am dreaming of the sun
Say good night
When the sun goes down, the birds on the trees
Are singing sweet for the night
When the sun says good night to the mountain
I am dreaming of the sun
Say good night
When the sun goes down, the birds on the trees
Are singing sweet for the night
When the sun says good night to the mountain
I am dreaming of the sun
Say good night
Rain
Rain, rain, rain, rain
Beautiful rain
Rain, rain, rain, rain
Beautiful rain
Oh come, never come, oh come, never come
Oh come to me beautiful rain

Source: Ladysmith Black Mambazo, *Intokozo*. Gallo Music Productions, 1987.

THE KINGDOM OF
KUSH

Ancient Artifacts and Accounts, 450 B.C.–A.D. 77

After soldiers of Kush conquered Egypt in 751 B.C., the Kushites established an empire that dominated part of the Nile River valley in what is today Sudan for the next 1,000 years. The Kushites built pyramids and a great capital city named Meroë [MUR oo ee]. They also developed their own written language. Unlike Egyptian hieroglyphics, whose symbols have been decoded, no one has been able to decode the language of Kush. As a result, we know far less about ancient Kush than we do about ancient Egypt. Our knowledge of Kush comes from ancient artifacts and written accounts by people who visited Kush long ago.

The pictures of engravings and artifacts on pages 80–81 were all found at the site of ancient Kush. You can also read several descriptions of Kush adapted from Greek and Roman writers. Notice that these writers often called the Kushites "Ethiopians." Although Greeks and Romans used Ethiopians as a general term for black Africans, in the following passages they are mostly referring to the Kushites. What do the artifacts and travelers' accounts tell you about ancient Kush? Think of each of the following items as a clue in a puzzle. What do these clues reveal about the Kushites?

Herodotus, about 450 B.C.

After the forty days' journey on land from Egypt one takes another boat and in twelve days reaches a big city named Meroë. This city is said to be the capital of the Ethiopians. The inhabitants worship only the Gods of Zeus and Dionysus, and hold them in great honor. There is an **oracle** of Zeus in the city which directs the Ethiopians when it commands them to go to war. The Ethiopians are said to be the tallest and handsomest men in the whole world. In their customs they differ greatly from the rest of mankind, and particularly in the way they choose their kings. They find out the man who is the tallest of all the citizens, and of strength equal to his height. They appoint this man to be their ruler.

oracle: temple

Diodorus Siculus, about 50 B.C.

Historians tell us that the Ethiopians were the first of all men. The proofs of this statement, they say, are obvious. Historians say that the black peoples of Kush were the first to be taught to honor the gods and to hold sacrifices and processions and festivals by which men honor the gods. It is generally held that the sacrifices practiced among the Ethiopians are those which are the most pleasing to heaven. As witness to this these historians call upon the poet who is perhaps the oldest and certainly the most respected among the Greeks. For in the *Iliad*, Homer describes both Zeus and the rest of the gods with him on a visit to Ethiopia. The gods share in the sacrifices and the banquet which were given annually by the Ethiopians for all the gods together.

Strabo, 25-24 B.C.

When Gallus was leader of Egypt, I accompanied him in 25 and 24 B.C. We traveled up the Nile as far as Syene and the frontiers of Kush. I learned that as many as 120 vessels were sailing from Myos Hormos, a port on the Red Sea, all the way to India. In older times under the Egyptians, only a very few ventured to undertake the voyage and to carry on trade in Indian merchandise.

Gold mask of Queen Malaqaye

:ꟼꓱꟼꓱ:ⱯⱯⱱꟷꟷ:ꟼⱭꟷⱯⱯꟼꟷꟷ:ꟷꟷꟷꟷꟷ:ꟷꟷ꟱Ɐ

**Pliny the Elder,
about A.D. 77**

Meroë had once enjoyed great fame and had maintained four thousand artisans.... The queens of the country bore the name Candace, a title that had passed from queen to queen for many years.

**Kush god carved on
the stone wall of a
temple at Meroë**

These accounts and artifacts provide evidence of a rich civilization widely admired by other peoples. They reveal that the Kushites traded far beyond their borders, created beautiful art, developed an original system of writing, were deeply religious, and chose both men and women as their rulers. In the A.D. 100s the Kush empire began to decline. The nearby kindom of Axum conquered the capital city of Meroë in 350 and the Kush empire gradually disappeared.

Source: Basil Davidson, *African Civilization Revisited*. Trenton, NJ: Africa World Press, 1991.
Basil Davidson, *Africa in History*. New York: Macmillan Publishing Company, 1974.

Observations
of a 14th-Century Traveler

by Ibn Battutah, 1352–1353

In 1352, 20 years after Mansa Musa died, a Moroccan writer named Muhammed Ibn Abdullah Ibn Battutah (1304–1369) visited the empire of Mali. A world traveler, Ibn Battutah had journeyed to India, China, and many parts of Africa, Europe, and southwest Asia. He found Mali one of the most interesting places he had ever visited. In a book he wrote in Arabic about his travels, Ibn Battutah described life in the royal palace and the customs of the people of Mali. As you read the excerpt below from Ibn Battutah's book, notice how King Mansa Sulayman of Mali, Mansa Musa's grandson, greets visitors. How does the king make himself appear great? How does this description by Ibn Battutah compare to the account of the Mali empire described in the document on page 84?

*O*n certain days the **sultan** [Mansa Sulayman] holds audiences in the palace yard, where there is a platform under a tree, with three steps; this they call the *pempi*. It is carpeted with silk and has cushions placed on it. [Over it] is raised the umbrella...made of silk, **surmounted** by a bird in gold, about the size of a falcon. The sultan comes out of a door in a corner of the palace....The sultan is preceded by his musicians, who carry gold and silver two-stringed guitars, and behind him come three hundred armed slaves. He walks in a leisurely fashion, affecting a very slow movement, and even stops from time to time. On reaching the *pempi* he stops and looks round the assembly, then ascends it in the **sedate** manner of a preacher ascending a **mosque**-pulpit. As he takes his seat the drums, trumpets, and bugles are sounded....

Among the admirable qualities of these people, the following are to be noted:

1. The small number of acts of injustice that one finds there; for the Negroes are of all peoples those who most **abhor** injustice. The sultan pardons no one who is guilty of it.

2. The complete and general safety one enjoys throughout the land. The traveler has no more reason than the man who stays at home to fear...thieves....

sultan: king

surmounted: topped

sedate: calm
mosque: Muslim house of worship

abhor: hate

3. The blacks do not **confiscate** the goods of [North Africans] who die in their country, not even when these consist of big treasures. They deposit them, on the contrary, with a man of confidence among the [North Africans] until those who have a right to the goods present themselves and take possession.

confiscate: seize

4. They make their prayers punctually; they **assiduously** attend their meetings of the faithful, and punish their children if these should fail in this. On Fridays, anyone who is late at the mosque will find nowhere to pray, the crowd is so great. Their custom is to send their servants to the mosque to spread their prayer-mats in the due and proper place, and to remain there until they, the masters, should arrive. These mats are made of the leaves of a tree resembling a palm, but one without fruit.

assiduously: devotedly

5. The Negroes wear fine white garments on Fridays. If by chance a man has no more than one shirt or a soiled **tunic**, at least he washes it before putting it on to go to public prayer.

tunic: short jacket

6. They **zealously** learn the Koran by heart.

zealously: enthusiastically

Ibn Battutah was one of the great travel writers of his time. His descriptions of life in the three different continents he visited in the 1300s are among the liveliest and most interesting travel books ever written. His descriptions of Mali are especially important because less than 100 years after his visit the empire began to decline. In the late 1400s the Songhai Empire conquered Mali, and the once-great Mali empire collapsed.

Source: Basil Davidson, *African Civilization Revisited*. Trenton, NJ: Africa World Press, 1991.

The Empire of Mali

by Al Omari, 1336

In the 1300s the western African empire of Mali controlled much of the world's gold supply. This gave the empire great wealth, and the wealthiest person of all was the king, or sultan. In 1324 the Mali king, Mansa Musa, made a pilgrimage to Mecca. All along his journey Mansa Musa gave gifts of gold to both rich and poor people. Twelve years later author Al Omari wrote down the remembrances of people who knew Mansa Musa. Al Omari wrote that Mansa Musa is the king who is "the most feared by his enemies and the most able to do good to those around him." What do you think the author meant by that comment?

The king of this country [Mansa Musa] . . . is the most important of the Muslim [black] kings; his land is the largest, his army the most numerous; he is the king who is the most powerful, the richest, the most fortunate, the most feared by his enemies and the most able to do good to those around him. . . .

The sultan of this country has **sway** over the land of the "desert of native gold," whence they bring him gold every year. . . .

sway: control

The sultan of this kingdom presides in his palace on a great balcony called *bembe* where he has a great seat of **ebony** that is like a throne fit for a large and tall person: on either side it is flanked by elephant tusks turned towards each other. His arms stand near him, being all of gold, **saber**, lance, quiver, bow and arrows. He wears wide trousers made of about twenty pieces [of stuff] of a kind which he alone may wear. Behind him there stand about a score of Turkish or other pages which are bought for him in Cairo: one of them, at his left, holds a silk umbrella **surmounted** by a dome and a bird of gold: the bird has the figure of a falcon. His officers are seated in a circle about him, in two rows, one to the right and one to the left; beyond them sit the chief commanders of his **cavalry**. In front of him there is a person who never leaves him and who is his executioner; also another who serves as intermediary [that is, official spokesman] between the **sovereign** and his subjects, and who is named the **herald**. In front of them again, there are drummers. Others dance before their sovereign, who enjoys this, and make him laugh. Two banners are spread behind him. Before him they keep two saddled and bridled horses in case he should wish to ride.

ebony: hard, dark wood

saber: heavy, curved sword

surmounted: topped

cavalry: mounted soldiers

sovereign: king
herald: messenger

By 1490 Mali's place as the most powerful kingdom in western Africa had been taken over by the kingdom of Songhai.

Source: Al Omari, *The African Past*. Boston: Little Brown, 1964.

Test of a Friendship

Yoruba Tale Retold by Barbara Walker, 1968

Griots, or storytellers, play an important role in many parts of West Africa. Griots tell stories and help to pass on their people's culture, values, and history. Often these stories and tales have an important message or lesson to teach. The tale below is from the Yoruba people of Nigeria. What is the griot's message in this tale?

*L*ong ago and far away there were two good friends named Olaleye [oh lah leh yeh] and Omoteji [oh moh teh jee]. Each had a farm directly across the footpath from the other, and day after day they would greet each other as they went about their work. Finally their great friendship raised a question in the heart of their wise neighbor, and he determined to test their friendship for one another.

Secretly, he made a hat for himself which was red on one side and green on the other. Then one day after putting on his new hat, he strolled along the footpath.

"Good morning!" he greeted Omoteji as the good fellow bent over the **yams** in his field.

yams: sweet potatoes

"Good morning," answered Omoteji, standing up to stretch himself a little from his bending. "I see you have a fine new red hat."

"Oh, yes," answered the other. "I am happy that you noticed it." And he set his new hat more firmly upon his head. He walked on along the footpath, and Omoteji returned to his work.

A few moments later, he saw Olaleye pulling weeds in his yam patch. "Good morning, Olaleye!" he called.

Olaleye looked up and returned the man's greeting. Then, "Oho," said he. "I see you have a fine new green hat."

"Yes, indeed," answered the neighbor. "I looked a long time before I found the one I wanted." After a moment's chatting with Olaleye, he went on his way down the footpath, well satisfied with himself.

When the sun stood at the **zenith**, Olaleye stopped his work and went to eat his lunch with his good friend Omoteji. As they ate, Omoteji said, "Did you notice the fine new red hat our neighbor had?"

zenith: highest point

"*Red* hat!" exclaimed Olaleye. "My friend, you must have been a little dazzled by the sun."

"What do you mean?" asked Omoteji.

"It wasn't a red hat our neighbor was wearing. It was a *green* hat," explained Olaleye. And he smiled at his friend's mistake.

"A green hat!" exclaimed Omoteji. "Oh, no, my friend. It was *not* green. It was red. I know, for I remarked on it to our neighbor."

"And so did I," returned Olaleye, becoming a little impatient.

Omoteji, irritated by his friend's impatience, continued to argue that the hat was red, while Olaleye for his part maintained that the hat was green. From words, the quarrel grew to blows, and Omoteji was still **reeling** from Olaleye's stout blow when their neighbor hurried toward them.

reeling: staggering

"What's this!" he exclaimed. "You two fighting! I thought you were the best of friends. How can friends come to blows this way?"

Olaleye and Omoteji, their excitement somewhat cooled by this interruption, stared at their neighbor. This time, Omoteji saw the green side of the hat, and Olaleye saw the red side.

"Oh, my friend Omoteji," said Olaleye quickly. "You were right, after all. Our neighbor's hat *is* red."

"Oh, no," returned Omoteji earnestly. "I was wrong and you were right. I must have been dazzled by the sun, after all. Our neighbor's new hat *is* green."

Their difference of opinion would shortly have led to blows again if their neighbor had not laughed. Taking off his hat, he showed them the red side and then the green one. "Look here, my friends," he said. "You were both right about the hat. But you were both wrong about your friendship. You are not the best of friends if you cannot examine both sides of a question without anger, whether it be a hat or whether it be something more important."

"You are right," declared Olaleye. "One never knows about a friendship until it has been put to a test. As for me, a hat can be either green or red. It doesn't matter, as long as I have my good friend, Omoteji."

"Nor does it matter to me," agreed Omoteji.

And **thenceforth** the two were stronger friends than ever.

thenceforth: from then on

In gathering together to hear and respond to griots' stories like the one above, many people in West Africa share their beliefs and pass down their traditions. West Africans also pass down their traditions by writing literature. For an example of West African literature, read the document on pages 192–194.

Source: Barbara Walker, *The Dancing Palm Tree and Other Nigerian Folktales.* Lubbock: Texas Tech University Press, 1990.

JI-NONGO-NONGO

African Riddles Collected by Verna Aardema, 1978

The oral tradition in Africa of storytelling by griots, which you read about in the document on pages 85–86, also includes riddles. Griots often entertain a crowd by telling riddles before beginning a tale. Besides providing fun, the riddles also describe acceptable ways of behaving or make wise observations about life. Verna Aardema, an author who specializes in African folklore, collected the following riddles from various groups of people throughout the continent. See if you can guess the answers to the riddles. The answers are printed upside down. What are some of the ideas and values expressed in the riddles?

Accra

When is it safe to play with the leopard cubs?

Answer: When their mother is far away.

Congo

Why shouldn't you grow pumpkins on the side of a hill?

Answer: Because when they are ripe, they would roll down.

Ga

What is soft and flat, but cannot be slept upon?

Answer: The surface of the lake.

What leaps down the mountain, but cannot climb back up?

Answer: The mountain stream.

What is it that you look at with one eye, but never with two?

Answer: The inside of a bottle.

Hausa

Why is a man like a pepper?

Answer: Until you have tested him, you can't tell how strong he is.

What lies down when it's hungry and stands up when its full?

Answer: A rice sack.

What looks at the valley, but never goes into it?

Answer: The hill.

Bantu

Who is it that always stands, and never sits down?

Answer: A tree.

Masai

What doesn't run from the prairie fire?

Answer: The bare spot.

I have two skins—one to lie upon and the other to cover me. What are they?

Answer: The ground and the sky.

Wolof

What is long but has no shadow?

Answer: The road.

Yoruba

What thing in the forest frightens even the lion?

Answer: The forest fire.

They cut off its head. They cut off its feet. And its middle calls the town together. What is it?

Answer: A drum.

What is long and can be shortened by the feet, but not with a hatchet?

Answer: The path.

What can the buffalo do that two strong men can not?

Answer: Grow horns.

Today, Africans are recording their rich oral tradition by collecting stories, poems, legends, and riddles and publishing them in books. At the same time others are keeping the oral tradition alive in storytelling sessions, often combined with music and dance.

Source: Verna Aardema, *Ji-Nongo-Nongo Means Riddles*. New York: Four Winds Press, 1978.

The Epic of Liyongo

Swahili Epic, 1600–1800

Arabic settlers who made their homes in Africa's coastal cities contributed much to eastern African culture. They brought with them the religion of Islam as well as many words from the Arabic language. In fact, the name of this eastern African civilization is "Swahili," Arabic for "people of the shore." Like all cultures, the Swahili people tell stories about their heroes—people who are beloved for their extraordinary deeds. The following excerpt tells about a Swahili hero named Liyongo. He was a warrior known for his bravery and skill, who is said to have lived in the 1600s or 1700s on the island of Pate, near Kenya. The ruler, or sultan, of Pate was jealous of Liyongo's popularity and wanted him killed. After the sultan's first attempt to kill Liyongo failed, the ruler became frustrated because the people admired Liyongo more than ever. As the excerpt begins, the sultan's men have thrown Liyongo in jail and sentenced him to death. However, the sultan did not count on Liyongo's cleverness, or the help of his mother and the servant, Saada, whose name means "happiness" in Arabic. How does Liyongo outsmart the sultan? Can you think of heroes from other cultures who are remembered in stories, poems, or songs?

The Sultan sent his **men-at-arms** about
a hundred in number.

They marched in column with
spear and bows and **battlestaves**
and they seized Liyongo and he
was put in jail. . . .

They sent a slave-messenger to
Liyongo and said Death is certain
they have sent me to tell you.

What is there that you wish? The
Sultan has sent me you will
receive it most certainly so that
you may make your farewells to
the world. . . .

And he replied, Do not be sure tell
the Sultan that I wish for a
'mwao' dance and for a **'gungu'**
tourney as well.

And when the Sultan's messenger
had left the cell there entered a
servant-[girl] and she brought him
food.

And when his (Liyongo's) mother for
certain sent good food the soldiers
would **deprive him of** it and
would eat the food.

Whenever they brought food to him
the soldiers **confiscated** it but
on this day he said (to the
[servant]-girl) Greet my mother
for me.

And he spoke (in secret) rhyme
Go and tell her let my mother
prepare these things that I have
told you of. . . .

men-at-arms: soldiers

battlestaves: wooden
weapons

'mwao' dance:
celebratory dance

'gungu' tourney: special
tournament

deprive him of: keep
him from having

confiscated: took

Let her make a loaf for me and put
inside a **file** So that I can cut
through these handcuffs and break
my chains.

Let me cross these walls and the
roof shall be broken through,
Let me kill men and as they
fight I will laugh.
Let me go into the reeds and creep
like a fierce snake, Let me enter
the forest and roar like a fierce lion.
I am like a lone tree alone in the
treeless wilderness Without
kinsfolk or friends, alone I am
left an orphan.
Only my mother is left, to whose
help's cry her answering will be lent.

Saada **perceived** his plan and his
mother set the fires to make
a loaf of bran and sent him
the bread.

This bread, understand was of about
eight pounds weight and she
placed the file inside and Liyongo
received her (the [servant]-girl).

When the soldiers saw that it was
made of bran they cursed Only
slaves eat loaves of bran take it
to him, go on, get in.

But Liyongo in his cell broke the
loaf in secret and he saw the
file inside and was filled with joy....

And when night was come and they
made ready for the dances and
according to custom prepared the
gongs, horns, and trumpets....

file: metal tool used for
grinding

perceived: understood

No sooner the people arrive in the
hall than there is a great **throng**
with the tall folk on tip-toe
and the short ones straining
their necks....

At that moment Liyongo arose and
calmed his heart and **suppressed**
his rage and he calmed himself
as he sang while the maidens
and youths danced around....

When the songs' refrain increased
and the drumming loudly swelled
he was cutting away there at
his handcuffs and chains.

While the clapping increased he was
cutting away quickly until when
the clapping stopped he said to
them, Lift up your eyes.

And pausing in their dance Liyongo
appeared and fear fell upon them
and they were lost in fright as
they ran away.

For they all ran away there was
no one left Liyongo came forth
and returned once again to the
mainland....

*Liyongo was safe for the moment, but the sultan's rage proved unstoppable. The sultan
befriended Liyongo's son and promised his daughter's hand in marriage if the boy would
kill his father. Liyongo's son betrayed Liyongo, stabbing him with a copper dagger while
he was asleep. Liyongo chased his son into the center of a nearby town, before he fell
beside the town well and died. The Epic of Liyongo is still sung today at Swahili feasts,
and people still mourn the hero when they hear of his death.*

Source: Ali A. Jahadhmy, ed., *Anthology of Swahili Poetry.* London: Heinemann, 1975.

The Hoca

**Two Turkish Tales Retold by
Barbara K. Walker, 1988, 1990**

Although the things that make people laugh vary from culture to culture, all cultures have a sense of humor. The Hoca, also called Nasreddin Hoca, is a favorite character in Turkish humor. In Turkish the word hoca *means a Muslim priest who is also a teacher. The Hoca in Turkish stories like the ones below, however, always manages to get himself into trouble. Yet in the end the Hoca usually finds a way to have the last word. Can you think of other characters similar to the Hoca?*

The Hoca and the Candle

One day during a particularly bitter winter, the Hoca and his friends sat in the coffeehouse discussing the weather. Plain talk gave way to boasting, and before long the Hoca puffed out his chest importantly. "You may think we are having a cold winter. As for me, I thrive on cold and snow. Why, when I was a boy, I used to go out in the middle of January and break the ice on the river so that I could have a good, brisk swim for myself. Pooh! This cold is *nothing*."

This claim was too exaggerated for the rest of them. Nudging a companion, the Hoca's best friend set out a fine challenge. "I say, Hoca. You like cold weather. I suppose you could stay out all night long in the cold without a coat or a blanket and nothing at all to warm yourself?"

"Of course," bragged the Hoca.

"No fire, no hot tea, no blanket, no coat?" The others seemed impressed.

"Well," said the ringleader, "we'll make a bargain with you. If tonight you can stay outside, with absolutely nothing extra to warm you, all night long, you'll be our guest at a fine dinner. Right, friends?"

"Right!" they chorused.

"On the other hand," the ringleader continued, "if you use any means at all of keeping yourself warm, you will entertain us for dinner. How about that, Hoca **effendi**?"

effendi: the wise one

"Fine, fine," agreed the Hoca.

That evening the Hoca's friends watched through the windows of their warm houses as the Hoca strolled here and there, studying the stars in the chill sky, and **repenting** a thousand times of his hasty, boastful tongue. Just as he was about to **concede** defeat, he spied a candle set in a window perhaps a hundred meters away. Fixing his eye on the candle glow, the Hoca felt the blood flow back through his stiffening veins. Thus he was able to endure the long night.

repenting: regretting
concede: admit

The next morning his friends, stepping outside into the frosty air, were amazed to find the Hoca calm and smiling, none the worse for his chill **vigil**. "Well, Hoca effendi, are you *sure* you used no means at all of warming yourself?" persisted the ringleader.

vigil: night

"No means at all," the Hoca declared, "unless you can call a candle a hundred meters away a means! I *did* see a candle burning, and its glow kept me equal to the torments of the cold."

"Aha!" exclaimed the challenger. "Hoca effendi, you must be our host at dinner, for you warmed yourself by that candle." No protest on the part of the Hoca was sufficient to move the **resolve** of his friends on the matter, so they were invited that evening to dinner at the Hoca's house.

resolve: determination

The group arrived in good time, and sat on **bolsters** in the Hoca's sparsely furnished living room, waiting for the delicious smells that must **herald** a fine meal. But, sniff as they would, they could detect not a hint of what was to be served for dinner. What's more, the Hoca kept excusing himself to go out to the kitchen and supervise the cooking, a most unusual procedure for him. As one hour succeeded another with still no sign of food, the men began to grumble among themselves, and at last the ringleader **chaffed** the Hoca about the delay.

bolsters: pillows

herald: announce

chaffed: teased

"Ah, my friends, you can come and see for yourselves that your dinner is being made ready," declared their host, and he led the way to the kitchen. Following him, they were amazed to find a large caldron suspended from the ceiling. A meter below the caldron burned a single candle.

"But, Hoca effendi," spluttered the ringleader, "surely you don't expect to heat that caldron with a *candle*? Why, the dinner would *never* get done!"

"Oh, I'm not so sure," answered the Hoca calmly. "If a candle a *hundred* meters away can keep me warm all night long, surely a candle one meter away can heat a caldron!"

Backward on the Donkey

One Friday as Nasreddin Hoca was getting ready to go to the mosque to read the lesson from the Koran to the congregation, he heard a *Tak! Tak! Tak!* at his door. As he opened the door, he found all the boys from his school standing in the courtyard. "What is this!" he exclaimed.

"Well, Hoca Effendi, we decided to go with you to the service today," said one. And the others agreed that this was so.

"I'll be happy to have you attend the service," said the Hoca, "but I'm not quite ready yet to leave. Just wait out there, and I'll be along in a minute or so."

The Hoca shut the door and quickly put on his long coat and his **ample turban**. Then he hurried to the door, opened it, slipped into his shoes beside the doorstep, and rushed across the courtyard to mount his little donkey. But in his haste, he mounted his donkey backward!

ample turban: large head covering

The boys began to grin and to nudge one another, wondering what the Hoca would find to say about his ridiculous mistake. As for the Hoca, he was wondering, too, but he kept a firm grasp on his wits as he glanced from one boy to another.

"I suppose you are all wondering," he said, "why I have seated myself backward on my donkey, but *I have my reasons*. If I were to seat myself forward on my donkey and ride ahead of you, I could not keep my eye on you. On the other hand, if I were to sit forward on the donkey and ride behind you so that I could watch you, that would be improper, for I am your master. Therefore, I am riding ahead of you *and* keeping my eye on you!"

People from the Turkish culture laugh at the Hoca, but it is in a kind way. He is sometimes smart and sometimes not so smart, but he is always a thoroughly lovable character. When a person from Turkey is asked to tell a story, most often it will be about the Hoca.

Sources: Barbara K. Walker, *A Treasury of Turkish Folktales for Children*. Hamden, CT: Linnet Books, 1988, and Barbara K. Walker, *The Art of the Turkish Folk Tale*. Lubbock, TX: Texas Tech University Press, 1990.

The Splendors of Hangzhou

by an Unknown Chinese Traveler, 1235

For thousands of years cities have been an important part of Chinese life. One of the oldest cities in China is Hangzhou (HAHNG joh). This city along the east coast of China served as the nation's capital in the twelfth and thirteenth centuries. During this period Hangzhou overflowed with markets, goods, and endless types of entertainment. The drawing on the next page, which was created by a Chinese artist living in Hangzhou during the 1200s, shows one of the city's many silk shops. In 1235 a Chinese traveler visited this fascinating city and described its attractions. As you read this traveler's account, think of what you might do if you had one day to spend in ancient Hangzhou. How do the attractions of thirteenth-century Hangzhou compare with attractions of cities today?

Markets

In the evening, with the exception of the square in front of the palace, the markets are as busy as during the day. The most attractive one is at Central Square, where all sorts of **exquisite artifacts**, instruments, containers, and hundreds of varieties of goods are for sale. In other marketplaces, sales, auctions, and exchanges go on constantly. In the wine shops and inns business also thrives. Only after the fourth drum does the city gradually quiet down, but by the fifth drum, court officials already start preparing for audiences and merchants are getting ready for the morning market again. This cycle goes on all year round without **respite**. . . .

exquisite artifacts: beautiful hand-crafted goods

respite: rest

Commercial Establishments

Various businesses are designated by the word "company" (*hang*), which is a taxation category **imposed** by the government and is used for all businesses dealing in **commodities**, regardless of their size. Even physicians and fortunetellers are included. Other trades sometimes also borrow the word "company" for their own use, such as liquor company and food company. Some businesses are called "gatherings" (*ho*), such as a flower gathering, fruit gathering, dried-fish gathering. . . . **Artisans** sometimes call their businesses "workshops" (*tso*), such as comb workshop, belt workshop, gold-and-silver plating workshop. There are some businesses that use unusual names; for example, shops dealing in the "seven treasures" (gold, silver, pearl, amber, etc.) may call themselves **curio** companies, whereas a bathhouse may be designated a fragrant-water company.

imposed: set up
commodities: goods

artisans: skilled workers

curio: rare goods

In general, the capital attracts the greatest variety of goods and has the best craftsmen. For instance, the flower company at Superior Lane does a truly excellent job of flower arrangement, and its caps, hairpins, and collars are **unsurpassed** in craftsmanship. Some of the most famous specialties of the capital are the sweet-bean soup at the **Miscellaneous** Market, the pickled dates of the Ko family, the thick soup of the Kuang family at Superior Lane, the fruit at the Great Commons marketplace, the cooked meats in front of Eternal Mercy Temple, Sister Sung's fish broth at Penny Pond Gate, the juicy lungs at Flowing Gold Gate, the "lamb rice" of the Chih family at Central Square, the boots of the P'eng family, the fine clothing of the Hsüan family at Southern Commons, the sticky rice pastry of the Chang family, the flutes made by Ku the Fourth, and the Ch'iu family's Tatar whistles at the Great Commons. . . .

unsurpassed: not topped

miscellaneous: varied

Entertainment Centers

The hundred games used to be the official entertainment of the old capital. The experts . . . can climb high poles, do somersaults, walk on stilts, juggle spears . . . play with swords, display horsemanship, and so on.

The various skills of the entertainers have their respective high-sounding names. Their acts include: kicking bottles, juggling plates, kicking musical stones, twirling drumsticks, kicking writing brushes, playing ball. There are also performances with trained insects, fish or bears, fireworks, fire shows, water shows, puppet shows, and marksmanship of all kinds.

Puppet shows include string-puppets, cane-top puppets, water-puppets, and flesh-puppets. The stories are usually fictitious and fantastic. Shadow plays originated in the old capital. At first the figures were made with white paper; later they were made of leather and painted various colors. The stories of the shadow plays are pretty much the same as those used by the storytellers; generally speaking, they are a mixture of truth and fiction. The loyal and righteous are given a handsome appearance, whereas the wicked and **treacherous** are depicted as monstrously ugly—a kind of **implicit** criticism that is easily understood by the people in the streets. The storytellers can be divided into four groups: those who specialize in social tales, mysteries, and miracle tales; those who deal with military adventures; those who **explicate sutras** by telling religious tales; and those who relate historical events....

treacherous: untrustworthy
implicit: understood

explicate: explain
sutras: sacred Buddhist teachings

Boats

The capital is encircled by a river on the left side and by West Lake on the right; thus the most convenient way to travel is by boat. The boats for hire on West Lake vary greatly in size. Some are 50 feet [15 m] long and have a capacity of more than 100 passengers; others are 20 to 30 feet [6 to 9 m] long and can take 30 to 50 passengers. All of them are exquisitely constructed, with carvings on the railings and paintings on the beams. They sail so smoothly that the passengers may forget that they are on water. These boats are for hire in all seasons and never lack patrons. They are also well equipped with everything; a tourist can get on board in the morning, drink wine, and enjoy himself; at dusk he may walk home by following a trail. It is not tiring but is rather expensive. Some wealthy families have their own pleasure boats, and these are even more exquisitely built and more luxuriously fitted out.

Dragon boat competitions are held in spring at the West Lake and in autumn at the Che River. The dragon boats are light and swift and make a grand **spectacle**....In early and mid-autumn there are swimmers in the Che River, who, **brandishing** pennants and poles, display the most breathtaking skills. I believe this is a unique attraction of the capital....

spectacle: show
brandishing: waving

Specialty Stores

Some famous fabric stores sell exquisite brocade and fine silk which are unsurpassed elsewhere in the country. Along the river, close to the Peaceful Ford Bridge, there are numerous fabric stores, fan shops, and **lacquerware** and porcelain shops. Most other cities can only boast of one special product; what makes the capital unique is that it gathers goods from all places. Furthermore, because of the large population and busy commercial traffic, there is a demand for everything. There are even shops that deal exclusively in used paper or in feathers, for instance.

lacquerware: varnished wood products

The treasures of Hangzhou and other parts of China were among the greatest in the world. After Marco Polo visited China in the late 1200s, tales of China's wealth began to spread to Europe. Europeans wanted these fabulous goods and luxuries, and a busy trade soon flourished. During the 1400s Europeans, who were eager for such treasures, began racing to find the shortest route to China and Asia.

Source: Patricia Buckley Ebrey, ed., *Chinese Civilization and Society*. New York: The Free Press, 1981.

The Travels of Marco Polo

Travel Journal, 1298

Marco Polo was born in Venice, Italy, in 1254. His father was a trader who traveled all over the world. In 1271, when Polo was 17, his father and his uncle took him on an expedition to Asia. When they reached the ruler Kubla Khan's court in Cambaluc, known today as Beijing, China, they had been on their journey for four years. Kubla Khan (1215–1294) liked Marco Polo and sent him on missions throughout the empire and beyond. After many adventures Polo finally returned to Italy and, in 1298, recorded his stories in a book. He describes some of the people he met, sights he saw, and stories he heard on his journeys. As you read the following excerpts, think about how this book might have been viewed by a European reader from Marco Polo's time. Why do you think this book is considered such an important historical record?

OF THE WHITE FEAST HELD ON NEW YEAR'S DAY AND OF THE NUMBER OF PRESENTS THEN BROUGHT

It is well **ascertained** that the Tartars date the **commencement** of their year from the month of February, and on that occasion it is customary for the Great Khan, as well as all who are **subject to** him, in their several countries, to clothe themselves in white garments, which, according to their ideas, are the **emblem** of good fortune. This is done in the hope that, during the whole course of the year nothing but what is fortunate may happen to them, and that they may enjoy pleasure and comfort.

Upon this day the inhabitants of all the provinces and kingdoms who hold lands or rights of **jurisdiction** under the Great Khan, send him valuable presents of gold, silver, and precious stones, together with many pieces of white cloth.... On this occasion great numbers of beautiful white horses are presented to the Great Khan; or if not perfectly white, it is at least the **prevailing** colour. In this country white horses are not uncommon.

It is moreover the custom in making presents to the Great Khan, for those who have it in their power to **furnish** nine times nine of the article of which the present consists. Thus, for instance, if a province sends a present of horses, there are nine times nine, or eighty-one head in the **drove**. And so also of gold, or of cloth, nine times nine pieces. His Majesty receives at this festival no fewer than a hundred thousand horses.

On this day it is that all his elephants, amounting to five thousand, are exhibited in procession, covered with **housings** of cloth, fancifully and richly worked with gold and silk, in figures of birds and beasts. Then follows a train of camels. When the whole are properly arranged, they pass in review before his Majesty, and form a pleasing spectacle.

ascertained: understood

commencement: beginning

subject to: ruled by

emblem: symbol

jurisdiction: rule

prevailing: most common

furnish: provide

drove: group of horses

housings: coverings

After dinner the musicians and theatrical performers exhibit for the amusement of the court. But on this occasion a lion is conducted into the presence of his Majesty, so tame, that it is taught to lay itself down at his feet. The sports being finished, every one returns to his own home.

OF THE ISLAND OF ZIPANGU AND THE GREAT KHAN'S ATTACK AGAINST IT

Zipangu [Japan] is an island in the eastern ocean, situated at the distance of about fifteen hundred miles from the main-land, or the coast of Manji.

It is of considerable size; its inhabitants have fair complexions, are well made, and are civilized in their manners. Their religion is the worship of **idols**. They are independent of every foreign power, and governed only by their own kings. They have gold in the greatest abundance, its sources being **inexhaustible**, but as the king does not allow its being exported, few merchants visit the country. Nor is it **frequented** by much shipping from other parts.

idols: images of gods

inexhaustible: unlimited

frequented: visited often

The extraordinary richness of the sovereign's palace, according to what we are told by those who have access to the place is a wonderful sight. The entire roof is covered with a plating of gold, in the same manner as we cover houses, or more properly churches, with lead. The ceilings of the halls are of the same precious metal; many of the apartments have small tables of pure gold, of considerable thickness; and the windows also have golden ornaments. So vast, indeed, are the riches of the palace, that it is impossible to **convey** an idea of them....

convey: explain

So great was the wealth of this island, that a desire was excited in the breast of the Great Khan Kublai, now reigning, to make the conquest of it, and to **annex it to his dominions**. In order to [do] this, he **fitted out** a numerous fleet, and [sent] a large body of troops, under the command of two of his principal officers.... The expedition sailed from the ports of **Zai-tun and Kin-sai**, and, crossing the [East China Sea and South China Sea], reached the island in safety.

annex it to his dominions: make it part of his empire

fitted out: prepared

Zai-tun and Kin-sai: present-day Chuan-chow and Hang-chow, China

A jealousy, however, arose between the two commanders, one of whom treated the plans of the other with contempt and resisted execution of his orders. Because of this they were unable to gain possession of any city or **fortified** place, with the exception of one only....

fortified: strengthened

It happened, after some time, that a north wind began to blow with great force, and the ships of the Tartars, which lay near the shore of the island, were driven **foul of** each other. It was then determined, in a council of the officers on board, that they ought to disengage themselves from the land; and accordingly, as soon as the troops were **re-embarked**, they set out to sea. The gale, however, increased to so violent a degree that a number of the vessels **foundered**. The people belonging to them, by floating upon pieces of the wreck, saved

foul of: into

re-embarked: boarded again

foundered: sunk

themselves upon an island lying about four miles from the coast of Zipangu.

The other ships, which, not being so near to the land, did not suffer from the storm, and in which the two chiefs were embarked, together with the principal officers, or those whose rank entitled them to command a hundred thousand or ten thousand men, directed their course homewards, and returned home to the Great Khan.

OF THE PROVINCE OF MAABAR

Leaving the island of Zeilan, and sailing in a westerly direction sixty miles, you reach the great province of Maabar, which is not an island, but part of the continent of the greater India, as it is termed, being the noblest and richest country in the world.

It is governed by four kings, of whom the **principal** is named Sender-bandi. Within his **dominions** is a fishery for pearls, in the gulf of a bay that lies between Maabar and the island of Zeilan, where the water is not more than from ten to twelve **fathoms** in depth, and in some places not more than two fathoms.

principal: most powerful

dominions: areas of rule

fathoms: six-foot units of measurement

The business of the fishery is conducted in the following manner. A number of merchants form themselves into separate companies, and employ many vessels and boats of different sizes, well provided with anchors. They engage and carry with them persons who are skilled in the art of diving for the oysters in which the pearls are enclosed. These they bring up in bags made of netting that are fastened about their bodies, and then repeat the operation, rising to the surface when they can no longer hold their breath. And after a short **interval** they dive again. The greater proportion of the pearls obtained from the fisheries in this gulf, are round, and of good lustre. . . .

interval: period of time

The gulf being infested with a kind of large fish, which often prove destructive to the divers, the merchants take the precaution of being accompanied by certain enchanters belonging to a class of [Brahmans], who, by means of their mystical art, have the power of **stupefying** these fish, so as to prevent them from doing mischief.

Brahmans: Hindus of the highest caste

stupefying: making senseless

What kind of fish do you think Marco Polo might be describing in the last paragraph? After returning to his home, Polo married and had three daughters. He died about 1323. Less than 200 years later, Polo's book helped inspire Christopher Columbus to look for a route to India by sea.

Source: Manuel Komroff, ed., *The Travels of Marco Polo.* New York: Horace Liveright, 1930.

The Tale of Genji

by Murasaki Shikibu, early 1000s

In the late tenth century, Japanese literature began to flower with stories and poems about the rituals and ceremonies of the island nation's palace life. Around the year 1000 Murasaki Shikibu (moor uh SAHK ee SHEE kee boo, 978–1031), a woman who worked for the empress, wrote Genji monogatari, which translates as The Tale of Genji (GEN JEE). This book, often considered the world's first novel, is about the adventures of a prince named Genji and numbers more than 4,000 pages. In the following excerpt the prince gets caught in a dangerous storm while he is away from the emperor's palace. What does this story tell you about the customs and beliefs of Japanese society in the eleventh century?

*I*t was the day of the serpent, the first such day in the Third Month. "The day when a man who has worries goes down and washes them away," said one of his men, admirably informed, it would seem, in all the **annual observances**.

Wishing to have a look at the seashore, Genji set forth. Plain, rough curtains were strung up among the trees, and a **soothsayer** who was doing the circuit of the province was **summoned** to perform the **lustration**.

Genji thought he could see something of himself in the rather large doll being cast off to sea, bearing away sins and **tribulations**. . . .

The bright open seashore showed him to wonderful advantage. The sea stretched placid into **measureless** distances. He thought of all that had happened to him, and all that was still to come. . . .

Suddenly a wind came up and even before the services were finished the sky was black. Genji's men rushed about in confusion. Rain came pouring down, completely without warning. Though the obvious course would have been to return **straightway** to the house, there had been no time to send for umbrellas. The wind was now a howling **tempest**, everything that had not been tied down was **scuttling** off across the beach. The surf was biting at their feet. The sea was white, as if spread over with white linen. Lightning flashed and thunder roared. Fearful every moment of being struck down, they finally made their way back to the house.

"I've never seen anything like it," said one of the men. "Winds do come up from time to time, but not without warning. It is all very strange and very terrible."

annual observances: yearly ceremonies

soothsayer: fortune teller

summoned: called

lustration: purifying ceremony

tribulations: sufferings

measureless: great

straightway: at once

tempest: storm

scuttling: scurrying

The lightning and thunder seemed to announce the end of the world, and the rain to beat its way into the ground; and Genji sat calmly reading a **sutra**. The thunder **subsided** in the evening, but the wind went on through the night.

"Our prayers seem to have been answered. A little more and we would have been carried off. I've heard that tidal waves do carry people off before they know what is happening to them, but I've not seen anything like this.". . .

sutra: sacred Buddhist teaching
subsided: lessened

Genji offered prayers to the king of the sea and countless other gods as well. The thunder was increasingly more terrible, and finally the gallery adjoining his rooms was struck by lightning. Flames sprang up and the gallery was destroyed. The confusion was immense; the whole world seemed to have gone mad. Genji was moved to a building out in back, a kitchen or something of the sort it seemed to be. It was crowded with people of every station and rank. The **clamor** was almost enough to drown out the lightning and thunder. Night descended over a sky already as black as ink.

clamor: noise

Presently the wind and rain subsided and stars began to come out. The kitchen being altogether too mean a place, a move back to the main hall was suggested. The **charred** remains of the gallery were an ugly sight, however, and the hall had been badly muddied and all the blinds and curtains blown away. . . .

charred: burned

[Genji] opened a **wattled** door and looked out. The moon had come up. The line left by the waves was white and dangerously near, and the surf was still high. There was no one here whom he could turn to, no student of the deeper truths who could **discourse** upon past and present and perhaps explain these wild events. All the fisherfolk had gathered at what they had heard was the house of a great gentleman from the city. They were as noisy and impossible to communicate with as a flock of birds, but no one thought of telling them to leave.

wattled: woven with poles and reeds

discourse: talk

"If the wind had kept up just a little longer," someone said, "absolutely everything would have been swept under. The gods did well by us."

Genji goes through many adventures before this 11th-century novel comes to a close. In addition to writing this novel, Murasaki Shikibu also kept a diary that reveals much about life in ancient Japan.

Source: Murasaki Shikibu, *The Tale of Genji*. New York: Vintage Books, 1990.

2-Rabbit, 7-Wind

Retold by Toni de Gerez, 1971

The Aztec people of central Mexico founded their capital city, Tenochtitlán, in 1325. It soon flourished, and the Aztecs developed a sophisticated civilization. The following poems were written during this period. One poem mentions the Toltec people, who first established cities in Mexico around 900. Honoring the Toltecs as their predecessors was an important part of the Aztec culture. The other poems reflect on other significant aspects of Aztec civilization—art, storytelling, and medicine. Doctors knew of over a thousand plants that could be used to treat patients. As you read, think of other occupations cultures need to build civilizations.

The Toltecs were wise
they **conversed** with their own hearts

they played their drums
they played their rattles
    they were singers
    they made songs
the Toltecs guarded the songs
in their memories

the Toltecs were wise
they conversed with their own hearts

conversed: talked together

The true artist is a *tlacuilo*
he paints with red-and-black ink
with black water
the true artist is wise
god is in his heart he paints god
    into things
he knows all colors
he makes shapes he draws feet
    and faces
he paints shadows
he is a Toltec
he has a dialogue with his own heart

The true storyteller is a *tlaquetzqui*
he says things boldly
with the lips and mouth of an artist
the true storyteller uses words of joy
flowers are on his lips
his language is strict
his language is noble

the bad storyteller is careless
he confuses words he swallows them
he says useless words
he has no dignity

The true doctor is a *tlamatini*
he is a wise man he gives life
he knows herbs stones trees roots
he examines he experiments he sets bones
he gives potions he bleeds his patients
he cuts and sews he stops the bleeding
    with ashes

The Aztec people were conquered by the Spanish in 1521. However, some Aztec traditions still survive today. The name Mexico comes from the name the Aztec called themselves. Today people around the world enjoy a food first introduced by the Aztec, made from cacao beans. This food is called chocolate. Perhaps this is one of your favorite treats.

Source: Toni de Gerez, *2-Rabbit, 7-Wind: Poems from Ancient Mexico Retold from Nahuatl Texts.* New York: Viking Press, 1971.

THE GLORY OF

THE INCAS

by Pedro de Cieza de León, 1553

Five hundred years ago the Inca ruled a vast empire that stretched 2,500 miles along the western coast of South America. They built thousands of miles of roads to connect their empire. They also built terraces on the steep slopes of the Andes Mountains. These terraces enabled them to grow crops that yielded abundant supplies of food. In the 1530s a young Spanish soldier named Pedro de Cieza de León (day SEEAY zah day lay OHN) traveled on horseback throughout the lands of the former Inca empire and kept a record of his journey. Cieza de León was impressed by the skill of Inca carvers. He was also amazed at how well the Inca distributed food so that no one would go hungry. The following excerpt is translated from a book published by Cieza de León in 1553. What are three things about the Inca that most impressed the author? Why did they impress him? When you are finished reading the text, study the illustrations. They were drawn by Felipe Guamán Poma de Ayala, a seventeenth-century Inca nobleman from the Andes Mountains. How do his drawings help illustrate Cieza de León's account?

There is no disputing the fact that when one sees the fine handicraft they have produced, it arouses the admiration of all who have knowledge of it. The most amazing thing is how few tools and instruments they have for their work, and how easily they produce things of finest quality. At the time the Spaniards conquered this kingdom, articles of gold, clay, and silver were discovered, the parts joined one to the other as though they had been created that way. The most amazing examples of silverwork, **statuettes**, and other larger things were seen, . . . I have seen dinner **services** made with the use of pieces of copper and two or three stones, so finely worked, and the goblets, platters, and **candelabra** all **embossed** with leaves and designs, that master workmen would have their work cut out for them to do as well with all the instruments and tools they have. Aside from the articles of silver, many of them make **medallions**, chains, and other things of gold. And little boys, who if you saw them you would not think knew how to talk yet, understand how to do these things. . . .

The *Orejones* [awr ay HOH nays] of **Cuzco** who supplied me with information are in agreement that in olden times, in the days of the Lord-Incas, all the villages and provinces of Peru were notified that a report should be given to the rulers and their representatives each year of the men and women who had died, and all who had been born, for this was necessary for the **levying** of the **tributes** as well as to know how many were available for war and those who could assume the defense of the villages. This was an easy matter, for each province at the end of the year had a list by the knots of the **quipus** [KEE pooz] of all the people who had died there during the year and how many deaths. This was reported with all truth and accuracy, without any **fraud** or **deceit**. In this way the **Inca** and the governors knew which of the Indians were poor, the women who had been widowed, whether they were able to pay their taxes, and how many men they could count on in the event of war, and many other things they considered highly important.

As this kingdom was so vast, as I have repeatedly mentioned, in each of the many provinces there were many storehouses filled with

statuettes: small statues
services: table settings

candelabra: branched candlesticks
embossed: decorated

medallions: large medals

Orejones: Incan nobles
Cuzco: capital of the Incan empire

levying: raising
tributes: payments to a ruler

quipus: special cords used for counting

fraud: cheating
deceit: trickery

Inca: title for the Incan emperor

supplies and other needful things; thus, in times of war, wherever the armies went they [drew] upon the contents of these storehouses, without ever touching the supplies of their **confederates** or laying a finger on what they had in their settlements. And when there was no war, all this stock of supplies and food was divided up among the poor and the widows. These poor were the aged, or the lame, crippled, or paralyzed, or those **afflicted** with some other disease; if they were in good health, they received nothing. Then the storehouses were filled up once more with the tributes paid the Inca. If there came a lean year, the storehouses were opened and the provinces were lent what they needed in the way of supplies; then, in a year of abundance, they paid back all they had received. . . .

No one who was lazy or tried to live by the work of others was **tolerated**; everyone had to work. Thus on certain days each lord went to his lands and took the plow in hand and cultivated the earth, and did other things. Even the Incas themselves did this to set an example, for everybody was to know that there should be nobody so rich that, on this account, he might **disdain** or **affront** the poor. And under their system there was none such in all the kingdom, for, if he had his health, he worked and lacked for nothing; and if he was ill, he received what he needed from the storehouses. And no rich man could deck himself out in more **finery** than the poor, or wear different clothing, except the rulers and headmen, who, to maintain their dignity, were allowed great freedom and privilege, as well as the *Orejones*, who held a place apart among all the peoples.

confederates: allies

afflicted: suffering

tolerated: permitted

disdain: look down on
affront: insult

finery: fancy clothing

From 1531 to 1535 Spanish troops led by Francisco Pizarro attacked and finally defeated the Inca empire. Today Cieza de León's writings survive as one of the finest accounts of what Inca life was once like.

Source: Victor Wolfgang von Hagen, ed., *The Incas of Pedro de Cieza de León*. Norman, OK: University of Oklahoma Press, 1959.

THE LAKOTA AND NATURE

by Luther Standing Bear, 1933

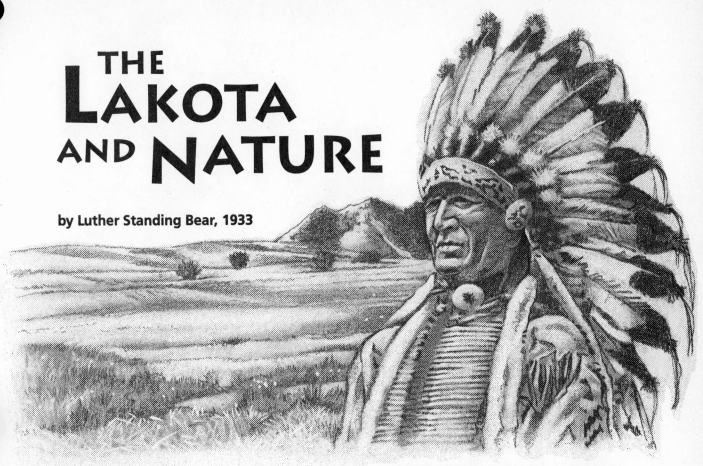

The ways North America's early settlers lived were as varied as the lands they inhabited. Yet Native American groups all over the continent were united by their deep respect for nature and the environment. In 1933 one Native American leader wrote a book about his people, the Lakota, and their roots in the land. Luther Standing Bear grew up on the grassy plains of what is now South Dakota. In the following excerpt from his book Land of the Spotted Eagle, *he explains why the Lakota feel such strong ties to the earth. According to Luther Standing Bear, what ties do the Lakota have to the earth and all of its creations?*

The Lakota was a true naturist—a lover of Nature. He loved the earth and all things of the earth, the attachment growing with age. The old people came **literally** to love the soil and they sat or **reclined** on the ground with a feeling of being close to a mothering power. It was good for the skin to touch the earth and the old people liked to remove their moccasins and walk with bare feet on the sacred earth. Their tipis were built upon the earth and their **altars** were made of earth. The birds that flew in the air came to rest upon the earth and it was the final **abiding** place of all things that lived and grew. The soil was soothing, strengthening, cleansing, and healing.

This is why the old Indian still sits upon the earth instead of propping himself up and away from its life-giving forces. For him, to sit or lie upon the ground is to be able to think more deeply and to

literally: actually
reclined: lay down

altars: places where religious services are performed
abiding: dwelling

feel more keenly; he can see more clearly into the mysteries of life and come closer in **kinship** to other lives about him. . . .

From **Wakan Tanka** there came a great unifying life force that flowed in and through all things—the flowers of the plains, blowing winds, rocks, trees, birds, animals—and was the same force that had been breathed into the first man. Thus all things were **kindred** and brought together by the same Great Mystery. . . .

The animals had rights—the right of man's protection, the right to live, the right to multiply, the right to freedom, and the right to man's **indebtedness**—and in recognition of these rights the Lakota never enslaved the animal, and spared all life that was not needed for food and clothing.

This **concept** of life and its relations was humanizing and gave to the Lakota an abiding love. It filled his being with the joy and mystery of living; it gave him **reverence** for all life; it made a place for all things in the **scheme** of existence with equal importance to all. The Lakota could despise no creature, for all were of one blood, made by the same hand, and filled with the **essence** of the Great Mystery. . . .

But the old Lakota was wise. He knew that man's heart, away from nature, becomes hard; he knew that lack of respect for growing, living things soon led to lack of respect for humans too. So he kept his youth close to its softening influence.

kinship: understanding

Wakan Tanka: the Creator

kindred: related

indebtedness: owing something to another

concept: idea

reverence: respect
scheme: plan

essence: heart and soul

The Lakota and other Native American groups have kept this deep respect for nature. Today many Americans are working to help protect the environment.

Source: Luther Standing Bear, *Land of the Spotted Eagle.* Lincoln, NE, and London, England: University of Nebraska Press, 1933.

KOKOOM

**Cree Tale Retold by
Garry Gregory J. Ladouceur, 1982**

For thousands of years, the Cree Indians have lived in Canada's north country, passing down tales from one generation to the next. Many of these tales describe the Cree's closeness to nature and try to explain the origins of the natural world. A Cree named Garry Gregory J. Ladouceur heard the tale called Kokoom from his father as a boy and later wrote it down. "Kokoom" refers to a kind grandmother who loves children. What does this folktale say about the Cree's feelings toward their elders?

In the old days before the world was as it is now, there was only the sun. Once the sun disappeared, however, the night was in blackness. There was no moon. Night was a particularly trying time for children who were **cowed** by the dark. In the community there lived [one] grandmother or "Kokoom" whom the children . . . loved and adored. They spent a great deal of time with her because she was kind and so interesting to be with. Gradually though, with the forces of time "Kokoom" became older, and . . . the children and "Kokoom" realized that she must soon leave. The children became very **distraught** as they came to realize the **inevitability** of "Kokoom's" death. "Kokoom" herself was also pained, not because she feared her own **mortality**, but because of the sorrow she knew the children would feel on her **passing**.

Before she died therefore, she gathered all the children of the village about her and she made a promise. Because of her great love for the children, "Kokoom" promised them that she would continue to protect and give them comfort even if she died.

When "Kokoom" finally died, the children were **disheartened** nonetheless. On the night of her death, however, "Kokoom" rose into the night skies and became the moon. It was obvious that the moon was "Kokoom" as she had a round face (My father explained that older Indian women generally have round faces), and a smile that one could see as shadows on the moon's features. "Kokoom" had kept her promise and is still keeping it today. Where the nights had previously been black and fearful and the "Cheepeyes" (fearful spirits of the forest) had had **free rein** and forced the children to hide in fear, night was now lit by "Kokoom." She always watches over her children.

cowed: scared

distraught: upset
inevitability: certainty
mortality: certainty of death
passing: dying

disheartened: saddened

free rein: complete freedom of movement

By writing down tales such as Kokoom, Garry Gregory J. Ladouceur helps preserve his Cree culture. He also enables other people to learn about Cree traditions and beliefs.

Source: Herbert Halpert, ed., *A Folklore Sampler from the Maritimes.* St. John's, Newfoundland, Canada: Memorial University of Newfoundland, 1982.

Sugar Mapling

by Jacqueline Sletto, 1992

The Ojibwa people, also known as the Anishinabe (ahn ish uh NAH bee), have lived in the Great Lakes region of North America for over five hundred years. The following excerpt from a magazine article describes the Ojibwa tradition of sugar mapling that continues today. Why does this Ojibwa family consider mapling important? Which traditions have remained the same for this Ojibwa family? Which have changed?

Through the long [Minnesota] winter, Lisa Erle and her family wait. Spring will come, they say. Just wait. And when at last the days lose their icy brilliance and the nights their bone-chilling cold, Lisa and her relatives gather again at the family's stand of sugar maple trees—called a "sugar bush"—on the White Earth Reservation. They have come to maple, **rendering** the sap of the sugar maple tree into syrup and sugar as their parents and grandparents and uncounted generations of Anishinabe before them have done....

rendering: making

The Anishinabe...were one of the woodland tribes who engaged in sugar mapling long before the **advent** of Europeans. Every year, when Lisa Erle and her family return to the sugar bush, they are **acutely** aware of the connections they are making with their past. "It's something you pass on to each generation," says Erle. "I'm glad my children can do something with me like I did with my parents and grandparents when I was a child."

advent: coming

acutely: very

The process begins when the family drills holes into their sugar maple trees and inserts spiles—four-inch-long tubes with sharpened ends fashioned from aluminum or tin piping—to draw off the sap....At the ends of the spiles, they hang collection vessels **fashioned** from plastic milk jugs, two-liter pop bottles, or coffee cans....

fashioned: made

When the temperature rises above 40°F during the day—usually in early March—sap begins flowing from the sugar maples' roots to their branches, triggering the budding process. At this time of year, temperatures sink to freezing again in the nighttime, however, and the sap rushes back down to the protection of the trees' roots....As the sap runs back and forth within the trees, some of it drips out of the spiles and into the containers.

Once the sap starts flowing, [Lisa] Erle and her family spend every weekend in the sugar bush, which is located on her grandfather's land. This last spring they tapped approximately seventy trees, and collected close to 150 gallons of sap. They boiled the sap over an open

fire in a cast-iron kettle that belonged to Lisa's grandparents—forty gallons at a time. After six or eight hours, most of the water in the sap has boiled away, leaving about a gallon of thick, rich maple syrup, called *zheewaagamaazigan* in Anishinabe. Lisa stops the process here, simply straining the syrup through **cheesecloth** and bottling it for use on wild rice pancakes or as a cooking sweetener for such foods as sweet potatoes and wild rice.... Although she could sell the syrup, as some Anishinabe in the area do, she prefers to keep it for her family and use it in her own cooking. "It's too precious to sell," she says. "It takes so long to make."

cheesecloth: loosely woven cotton

Mapling is **laborious**, but Lisa [and her] family have an easy time of it compared to the processing problems encountered by Anishinabe in the old days. Traditionally, they slashed the maples with axes and then inserted a flattened wooden chip, reed, or piece of bark into the gash, which allowed the sap to drip neatly into birchbark containers sealed with **pitch** propped at the foot of the tree....

laborious: hard work

In the old days, all family members would assist in tapping the trees, just as Lisa Erle's family does today, but once the sap started to run and the boiling **began in earnest**, the women were in charge. They supervised the processing from the shelter of a specially constructed sugaring lodge covered with birchbark, furnished inside with built-in platforms along the walls where the family slept at night. The mapling fire, lit just outside the lodge door, burned all day and night as the women boiled the sap down to sugar. The men contributed to the **endeavor** by chopping the firewood and carrying the sap to the fire in large birchbark pails.

pitch: sticky substance from a tree

began in earnest: got underway

endeavor: work

Boiling posed something of a problem before Europeans brought iron kettles. The Anishinabe—known among neighboring tribes as "The Birch-bark People"—fashioned special deep birchbark troughs for boiling. They would heat stones to red-hot and then drop them in the troughs, continually adding new stones and removing cooled ones to keep the sap boiling steadily....

Although mapling was not easy, the Anishinabe thought the effort worthwhile to obtain one of their favorite foods. Like the other woodland tribes, they ate maple sugar throughout the year with almost every meal, causing surprised Europeans to comment on their **penchant** for sweets....

penchant: strong liking

[Lisa's grandfather] tells the story of how the Anishinabe learned about the goodness of maple sap. "They saw a bear scraping at a tree and licking off the sap," he says. "So they tasted the sap, too, because they knew that the bear is the wisest of animals, and if he found the sap good, then it must be."...

"I really like [sugar mapling]," says Lisa.... "It's the family time together. I grew up with this, and I want to continue the tradition."

Lisa Erle and her family enjoy their memories and the maple treats they have made for the rest of the year. What traditions does your family share?

Source: *Native People's Magazine* (Fall 1992, Vol.6, No.1). Phoenix: Media Concepts Group Inc., 1992.

Loneliness Song

by an unknown Navajo woman, 1864

The Navajo were among the diverse groups of Native Americans living in North America before the Europeans arrived. Beginning in the 1700s the Navajo settled in what is today western New Mexico and Arizona. Over the next century they were involved in many land disputes with European settlers as well as other Native American peoples—the Hopi and the Zuni. In 1863 the United States government sent in troops under the leadership of General Kit Carson to force the Navajo from their homes. Many Navajo died when they were forced to march over 300 miles east, where they were imprisoned in a fort. The march became known as "The Long Walk." "Loneliness Song" is believed to have been created in 1864 by an unknown Navajo woman. The songwriter does not mention "The Long Walk." Do you think her song may have been partly inspired by the recent experiences of her people? If so, why?

Navajo Indian Song

Navajo: She _____ na' sha, she _____ na' sha,
English: As _____ I walk, as _____ I walk,

She _____ na' sha, B' keh, huh zho-la he-yah heyn' neh' yuh.
As _____ I walk, O may my path be beau-ti - ful for me.

Ah' ah' luh, ah' ah' luh koh' nuh sha. _____
Or I'm a-lone in my lone - li-ness. _____

In 1868 a peace treaty was signed and the Navajo settled on a reservation that today covers 16 million acres in New Mexico, Arizona, and Utah. While the Navajo are known as farmers and ranchers, they also operate the largest Native American newspaper in the United States and the only Native American-run college—Navajo Community College. Navajo craftspeople are famous for their beautiful silver and turquoise jewelry and their unique handwoven blankets.

Source: *Music and You, Grade 5*, Macmillan/McGraw-Hill, 1991.

114

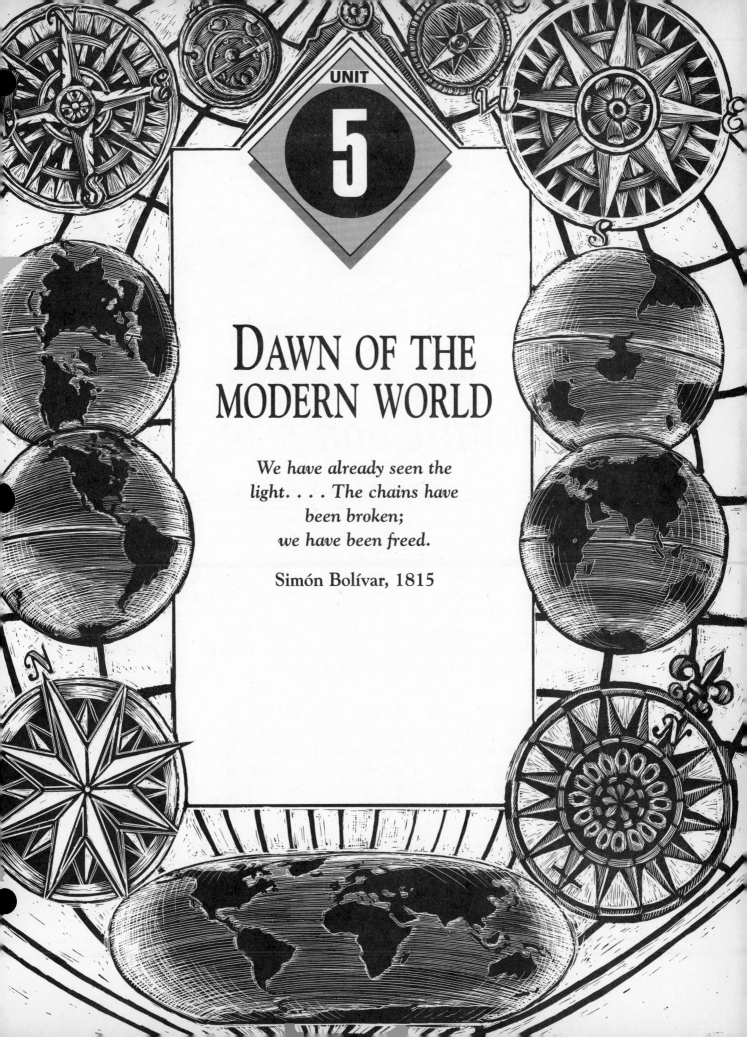

UNIT 5

DAWN OF THE MODERN WORLD

*We have already seen the
light. . . . The chains have
been broken;
we have been freed.*

Simón Bolívar, 1815

Captain Cook's Journal

by James Cook, 1770

In 1768 a British sea captain named James Cook set out on an expedition to find a giant continent that many Europeans believed existed in the Southern Hemisphere. In the course of his three-year journey, Captain Cook explored many islands, such as Tahiti, New Zealand, and Tasmania. He also explored the eastern coast of Australia. In a journal that he kept of his voyage, Cook described the great coral reefs, the beautiful fish and animals, and the Aborigines (ab uh RIHJ uh neez), the original inhabitants of Australia. Below is an excerpt from Captain Cook's journal. What are some of the skills and traits of the Aborigines that impressed him? Why do you think the Aborigines had little interest in trading with Captain Cook and his crew?

Land animals are scarce, so far as we know [they are limited] to a very few species. . . . The sort which is in the greatest plenty is the kangaroo. . . , so called by the Natives; we saw a good many of them [as they were] eating. Here [in Australia] are likewise lizards, snakes, scorpions, . . . etc., but not in any [large numbers]. Tame animals they have none but dogs, and of these we saw but one, and therefore [they] must be very scarce. . . .

The land **fowls** are **bustards**, eagles, hawks, crows, such as we have in England, **cockatoos** of 2 sorts, white and brown, very beautiful birds of the parrot kind, . . . pigeons, doves, quails, and several sorts of smaller birds. The sea is . . . well stocked with fish of various sorts. . . . Here are also upon the shoals and reefs great

fowls: birds
bustards: Australian birds
cockatoos: a type of parrot

numbers of the finest green turtle in the world, and in the river and salt creeks are some alligators.

The Natives of this country are of a middle **stature**, [with] straight bodies and slender limbs; their hair [is] mostly black [and] they all wear it cut short; their beards, which are generally black, they likewise [keep] short. . . . Their features are far from being disagreeable, and their voices are soft and **tunable**.

I do not look upon them to be a warlike people; on the contrary, I think them a **timorous** and inoffensive race, no ways inclined to cruelty, neither are they very numerous. They live in small parties along by the sea coast, the banks of lakes, rivers, creeks, etc. They seem to have no fixed **habitation**, but move about from place to place in search of food. . . . They have wooden fish **gigs**, with 2, 3, or 4 prongs, each very **ingeniously** made, with which they strike fish. We have also seen them strike both fish and birds with their darts. With these they likewise kill other animals; they have also wooden **harpoons** for striking turtles, but of these I believe they get but few, except at the seasons [the turtles] come ashore to lay [eggs]. . . .

From what I have said of the natives of **New Holland** they may appear to some to be the most **wretched** people upon earth; but in reality they are far more happy than we Europeans, being wholly unacquainted not only with the **superfluous**, but with the necessary conveniences so much sought after in Europe; they are happy in not knowing the use of them. They live in a **tranquility** which is [based on the equal treatment of all members in their society]. The earth and sea of their own accord furnish them with all things necessary for life. They **covet** not magnificent houses, household-stuff, etc.; they live in a warm and fine climate, and enjoy every wholesome air, so that they have very little need of clothing; and this they seem to be fully sensible of, for many to whom we gave cloth, etc., left it carelessly upon the sea beach and in the woods, as a thing they had no manner of use for; in short, they seemed to set no value upon anything we gave them, nor would they ever part with anything of their own for any one article we could offer them. This, in my opinion, argues that they think themselves provided with all the necessarys of life, and that they have no **superfluities**.

stature: height

tunable: melodic, attractive

timorous: shy

habitation: home

gigs: pronged spears
ingeniously: cleverly

harpoons: long spears

New Holland: early name for Australia, which was claimed by Holland, or the Netherlands
wretched: miserable
superfluous: luxurious, wasteful
tranquillity: state of peace
covet: want

superfluities: unneeded possessions

Captain James Cook claimed eastern Australia for Great Britain in 1770. During his voyages Cook mapped many islands in the Pacific Ocean and explored the coast of North America from Oregon to Alaska. He was killed in Hawaii in 1789. One year earlier, in 1788, the first English colonists—many of them convicts—began arriving in Australia, and thousands of free settlers came in the 1800s.

Source: *Captain Cook's Journal During His First Voyage Round the World*. London: Elliot Stock, 1893.

BATTLE OF TENOCHTITLÁN

by Aztec Historians, 1521

Beginning around 1325, the Aztec ruled a powerful empire in the Central Valley of Mexico. In 1519, however, Hernando Cortéz and his army of Spanish soldiers arrived in the Aztec capital of Tenochtitlán. At first the Aztec ruler Moctezuma permitted the Spaniards to enter the city peacefully. The Spaniards, however, were not interested in peace but rather in the vast quantities of Aztec gold and silver stored at Tenochtitlán. The Spaniards attacked the Aztec and, in 1521, laid siege to the city for 85 days. Aztec historians recorded these events in pictographs, a form of writing in which pictures are used to represent events and ideas. Aztec pictographs were written on amatl (ah MAHT ul), a type of paper that was made by pounding the inner bark of a wild fig tree. The pictograph on the next page, based on the Aztec calendar, tells the history of the Spanish conquest. The three boxes at the top of the pictograph contain Aztec symbols that stand for three different years. Study the other images and try to determine what they mean. Then compare your ideas to the explanation below.

On the left side of the pictograph, the soldier on a horse carrying a sword, shield, and cross represents the Spaniards landing in Mexico in the Aztec year of 1-Reed. It is believed that the event in this picture took place in 1519, because a reed, which is pictured in the box above the soldier, is one of the symbols used by Aztecs in naming that year. The Aztecs used a calendar year fixed at 365 days, much as the United States and many other countries do today.

Beside the Spanish soldier is an Aztec official who is greeting him. The official is shown offering the soldier a gift, which indicates that at first the Aztecs welcomed the Spaniards. The faces in the row of images at the bottom of the pictograph show the different Indian groups allied with the Aztecs.

The next scene shows that during the year of 2-Flint, or 1520, a fight took place in the Aztec capital. The pictograph shows Aztec priests being cut down in battle by the Spaniards' steel swords on the steps of the city's main pyramid. This pyramid—the most important building in Tenochtitlán—housed the two main temples dedicated to Aztec gods. These are shown by the two sets of steps leading up the pyramid. Try to find the image of the cactus and stone joined to a temple, which was another symbol for Tenochtitlán. Although the Spaniards' first attempt to capture Tenochtitlán was unsuccessful, they later conquered the city on the day 1-Serpent of the year 3-House, or 1521.

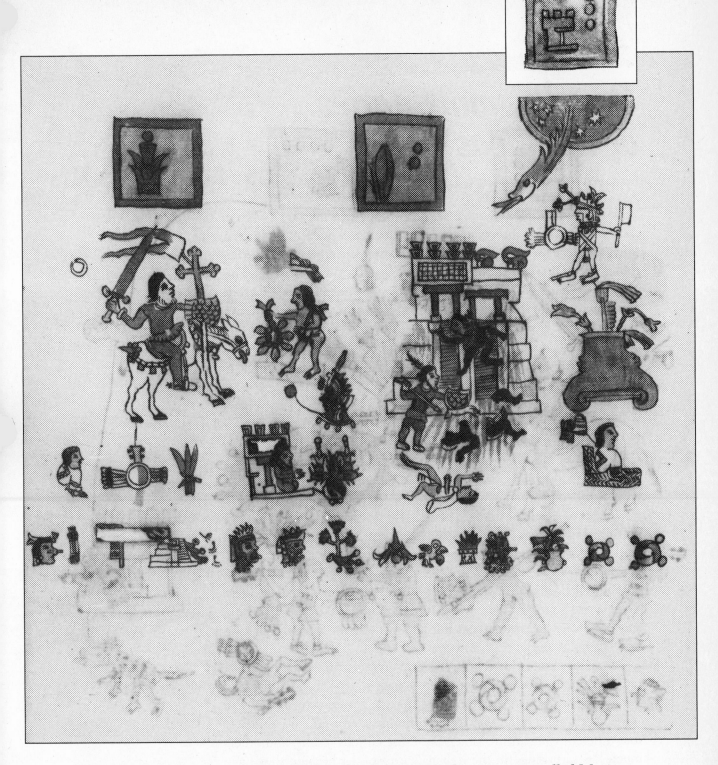

After defeating the Aztec at Tenochtitlán, the Spaniards built a new city, called Mexico City, on top of the Aztec ruins. Today Mexico City is the capital of Mexico. This pictograph preserves the memory of Tenochtitlán and helps us to understand the Spanish conquest from an Aztec point of view. Suppose you were asked to make a pictograph of an event in your life or that of your classroom or country. What symbols might you use?

Royal Commentaries of the Incas

by Garcilaso de la Vega, El Inca, 1612

When Spanish explorers came to the Americas in the late 1400s and early 1500s, they were introduced to many cultural traditions and natural features of the Americas that they had never seen before. In turn, the Spanish brought with them parts of their culture that were unfamiliar to the people that lived in the Americas. The following selection tells of some animals and plants the Spanish introduced to the Americas, along with ideas about how to use them. Is it easy for a culture to accept another culture's ideas? Would some ideas be easier to accept than others?

As it will be agreeable for those of this and future generations to know what things were not found in Peru until the Spaniards conquered it, I have thought fit to devote a separate chapter to them, so that the reader may see and understand how many things that are apparently necessary to human life the Indians were able to do without. And they were very satisfied without them. In the first place, they had neither horses nor mares for warfare or festivities; neither cows nor oxen for ploughing and sowing; neither camels, [donkeys], nor mules as beasts of burden; neither the **coarse** Spanish sheep nor **merinos** for wool and meat; neither goats nor pigs for dried meat and leather; nor even **pedigree** dogs for hunting, such as greyhounds, beagles, retrievers, setters, pointers, spaniels, **whippets,** or mastiffs to guard their flocks, or even the pretty little creatures called lap dogs. There were a great many of what in Spain are called **curs,** large and small. Neither had they wheat nor barley, nor wine nor oil, nor fruit nor vegetables of the Spanish varieties....

coarse: rough
merinos: Spanish sheep
pedigree: bred
whippets: slender dogs

curs: mutts

Some Spaniards have taken such an interest in agriculture, as I have been told, that they have **grafted** Spanish fruit trees on those of Peru, producing wonderful fruit to the great astonishment of the Indians on finding that one tree can be made to bear two, three, or four different fruits in the same year: these curious results, and others much less surprising, fill the Indians with wonder because they have never attempted such things.

grafted: combined

Garcilaso de la Vega, who wrote this selection, was a Peruvian historian. He was born in Cuzco, Peru, in 1539. His father was one of the Spanish people who helped conquer Peru, and his mother was a princess of the Inca people. De la Vega died in 1616.

Source: Garcilaso de la Vega, El Inca, Harold Livermore, trans., *Royal Commentaries of the Incas and General History of Peru, Part One.* Austin: University of Texas Press, 1966.

TEARS OF THE INDIANS

by Bartolomé de Las Casas, 1542

When Spanish colonists arrived in what is today called Latin America, they set up the encomienda system, which used enslaved Indians as forced labor. This system, as well as the diseases brought by Europeans, caused the deaths of many Native Americans in the early 1500s. Bartolomé de las Casas (1474–1566) was a Spanish priest who supported the encomienda system at first but then turned against it. In fact, Las Casas was so upset about the behavior of the Spanish colonists that he wrote letters to Spain's rulers, protesting the mistreatment of Indians. In the excerpt below, translated from a book he wrote in 1542 about the colonies, Las Casas presents his views about how the Spaniards' actions were destroying the Indians and their civilization. According to Las Casas, what effect did Spanish colonization have on the Indians? What evidence does he give to support his claim?

There were ten kingdoms [on the continent of North America] as large as the kingdom of Spain, Aragon, and Portugal, **encompassing** over a thousand square miles [2,600 sq km]. Of all this the inhumane and **abominable** villainies of the Spaniards have made a wilderness, for though it was formerly occupied by vast and **infinite** numbers of men [women and children] it is stripped of all people. And we dare assert with confidence that in those forty years during which the Spaniards have exercised their abominable cruelties and detestable **tyrannies** in those parts, over twelve million souls innocently **perished**, women and children being included in the sad and fatal list. Moreover I truly believe that I should be speaking within the truth if I were to say that over fifty millions were **consumed** in this massacre.

encompassing: including

abominable: terrible

infinite: endless

tyrannies: abuses of power

perished: died

consumed: killed

As for those that came out of Spain, boasting themselves to be Christians, they had two ways of **extirpating** the Indian nation from the face of the earth: the first was by making bloody, unjust, and cruel wars against them, the second was by killing all those that so much as sought to recover their liberty, as some of the braver sort did. And as for the women and children that were left alive, the Spaniards laid so heavy and **grievous** a **yoke of servitude** upon them that the condition of beasts was much more tolerable.

All the various other torments and inhumanities which they **employed** to the ruin of these poor nations may be included under these two headings.

What led the Spaniards to these **unsanctified impieties** was the desire for gold to make themselves suddenly rich, in order to obtain dignities and honors that were in no way fit for them. In a word their **covetousness**, their ambition which could not be exceeded by any people under heaven, the riches of the country, and the patience of the people gave occasion for this devilish **barbarism**. For the Spaniards so despised them (I now speak what I have seen without the least untruth) that they used them not like beasts, for that would have been tolerable, but looked upon them as if they had been but the **dung** and filth of the earth, and so little did they regard the health of their souls that they permitted this great **multitude** to die without the least light of religion. Nor is this less true than what I have said before and what those tyrants and hangmen themselves do not deny . . . namely, that the Indians never gave them the least cause for such violence but received them as angels sent from heaven, until the excessive cruelties and torments and slaughters moved them to take arms against the Spaniards. . . .

extirpating: wiping out

grievous: painful
yoke of servitude: state of slavery

employed: used

unsanctified impieties: wicked deeds

covetousness: greed

barbarism: uncivilized acts

dung: manure

multitude: large number

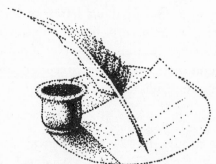

During the early 1500s Bartolomé de Las Casas's voice of protest was heard by the Spanish king. In 1516 Las Casas was appointed "Protector of the Indians." He made the cause of protecting the rights of Indians his lifelong crusade. Due to Las Casas's efforts, the New Laws—royal decrees prohibiting forced labor of the Indians—were issued in 1542, the same year his book appeared. But the Spaniards soon replaced the Indians with enslaved people from Africa. To learn about the first slaves in Latin America who rebelled and gained their freedom, read the document on page 133.

Source: Adapted from the translation by John Phillips, from Bartolomé de Las Casas, *The Tears of the Indians, Being an Historical and True Account of the Cruel Massacres and Slaughters of above Twenty Millions of Innocent People* (London, 1656), in Charles Gibson, ed., *The Spanish Tradition in America.* New York: Harper, 1968.

The Legacy Of Columbus

by Sarah Elder Hale, 1992

When Christopher Columbus (1451–1506) came to the Americas in 1492, the land that was the "New World" to him was an old world to the cultures that had lived there over the past 10,000 years. The following selection is an editorial that was written on the 500th anniversary of Columbus's arrival in the Americas. As the author points out, without that time of change and exchange between cultures, we would not have the diverse cultural heritage we enjoy today. What things in your daily life came from other cultures? How has the world changed since the time of Columbus?

Most of you know that 1992 marks the five hundredth anniversary, the quincentennial, of Christopher Columbus's voyage across the "Ocean Sea" and his arrival in what was later called the Americas. Columbus's mission was to find a westward route to the rich lands of India, the Spice Islands, Cipangu (Japan), and other Asian ports and to carry with him the message of Christianity. He did not know that two continents lay between him and Asia. His accidental "discovery" of lands and peoples unknown to Europeans changed the world.

In 1492, Columbus started an exhange of cultures, resources, and ideas that continues to this day. Food, animals, customs, and diseases crisscrossed the Atlantic in the years following Columbus's first voyage. Unfortunately, the native peoples suffered greatly under Spanish **colonialism**. It was a dramatic encounter between two civilizations, an encounter that changed forever the course of history.

colonialism: conquering

We use the words "change" and "exchange" often in history. Without change, we could not further our understanding of the world around us, and without exchange, cultures would become **isolated** and **stagnant**. In 1992, every American should take time to reflect on what Columbus's voyage has meant to this country and the world. Some will celebrate the **intermingling** of cultures; others will protest these celebrations and mourn what was lost when Columbus landed in America. But we also should look ahead. What will people's understanding of the world (or the universe) be five hundred years from now, and what will historians think of those who lived in 1992?

isolated: separate

stagnant: inactive and unchanging

intermingling: mixing

Both the European and Native American cultures have given us traditions that still exist today. The Americas—especially the United States—continue to become more and more culturally diverse as we communicate and trade with people in all parts of the world, and as people immigrate. In what ways do you think the world may change in the next 500 years?

Source: *Cobblestone Magazine* (January, Vol. 13, No. 1). Peterborough, NH: Cobblestone Publishing, Inc., 1992.

CAPTURED!

by Olaudah Equiano, 1789

When Europeans arrived in Africa in the late 1400s, they greatly expanded the slave trade that Arab merchants had been carrying on for hundreds of years. They also began to forcibly transport Africans overseas to the Americas. In 1756 Olaudah Equiano (AHL uh duh ih kwee AH nah, 1745–1797) was an 11-year-old boy living in the village of Benin in what is today Nigeria. One day slave traders came to his village and changed his life forever. In his autobiography Equiano described this fateful day and what happened afterward. As you read the following excerpt from his autobiography, think of the experiences he describes. How does he manage to endure?

One day, when all our people were gone out to their works as usual, and only I and my dear sister were left to mind the house, two men and a woman got over our walls, and in a moment seized us both; and, without giving us time to cry out, or make resistance, they **stopped** our mouths, and ran off with us into the nearest wood. Here they tied our hands, and continued to carry us as far as they could, till night came on, when we reached a small house, where the robbers halted for refreshment, and spent the night. We were then unbound; but were unable to take any food; and, being quite overpowered by fatigue and grief, our only relief was some sleep, which **allayed** our misfortune for a short time.

stopped: stuffed something into

allayed: eased

The next morning we left the house, and continued travelling all the day. For a long time we had kept [to] the woods, but at last we came into a road which I believed I knew. I had now some hopes of being **delivered**; for we had advanced but a little way before I discovered some people at a distance, [and] I began to cry out for their assistance; but my cries had no other effect than to make them tie me [tighter] and stop my mouth, and then they put me into a large sack. They also stopped my sister's mouth, and tied her hands; and in this manner we proceeded till we were out of the sight of these people.

delivered: rescued

When we went to rest the following night they offered us some **victuals**; but we refused them; and the only comfort we had was in being in one another's arms all that night, and bathing each other with our tears. But alas! We were soon deprived of even the smallest comfort of weeping together. The next day proved a day of greater sorrow than I had yet experienced; for my sister and I were then separated, while we lay clasped in each other's arms: it was in vain that we **besought** them not to part us: she was torn from me, and immediately carried away, while I was left in a state of **distraction** not to be described. I cried and grieved continually; and for several days did not eat any thing but what they forced into my mouth. . . .

From the time I left my own nation I always found somebody that understood me till I came to the sea coast. The languages of different nations did not totally differ, nor were they so **copious** as those of the Europeans, particularly the English. They were therefore easily learned; and, while I was journeying thus through Africa, I **acquired** two or three different **tongues**.

In this manner I had been travelling for a considerable time, when one evening, to my great surprise, whom should I see brought to the house where I was but my dear sister? As soon as she saw me she gave a loud shriek, and ran into my arms—I was quite overpowered: neither of us could speak, but, for a considerable time, clung to each other in mutual embraces, unable to do any thing but weep. Our meeting affected all who saw us; and indeed I must acknowledge, in honour of those **sable** destroyers of human rights, that I never met with any ill treatment, or saw any offered to their slaves, except tying them, when necessary, to keep them from running away. When these people knew we were brother and sister, they **indulged** us to be together; . . . and thus for a while we forgot our misfortunes in the joy of being together; but even this small comfort was soon to have an end; for scarcely had the **fatal** morning appeared, when she was again torn from me forever! I was now more miserable, if possible, than before. . . .

I continued to travel, sometimes by land, sometimes by water, through different countries, and various nations, till, at the end of six or seven months after I had been kidnapped I arrived at the sea coast.

After arriving on the west coast of Africa, Olaudah Equiano was sold to European slave traders. They transported him overseas to Barbados. Equiano was one of more than 14 million Africans captured and carried by force to the Americas from the late 1400s to the 1800s. Equiano, however, was more fortunate than most. A British sea captain later bought him and made him a sailor. Although enslaved, Equiano managed to earn money and bought his freedom in 1766. As a free man, he traveled the world and explored the northern Arctic. Years later he settled in England and wrote his autobiography. The book was widely read in the 1790s and helped the growth of the antislavery movement.

victuals: food

besought: begged

distraction: worry

copious: full of words

acquired: learned
tongues: languages

sable: dark

indulged: allowed

fatal: dreaded

Source: Olaudah Equiano, *The Interesting Narrative of the Life of Olaudah Equiano, or Gustavus Vassa, the African. Written by Himself.* London: W. Durell, 1791.

Jonathan Down Under

by Patricia Beatty, 1982

Australia was originally colonized by the English in 1788 as a place to send their convicts. In time, the colony became a land of opportunity for non-convicts as well. When gold was discovered in Australia in 1851, many more free settlers arrived in Australia to strike it rich. Whether to farm, raise sheep, or search for gold, Europeans and Americans flocked to Australia to try their luck in this distant land. For many, Australia was a rough place. With its dry climate and an abundance of people accustomed to lives of crime, this land offered opportunity but no guarantees. This excerpt from Patricia Beatty's story captures the excitement and uncertainty of a young boy searching with his father for their fortunes in the Australian "Down Under." How do you think Jonathan's thoughts on Australia differ from his father's?

As they continued sailing south, it grew somewhat cooler, and the sailors who had sweated in cotton shirts and duck trousers **donned** jackets for warmth. The *Wendover* raced under full sail beneath a sky of such an eye-aching blue that it dazzled Jonathan and made his father say that he had never seen such a color. Nearing the east coast of Australia, the **whaler** battled rough seas and head winds, while the wind screeched in her rigging like a woman crying for a lost child.

One evening when the head winds had died down a bit, Jonathan, standing at his usual post at the rail, saw seabirds flying out of the south. Some perched atop the swaying **mastheads** of the *Wendover*. Members of the crew saw them too and clapped each other on the back. One man shouted out, "Land's near now!"

The next morning, after nearly three months of travel aboard two ships, Jonathan saw land off the starboard bow. It was only a

donned: put on

whaler: vessel used for hunting whales

masthead: top of the ship's pole that holds the sail

126

blue-purple stain on the horizon then, but hour by hour it grew more distinct. By sunset of that day Jonathan could smell it, and what a strange scent Australia was, so **pungent** it made his nose wrinkle.

He called his father from his game of solitaire in the **foc'sle** to smell it too. Charlie Cole filled his nose with the odor, laughed, and cried, "Yes, it's land all right! Land can be smelled. They say the scent of flowers from a tropical island carries for miles out to sea. I heard the second mate say not five minutes ago that we're in the Bass Strait between the mainland of Australia and the big island of Van Diemen's Land to the south. That's the scent of gold you smell.

"You know, son, I just thought of something. It could be lucky for you here. Americans aren't only called Yankees by people in other lands but sometimes Brother Jonathans. You're already a Jonathan, so here you might be Brother Jonathan Down Under or just plain Johnny Down Under."

"That could be, Pa."

As he stared at the line of land on the horizon, Jonathan wondered about the Australians and the reception he and his father might get from them. He knew his American history from school. England ruled Australia, and America and England had fought two wars. Grandfather Cole had fought in that last war of 1812 and had carried a musket ball from it **embedded** in his shoulder. Perhaps the Australians wouldn't like foreigners digging in their land. Some American miners he'd known in California had resented the Chileans, Mexicans, and Europeans who had filed claims and dug for American gold.

Jonathan said, "Pa, the Australians might not want us."

Charlie Cole laughed. "The whole world flocks to every gold strike. If they don't know it yet, the Australians will soon find that out. I'll bet there'll be other Americans in Ballarat ahead of us. We won't be the only Brother Jonathans."

The boy said nothing. Instead he thought of the song the *Wendover's* sailors had sung that very morning. It had been a rousing **chantey**, but the words had disturbed him. It was as though they had been aimed at him, as over and over they sang: "Leave her, Johnny, leave her."

In the morning Jonathan spied the little pilot ship sailing toward the *Wendover* in response to her flag signaling that a pilot was needed. He stayed at the rail to see the pilot come up the **Jacob's ladder** and guide the whaler through the dangerous passage between the narrow rocky heads at Port Phillip into Hobson's Bay. A southerly wind took the *Wendover* **scudding** past the narrows of the heads and swiftly over rough water into the bay.

Jacob's ladder: a ladder of rope and wood

scudding: to sail quickly

At dawn of the next day Jonathan was again on deck, straining his eyes for a closer view of this new continent, expecting to see the city of Melbourne rise up on hills before him like San Francisco. He saw only a dark irregular shoreline that resolved itself into houseless hills and deep green forest, and then into a number of settlements scattered along the bay's wide shores. One settlement was sure to be Melbourne. Jonathan saw that not all ships had come through the heads safely. Wrecks littered the shores of the bay. Other vessels, their masts naked of sails, lay at anchor a distance from the beaches. Jonathan thought these ships strange looking. Their hulls were neither red nor black but yellow. Near them lay a black, sleek-hulled **sloop** with gunports for cannon below her top deck.

sloop: a ship or boat with one mast and two sails

As Charlie Cole came out of the foc'sle, Jonathan asked, "What are the yellow ships?"

The agile little pilot who had stayed aboard the *Wendover* overnight answered Jonathan's question, startling him. "The hulks? They're convict ships. Convicts who build the stone wall at Gellibrand Point by day sleep aboard 'em at night—convicts sent out here to Australia from old England. I was one meself. Good day to ye."

Both Coles stared at the man, who laughed softly and added, "There'll be many ticket-of-leave men like myself at the mines and some far worse than me who never stole nothin' more in old England than thirteen boots."

"Thirteen pairs of boots?" asked Charlie Cole.

"Naw, thirteen boots."

"Why thirteen?"

Just before he swung out over the side, the Australian pilot grinned and said, "That's a thing for ye new chum Yankees to ponder while ye break yer backs at Ballarat along with ten thousand other diggers." And he was gone, down to his own boat waiting below, leaving the Coles looking at one another in astonishment.

Charlie Cole didn't talk about the thirteen boots. Instead he said, "This could turn out to be a queer country, Johnny. You know, it's early summer here now, though it's coming on to snowtime in Massachusetts. Summer means hot weather anywhere, though here the seasons happen to be upside down for us. One good thing about summer—we don't have to buy cold weather duds to take to the goldfields. We'll outfit for the mines in Melbourne. I heard the captain say Melbourne's supposed to be a real city, and it will be easy to get what we need there. It isn't as if we don't know just what a prospector needs anywhere, eh?"

"No, Pa. We know," said Jonathan, holding on to the rigging as he watched the pilot ship sail away, heading south to guide another ship through the **heads**. He was thinking of the pilot's words about convicts and ex-convicts in Australia. Surely they were criminals—murderers and thieves. What kind of land would this be if it held many who were criminals? A queer land indeed, and likely a dangerous one!

head: land that reaches into the ocean

In Patricia Beatty's story, Jonathan and his father encounter many obstacles in Australia. Their stuggles are similar to those encountered by the many people who come to a land unkown to them. How would you feel about such a venture?

Source: Patricia Beatty, *Jonathan Down Under*. New York: William Morrow and Company, Inc., 1982.

LABOURING WITH THE HOE

by Frank Macnamara, early 1820s

*The author of this poem, Frank Macnamara, was known to many as "Frank the Poet."
He was sent as a convict to Australia in the early 1820s, possibly for the crime of forgery.
It has been noted that he was well-liked by both the other convicts and the free settlers.
In this poem, he provides us with much information about the fate of convicts in
Australia. Why might the settler in the second stanza use a threatening voice?*

I was convicted by the laws of England's hostile crown,
Conveyed across those swelling seas in slavery's **fettered** bound,
For ever banished from that shore where love and friendship grow,
That loss of freedom to **deplore** and work the labouring hoe.

fettered: confined, locked-up

deplore: regret

Despised, rejected and oppressed in tattered rags I'm clad—
What anguish fills my aching breast and almost drives me mad
When I hear the settler's threatening voice say, "Arise! to labour go;
Take **scourging**, convicts, for your choice or work the labouring hoe."

scourging: to punish severely

Growing weary from compulsive toil beneath the noontide sun
While drops of sweat bedew the soil my tasks remains undone;
I'm flogged for wilful **negligence**, or the tyrants call it so—
Ah what a doleful **recompense** for labouring with the hoe.

negligence: the state of not paying attention

recompense: payment, reward

Behold you lofty woodbine hills where the rose in the morning shines,
those crystal brooks that do distil and mingle through those vines—
There seems to me no pleasures gained, they but **augment** my woe
Whilst here an outcast doomed to live and work the labouring hoe.

augment: make larger

You generous sons of **Erin's isle** whose heart for glory burns,
Pity a wretched exile who his long-lost country mourns;
Restore me, Heaven, to liberty whilst I lie here below;
Untie that clue of bondage and release me from the hoe.

Erin's isle: Ireland

*In the last two lines of the last stanza, the poet makes a request. How do you think he
expects Heaven to release him "from the hoe"?*

Source: Frank Macnamara, *Labouring with the Hoe,* from *Old Bush Songs and Rhymes Of Colonial Times*
by Douglas Stewart and Nancy Keesing, from the Collection of A.B. Paterson. Sydney, Australia: Angus &
Robertson, Ltd., 1964.

Oodgeroo

(Paperbark Tree) by Oodgeroo Noonuccal, 1972

The author of this story, Oodgeroo, grew up on an island off the coast of Queensland, Australia, and is proud of her Aboriginal heritage. Here she tells how she became a writer, using the form of a traditional Aboriginal folk tale. The images and symbols in this story make it rich and interesting. Symbols help the reader connect to the meaning of a story. What symbols are used in this story? What do they mean to you?

In the new **dreamtime** there lived a woman, an Aborigine, who longed for her lost tribe and for the stories that had belonged to her people; for she could remember only the happenings of her own Dreamtime. But the old Dreamtime had stolen the stories and hidden them. The woman knew that she must search for the old stories—and through them she might find her tribe again.

dreamtime: a time of creation

Before she set off, she looked for her yam stick and **dilly bag**, but Time had stolen these, too. She found a sugar bag that the ants had left and which Time had forgotten to destroy, and she picked it up and carried it with her wherever she went. Time laughed at her efforts; he thought her new dilly bag was useless.

dilly bag: a bag for collecting special things

One day, as she searched, the woman came upon the ashes of a fire her own tribe had kindled long ago. Tears came to her eyes, for she yearned for her tribe and felt lonely. She sat down by the ashes and ran her fingers through the remains of the fire that had once glowed there. And as she looked at the ashes, she called to Biami the Good Spirit to help her find her tribe.

Biami told her to go to the paperbark trees and ask them to give her some of their bark. The paperbark trees loved this woman who had lost her tribe, and they gave her their bark. They knew she was not greedy and would not take more than she needed. So she put the bark in her dilly bag.

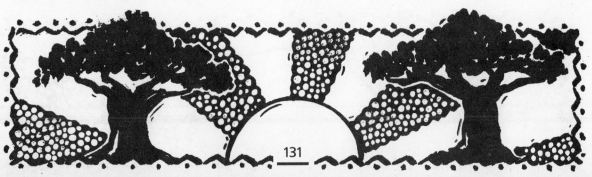

Then Biami told the woman to return to the dead fire of her tribe, collect all the charred sticks, and place these, too, in her bag—and to do this each time she came upon the dead fire of any lost tribe.

Time did not understand what the woman was doing, so he followed her.

She traveled far and wide over the earth, and each time she came upon the dead fire of a lost tribe, she would gather the charred sticks, and when at last her bag was filled with them, she went to the secret dreaming-places of the old tribes. Here she rested and again called to Biami, and asked him to help her remember the old stories, so that through them she might find her tribe.

Biami loved this woman, and he put into her mind a new way in which she might find those stories and her tribe. The woman sat down and drew from her bag the charred pieces of stick she had taken from the dead fires and placed the paperbark flat upon the ground. She drew the sticks across the paperbark and saw that they made marks on its surface.

So she sat for many years, marking the paperbark with the stories of the long-lost tribes, until she had used up all the charred **remnants** she had gathered and her bag was empty. In this way she recalled the stories of the old Dreamtime and through them entered into the old life of the tribes.

remnants: something remaining, scrap

And when next the paperbark trees filled the air with the scent of their sweet, honey-smelling flowers, they took her into their tribe as one of their own, so that she would never again be without the paperbark she needed for her work.

They called her Oodgeroo. And this is the story of how Oodgeroo found her way back into the old Dreamtime. Now she is happy, because she can always talk with the tribes whenever she wants to. Time has lost his power over her because Biami has made it so.

Many Aborigines have a close relationship to the natural world. What are some examples of this in the story? Why do you think the paperbark trees love the woman?

Source: Oodgeroo, *Dreamtime: Aboriginal Stories*. New York: Lothrop, Lee & Shepard Books, 1972.

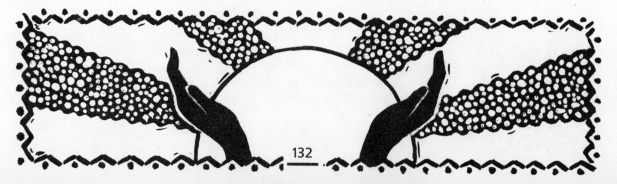

FIGHTING FOR FREEDOM

by Toussaint L'Ouverture, 1795

The Caribbean island of Hispaniola, which today includes the two nations of Haiti and the Dominican Republic, was the first place in the Americas to be colonized by Europeans. As early as the 1490s, Spaniards began enslaving the island's original people. When they died out, Europeans brought millions of Africans across the Atlantic Ocean by force over the next 300 years to work as slaves. Life under slavery was harsh. In 1791 enslaved Haitians began an uprising against their white rulers. The leader of this revolt was Toussaint L'Ouverture (too SAN loo vur TYUR, 1744–1803). Toussaint fought both the French who controlled Haiti and the Spanish and British who controlled the eastern part of Hispaniola. In 1795 Toussaint gave the following speech to rally fellow Haitians against the British. How does Toussaint defend the Haitians' struggle for freedom?

That my hopes for you, my friends, will not prove to be in vain, show yourselves to be men who know what liberty means and are prepared to defend it. The army is about to march, take, my friends, the **resolution** not to return home until you have chased from the Colony the English and the **Emigrés**, only then can you enjoy the sweetness of liberty, the justice of the republic and of our country, which you know cannot be possible if your enemies still occupy this land of freedom. Let not **fatigue**, the mountains nor the cliffs prevent you, we must conquer and it is now the time. . . .

resolution: vow

Emigrés: French allies of the British

fatigue: tiredness

It is not for fortune or for riches that we fight, there will be time to think of that when we have chased these enemies from our shores, it is for liberty which is the most precious of all earthly possessions, which we must preserve for our children, our brothers, and our comrades. God, who created all to be free has made it clear that it is our duty to preserve it for all who come after us.

It is my intention and my **resolve** not to cease the fight until I have driven the English and the Emigrés entirely from our shores. Let us leave them nothing which they once possessed. We will make our land flourish once more for this is the foundation and the structure of our liberty.

resolve: firm purpose

After many years of fighting against British, French, and Spanish troops, General Toussaint L'Ouverture led his army to victory and ended slavery in Haiti. As a result of this 13-year revolution, Haiti became an independent nation in 1804. Haiti was the first European-controlled area in Latin America to regain independence. To learn about how other Latin Americans fought for independence in the early 1800s, read the next document on pages 134–135.

Source: Wenda Parkinson, *"This Gilded African": Toussaint L'Ouverture.* London: Quartet Books, 1978.

Letter from Jamaica

by Simón Bolívar, 1815

In the early 1800s Spain still ruled most of Latin America and many people were poor or enslaved. After the revolution in Haiti, which was described in the document on page 133, the desire for independence swept across the region. Simón Bolívar (1783–1830), who as a boy had learned about the ideas of freedom around the world, rallied Latin Americans to fight for independence from Spain. At first Bolívar's efforts were unsuccessful, and he was forced to retreat to the island of Jamaica in 1815. While there, he wrote the following letter to an English friend, in which he predicted that South America would succeed in winning its independence. What do you think Bolívar meant by destiny?

September 6, 1815

Success will crown our efforts, because the destiny of America has been **irrevocably** decided; the tie that bound her to Spain has been **severed**. Only a **concept** maintained that tie and kept the parts of that immense monarchy together. That which formerly bound them now divides them. The hatred that the peninsula [of Spain] has inspired in us is greater than the ocean between us. It would be easier to have the two continents meet than to **reconcile** the spirits of the two countries. The habit of obedience; a community of interest, of understanding, of religion; mutual goodwill; a tender regard for the birthplace and good name of our forefathers; in short, all that gave rise to our hopes, came to us from Spain. . . . At present the **contrary** attitude persists: we are threatened with the fear of death, dishonor, and every harm; there is nothing we have not suffered at the hands of that unnatural step-mother—Spain. The veil has been torn **asunder**. We have already seen the light, and it is not our desire to be thrust back into darkness. The chains have been broken; we have been freed, and now our enemies seek to

irrevocably: impossible to change
severed: broken
concept: idea

reconcile: bring together

contrary: opposite

asunder: apart

enslave us anew. For this reason America fights desperately, and seldom has desperation failed to achieve victory. . . .

With respect to heroic and **hapless** Venezuela, events there have moved so rapidly and the **devastation** has been such that. . . [a] few women, children, and old men are all that remain. Most of the men have perished rather than be slaves; those who survive continue to fight furiously on the fields and in the inland towns, until they **expire** or hurl into the sea those who, **insatiable** in their thirst for blood and crimes, rival those first monsters who wiped out America's. . .[earliest people]. . . .

16,000,000 Americans either defend their rights or suffer **repression** at the hands of Spain, which although once the world's greatest empire, is now too weak, with what little is left her, to rule the new hemisphere or even to maintain herself in the old. . . . What madness for our enemy to hope to reconquer America when she has no navy, no funds, and almost no soldiers! . . .

Americans today, and perhaps to a greater extent than ever before, who live within the Spanish system occupy a position in society no better than that of serfs destined for labor, or at best they have no more status than that of mere consumers. . . . In short, do you wish to know what our future held?— simply the cultivation of the fields of indigo, grain, coffee, sugar cane, cacao, and cotton; cattle raising on the broad plains; hunting wild game in the jungles; digging in the earth to mine its gold— but even these limitations could never satisfy the greed of Spain.

So negative was our existence that I can find nothing comparable in any other civilized society, examine as I may the entire history of time and the politics of all nations. Is it not an outrage and a violation of human rights to expect a land so splendidly **endowed**, so vast, rich, and populous, to remain merely passive?. . .

More than anyone, I desire to see America **fashioned** into the greatest nation in the world, greatest not so much by virtue of her area and wealth as by her freedom and glory. . . .

From the **foregoing,** we can draw these conclusions: The American provinces are fighting for their freedom, and they will ultimately succeed.

hapless: unlucky
devastation: ruin

expire: die
insatiable: unable to be satisfied

repression: mistreatment

endowed: plentiful in resources

fashioned: shaped

foregoing: points stated before

After returning to South America, Bolívar led his troops on a difficult march across the steep, snow-covered Andes Mountains. His forces surprised the Spanish army in Colombia and defeated them in a battle that was the turning point in the struggle for independence. By 1824, with Bolívar's help, the Spanish colonies in South America had broken free from the Spanish empire. For his bold and heroic actions, South Americans remember Simón Bolívar as "The Liberator."

Source: Harold A. Bierck, Jr., ed., *Selected Writings of Bolívar.* New York: The Colonial Press, Inc., 1951.

WORKING IN THE MINES

by Ann Eggley and Elizabeth Eggley, 1842

One of the results of the Industrial Revolution, which began in England in the 1700s, was the use of child labor. Children as young as six often worked more than 12 hours a day in crowded mines and factories. In 1842 the British government began an investigation into the effects of child labor. Among the workers interviewed were two teenage sisters, Ann and Elizabeth Eggley. They both worked in the coal mines as "hurriers," people who pushed carts loaded with coal ore that weighed hundreds of pounds. As you read excerpts from their testimony to government officials, notice how the Eggleys feel about their work. Why do you think some people wanted to outlaw child labor?

Ann Eggley, 18 years old

We go [to work] at four in the morning, and sometimes at half-past four. We begin to work as soon as we get down. We get out after four, sometimes at five, in the evening. We work the whole time except an hour for dinner, and sometimes we haven't time to eat. I **hurry** by myself, and have done so for [a long time]. I know the **corves** are very very heavy. They are the biggest corves anywhere about. The work is far too hard for me; the sweat runs off me all over sometimes. I am very tired at night. Sometimes when we get home at night we have not power to wash us, and then we go to bed. Sometimes we fall asleep in the chair. Father said last night it was both a shame and a disgrace for girls to work as we do, but there was **nought** else for us to do. I have

hurry: push carts loaded with coal

corves: carts used in the mines

nought: nothing

136

tried to get **winding** to do, but could not. I begun to hurry when I was seven and I have been hurrying ever since. I have been 11 years in the pit. The girls are always tired. I was **poorly** twice this winter; it was with headache. I hurry for Robert Wiggins; he is not **akin** to me. I **riddle** for him. We all riddle . . . except the littlest. . . . We don't always get enough to eat and drink, but we get a good supper. I have known my father [to] go at two in the morning to work . . . and he didn't come out till four [in the afternoon]. I am quite sure that we work constantly 12 hours except on Saturdays. We wear trousers and our **shifts** in the pit, and great big shoes. . . . I never went to a dayschool. . . . I walk about and get the fresh air on Sundays. I have not learnt to read.

winding: raising coal to the surface of the mine

poorly: ill

akin: related

riddle: separate materials

shifts: loose shirts or dresses

Elizabeth Eggley, 16 years old

I am sister to the last witness. I hurry in the same pit, and work for my father. I find my work very much too hard for me. I hurry alone. It tires me in my arms and back most. We go to work between four and five in the morning. If we are not there by half past five we are not allowed to go down at all. We come out at four, five, or six at night as it happens. We stop in generally 12 hours, and sometimes longer. . . . I am sure it is very hard work and [it] tires us very much; it is too hard for girls to do. We sometimes go to sleep before we get to bed. We haven't a very good house; we have but two rooms for all the family. I have never been to school except four times. . . . I cannot read. . . .

The testimony of the Eggley sisters and other young workers made people in England more aware of the horrors of child labor. As a result of their testimony, Parliament passed new laws forbidding the employment of children under the age of 10 in the mines. Child labor, however, such as that described by the Eggleys, continued to exist in England for many more years.

Source: Erna Olafson Hellerstein, Leslie Parker Hume, and Karen M. Offen, eds., *Victorian Women*. Stanford, CA: Stanford University Press, 1981.

PROGRESS IN INDUSTRY

Advertisement, 1887

The Industrial Revolution began in England in the 1700s. Advancements in technology and manufacturing during this period made great changes in people's lives. The advertisement on this page is for a company that sold products that were developed during the Industrial Revolution. The locomotive was one of the great technological advances of this time. The first successful locomotive in the United States pulled its first train of cars on the South Carolina Railroad in December 1830. About a decade later the telegraph was invented by Samuel Morse (1791–1872). Many people were doubtful about the speed and usefulness of Morse's new invention. However, when the first telegraph message was sent from Washington, D.C., to Baltimore in May 1844 with news of the vice presidential nomination, everyone was impressed. The telegraph message arrived one and one-half hours ahead of the train that also carried the news! How does the advertisement below reflect the progress and excitement of the Industrial Revolution?

By 1900 the Industrial Revolution had spread to many countries throughout the world. How did the revolution change the way people traveled and the way they communicated? How would the world be different today if there had been no Industrial Revolution?

Source: Henry V. Poor, *Manual of the Railroads of the United States for 1887.* New York: Poor's Railroad Manual Co., 1887.

CLARA'S DIARY

by Clara Whitney, 1875–1887

Beginning about 1630, Japan chose to have very little contact with other nations. The borders began to open again in the 1850s, and by the early 1870s, many Japanese students came to the United States to attend college and gain skills they could take back to their country. During this period, called the "Meiji Restoration," there was a rise in industry in Japan that would forever change the country. In 1875 a 15-year-old American girl named Clara Whitney moved from Newark, New Jersey to Tokyo, Japan, where her father, William Whitney, planned to open a national business college. The following excerpts are from Clara's diary, which she kept throughout her life. What cultural traditions did Clara witness? What signs of cultural changes did she record?

Sunday, February 6, 1876:...After walking a short time we came to the [Shinto] temple which was not a large one, however. Several brass bells, shaped like large sleigh bells but having long ropes attached to them, hung around the porch.

This was the manner of worship. At a stand nearby the worshipers bought rice cakes wrapped up in little papers, further on they bought beans, and at the temple gate was a large tank of water for washing the hands and face before entering into the presence of the god. After washing they go up to the bells (if they can get to them) and pull long and well to attract the attention of the god. If they cannot reach the bells, they stand a ways off and throw beans and rice cakes in papers— the former are thrown into the temple or shrine, and the latter lodged on the roof. The people then clap their hands and bow their heads as they pray....

Friday, November 3, 1876: Today is His Majesty's birthday....How gay the streets were! Flags of all descriptions floated gaily from every window and door. Large flags, small flags, middle-sized flags, good flags, bad ones, and any kind of rag with a red spot on it were taken by our enthusiastic friends—the Japanese. Some of these emblems were evidently homemade. How they bristled out from every **casement**! What long avenues of "Rising Suns" [flags] we passed! At home we were not behind in style by any means, for we had two tall flags on our upper **verandah** guarding our homemade American **signal**. Mama said that as the sun in the center of the Japanese flag looks so much like the full moon, our stars harmonize very well with it....

casement: window

verandah: porch
signal: flag

Thursday, August 23, 1877: We went to the National Exhibition this afternoon and, though not as large as we expected, it was still a very fine affair. We went rather late, so that we had very little time to see all the sights. The Art Gallery was perfectly fascinating to me and appeared to be most attractive to the Japanese also, for it was full of people, some of whom in their flowing dresses and spread-out fans looked like statues themselves. It was with difficulty that I tore myself away from all the loveliness. We entered the Eastern Hall and found ourselves in the midst of cotton, canned fruit and other uninteresting things—although there was a nice bedroom set there. In the Machinery Hall we saw a loom invented by a Japanese. The Horticultural Hall was made up of dwarf pine trees and other botanical monstrosities. In the Agricultural Hall were very interesting collections of seeds and fruits from different provinces. The zoological section was not interesting because of the fierce-looking cows and horses there. But next to the Art Gallery, the Western Hall was the best, for in this were fine china, lacquered work, enameled ware, inlaid furniture and thousands of other pretty things.

Monday, March 25, 1878:...It is the day of the opening of the Central Telegraph Company and the building opposite us is decked with flags, lanterns, and evergreen arches, making a very pretty show....There was a display of acrobatic feats by the firemen in front of the building. They came rushing over the bridge, shouting and bearing aloft the fireman's signal—a big banner of silver paper. Six men in succession ascended a ladder and performed marvelous feats of acrobatic skill. One man fell off, bumped his nose, and fainted.

Saturday, April 25, 1884: Today I met the Emperor of Japan. His Majesty sent invitations to the **legations** and to members of the Japanese aristocracy to come and visit him at the **Hamagoten** to see the cherry blossoms and to take lunch with him....At last,... we were called to the space near the lake once more and bidden to form ourselves into a line, as His Majesty and the Empress were on their way....The brilliant imperial procession then approached. At its head walked the Emperor in French military uniform....He shook hands with the ministers and their ladies, bowed gracefully and smiled as he was made to understand their polite speeches through an interpreter....The Empress came next in beautiful **brocade** robes, the outer one of deep lovely blue and brocaded with many rich designs....Her Majesty also shook hands and made some pleasant remarks in reply to the polite speeches of the ministers....It was a striking picture....

legations: foreign diplomats
Hamagoten: palace

brocade: heavy fabric with raised designs

In 1886 Clara Whitney married Kaji Umetaro, the son of a family friend, and a native of Japan. They had six children. Clara returned to live in the United States in 1900.

Source: Clara A.N. Whitney, *Clara's Diary: An American Girl in Meiji Japan.* Tokyo: Kodansha International, Ltd., 1978.

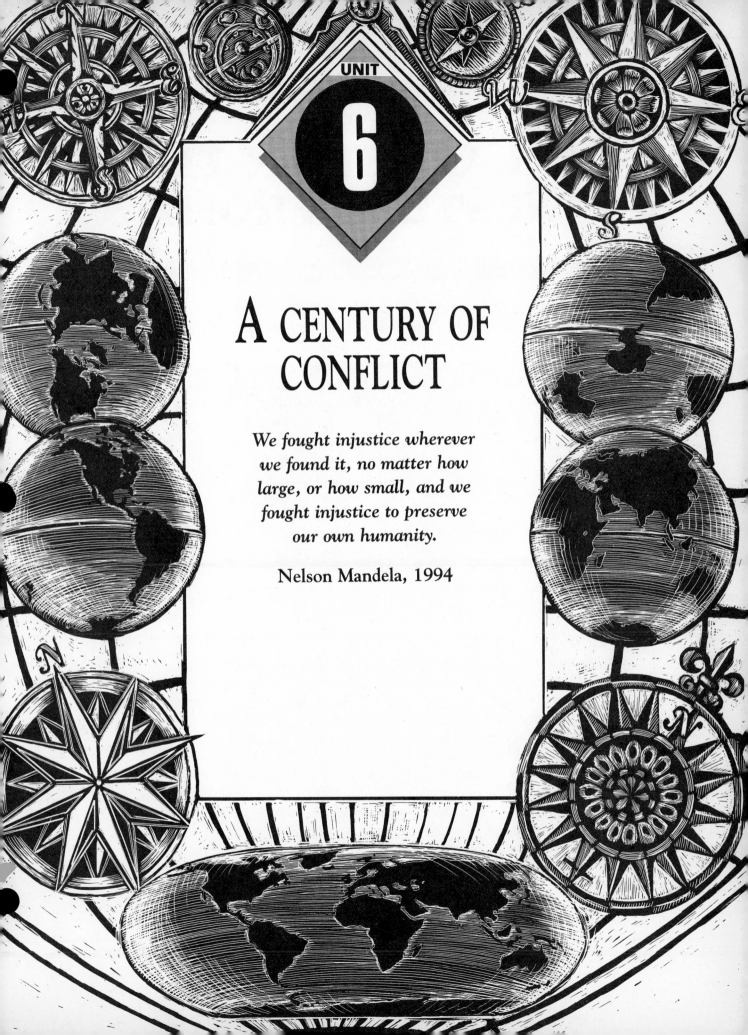

UNIT 6

A CENTURY OF CONFLICT

We fought injustice wherever we found it, no matter how large, or how small, and we fought injustice to preserve our own humanity.

Nelson Mandela, 1994

ALL QUIET ON THE WESTERN FRONT

by Erich Maria Remarque, 1929

World War I was the first major conflict of the 20th century. From 1914 to 1918, millions of soldiers engaged in a new style of fighting called trench warfare. Rather than face each other on large battlefields, soldiers on both sides dug trenches, or deep ditches. From these trenches, soldiers fired guns and threw hand grenades in hopes of driving out the enemy. Trench warfare led to many deaths but few victories. In 1929 a former German soldier named Erich Maria Remarque (1898-1970) wrote a novel describing his experiences in World War I. As you read the following excerpt from All Quiet on the Western Front, *notice how Remarque re-creates the experience of trench warfare. How do you think the narrator feels about war?*

Quiet, I squat in a **shell-hole** and try to locate myself. More than once it has happened that some fellow has jumped joyfully into a trench, only then to discover that it was the wrong one.

shell-hole: crater formed by an exploded bomb

After a little time I listen again, but still I am not sure. The confusion of shell-holes now seems so **bewildering** that I can no longer tell in my **agitation** which way I should go. Perhaps I am crawling parallel to the lines, and that might go on forever. So I crawl round once again in a wide curve.

bewildering: confusing
agitation: nervousness

These [awful] rockets! They seem to burn for an hour, and a man cannot make the least movement without bringing the bullets whistling round.

But there is nothing for it, I must get out. **Falteringly** I work my way farther, I move off over the ground like a crab and rip my hands sorely on the jagged splinters, as sharp as razor blades. Often I think that the sky is becoming lighter on the horizon, but it may be merely my imagination. Then gradually I realize that to crawl in the right direction is a matter of life or death.

falteringly: unsteadily

A shell crashes. Almost immediately two others. And then it begins in earnest. A bombardment. Machine-guns rattle. Now there is nothing for it but to stay lying low. Apparently an attack is coming. Everywhere the rockets shoot up. **Unceasing.**

unceasing: unending

I lie huddled in a large shell-hole, my legs in the water up to the belly. When the attack starts I will let myself fall into the water, with my face as deep in the mud as I can keep it without suffocating. I must pretend to be dead.

Suddenly I hear the **barrage** lift. At once I slip down into the water, my helmet on the **nape** of my neck and my mouth just clear so that I can get a breath of air.

I lie motionless;—somewhere something clanks, it stamps and stumbles nearer—all my nerves become taut and icy. It clatters over me and away, the first wave has passed. I have but this one shattering thought: What will you do if someone jumps into your shell-hole?— Swiftly I pull out my little dagger, grasp it fast and bury it in my hand once again under the mud. If anyone jumps in here I will go for him. It hammers in my forehead; at once, stab him clean through the throat, so that he cannot call out; that's the only way; he will be just as frightened as I am; when in terror we fall upon one another, then I must be first.

Now our **batteries** are firing. A shell lands near me. That makes me savage with fury, all it needs now is to be killed by our own shells; I curse and grind my teeth in the mud; it is a raving frenzy; in the end all I can do is groan and pray.

The crash of the shells bursts in my ears. If our fellows make a counter-raid I will be saved. I press my head against the earth and listen to the muffled thunder, like the explosions of quarrying—and raise it again to listen for the sounds on top.

The machine-guns rattle. I know our barbed wire entanglements are strong and almost undamaged;—parts of them are charged with a powerful electric current. The rifle fire increases. They have not broken through; they have to retreat.

I sink down again, huddled, strained to the uttermost. The banging, the creeping, the clanging becomes audible. One single cry yelling amongst it all. They are raked with fire, the attack is **repulsed**.

barrage: sound of exploding bombs

nape: back

batteries: guns

repulsed: driven back

More than 8 million soldiers died in World War I. Many people called this conflict "the war to end all wars." But only 20 years after the end of World War I, an even more horrible war would break out in Europe. For a description of one part of this war, read the document on pages 146–149.

Source: Erich Maria Remarque, *All Quiet on the Western Front*. New York: Fawcett Crest, 1989.

THE ENDLESS STEPPE

by Esther Hautzig, 1968

Under the rule of the Soviet government, the ownership of a business by an individual was considered a crime. When the Soviet army occupied the city of Vilnius, Lithuania, in June 1940, Esther Rudomin (b. 1930) and her whole family were arrested and sent to Siberia because her father had run his own business and, therefore, was considered an "enemy of the people." Siberia has long, bitterly cold winters, so few people live there voluntarily. For centuries Russian governments have used Siberia as a place to send criminals and political enemies. Steppes are the huge, grassy plains found in Siberia. The Rudomin family worked as slave laborers there for five years. As you read an excerpt from Esther's book, think about what it would be like to live and work under similar conditions. What kinds of things did Esther look for to give her comfort and strength to bear her hardship?

The next morning a whistle blew. At six o'clock that morning it was like a whip that lashed everyone to his feet. Since no one had undressed that first night, [getting ready] consisted of straightening a skirt, pulling a trouser belt, smoothing a dirty head of hair. Later, those who had brought sheets or comforters would use them as dressing rooms, squirming beneath them; those less fortunate would use coats—or the outhouse.

Popravka stamped into the room. In the early-morning light, he looked more hateful than ever, as if he had been brewing **venom** in his sleep.

Popravka: the head guard

venom: poison

"Women dynamiters—right. Men miners—left. Men truckers—forward. Children and old women—back of me."

In my view, we were all children, every last one of us. Who ever ordered grownups around this way? old grownups? **civilian** grownups?

civilian: nonmilitary

We did as we were told: there were no rebels among us, not then, not later. Outside, the steppe was vast and silent—not even a bird was overhead that morning—and it became Popravka's **accomplice** in reducing us to insects.

accomplice: helper

"When the whistle blows again," Popravka informed us, "some hours from now, go to the director's office. You will get bread there."

I watched Mother go off to dynamite, Father to drive a cart, and Grandmother to shovel. There was not so much as a second to say good-by. Until now, we had been together day and night for six weeks, been inseparable. Now suddenly I was alone. And **desolate**. I had been reared in the midst of a **clan**, I had had **Miss Rachel** as my constant companion. Under the best of circumstances, I was not a child who made friends easily. I felt **dismembered**.

desolate: miserable

clan: family

Miss Rachel: the Rudomins' former nanny

dismembered: torn apart

144

Left behind, standing **forlornly**, we were about a dozen children—once again none of them my age—each more **bedraggled** and dirtier than the next. One little girl, still somewhat plump after six weeks of near starvation, began to howl; an older girl, obviously her sister, tried to comfort her without success. Just then the boy who had smiled when he brought us our water joined us. He looked over his shoulder before going up to the little girl. Pulling his lower lids down and poking his nose up, he made a pig face for her; he also grunted. It worked; she smiled through her tears, and we all felt better.

forlornly: unhappily
bedraggled: messy

He led us to the potato patch and on the way he shed the role of happy-go-lucky, smiling young boy and became a serious and stern young man as he lectured us: We were to do our work well. No! That would not be good enough, we were to do our work to perfection. If we did not weed properly, there would be no potatoes next winter; if there were no potatoes, we would all starve. Did any among us enjoy starving? he inquired severely. "No!" we cried out from the bottom of our empty bellies.

After World War II, Esther Rudomin and her family went back to Lithuania for a short time and then moved to the United States. While sailing to the United States, Rudomin met her future husband, a concert pianist. She soon became Esther Hautzig. Besides her own story of growing up in Siberia, Hautzig has written many other books for young people. She now lives in New York City.

Source: Esther Hautzig, *The Endless Steppe: Growing Up in Siberia*. New York: Thomas Y. Crowell, 1968.

The Diary of Anne Frank

by Anne Frank, 1942–1944

During World War II Nazi Germany attempted to wipe out the entire Jewish population of Europe. In what became known as the Holocaust, the Nazis arrested millions of Jews and sent them to concentration camps where they were starved, tortured, and murdered. To try to save their lives, many Jews fought or fled, while others tried to hide. One of those who hid was a 13-year-old German girl named Anne Frank (1929–1944) living in the Netherlands. With her sister, parents, and four other people, Anne hid in a tiny attic over her father's place of business in Amsterdam. They were helped by Dutch friends who brought them food and other supplies. While in hiding, Anne kept a diary written in Dutch that described her life, her surroundings, and Nazi horrors during World War II. Below is an excerpt from an English translation of Anne Frank's diary. How does her diary express the fears that she and her family had to face every day? How does Anne feel about the war, the world, and the goodness of human beings?

Saturday, 11 July, 1942

Daddy, Mummy, and **Margot** can't get used to the sound of the Westertoren clock yet, which tells us the time every quarter of an hour. I can. I loved it from the start, and especially in the night it's like a faithful friend. I expect you will be interested to hear what it feels like to "disappear"; well, all I can say is that I don't know myself yet. I don't think I shall ever feel really at home in this house, but that does not mean that I **loathe** it here, it is more like being on vacation in a very peculiar boardinghouse. Rather a mad idea [mad way of looking at being in hiding], perhaps, but that is how it strikes me. The "Secret Annexe" is an ideal hiding place. Although it leans to one side and is damp, you'd never find such a comfortable hiding place anywhere in Amsterdam, no, perhaps not even in the whole of **Holland.**

Our little room looked very bare at first with nothing on the walls; but thanks to Daddy who had brought my film-star collection and picture postcards on beforehand, and with the aid of paste pot and

Margot: Anne's sister

loathe: hate

Holland: another name for the Netherlands

brush, I have transformed the walls into one gigantic picture. This makes it look much more cheerful, and, when the **Van Daans** come, we'll get some wood from the attic, and make a few little cupboards for the walls and other odds and ends to make it look more lively.

Margot and Mummy are a little bit better now. Mummy felt well enough to cook some soup for the first time yesterday, but then forgot all about it, while she was downstairs talking, so the peas were burned to a cinder and utterly refused to leave the pan. **Mr. Koophuis** has brought me a book called *Young People's Annual*. The four of us went to the private office yesterday evening and turned on the radio. I was so terribly frightened that someone might hear it that I simply begged Daddy to come upstairs with me. Mummy understood how I felt and came too. We are very nervous in other ways, too, that the neighbors might hear us or see something going on. We made curtains straight away on the first day. Really one can hardly call them curtains, they are just light, loose strips of material, all different shapes, quality, and pattern, which Daddy and I sewed together in a most unprofessional way. These works of art are fixed in position with drawing pins, not to come down until we emerge from here.

There are some large business premises on the right of us, and on the left a furniture workshop; there is no one there after working hours but even so, sounds could travel through the walls. We have forbidden Margot to cough at night, although she has a bad cold, and make her swallow large doses of codeine. I am looking for[ward to] Tuesday when the Van Daans arrive; it will be much more fun and not so quiet. It is the silence that frightens me so in the evenings and at night. I wish like anything that one of our protectors could sleep here at night. I can't tell you how oppressive it is *never* to be able to go outdoors, also I'm very afraid that we shall be discovered and be shot. That is not exactly a pleasant prospect. We have to whisper and tread lightly during the day, otherwise the people in the warehouse might hear us.

Someone is calling me.

Friday, 9 October, 1942

I've only got dismal and depressing news for you today. Our many Jewish friends are being taken away by the dozen. These people are treated by the **Gestapo** without a shred of decency, being loaded into cattle trucks and sent to Westerbork, the big Jewish [concentration] camp in **Drente**. Westerbork sounds terrible: only one washing **cubicle** for a hundred people and not nearly enough **lavatories**. There is no separate accommodation. . . .

It is impossible to escape; most of the people in the camp are branded as inmates by their shaven heads and many also by their Jewish appearance.

If it is as bad as this in Holland whatever will it be like in the distant and barbarous regions they are sent to? We assume that most of them are murdered. The English radio speaks of their being gassed.

Van Daans: family in hiding that shared the "secret annexe" with the Franks.

Mr. Koophuis: Dutch man who helped the Franks

Gestapo: secret police force of Nazi Germany

Drente: town in the Netherlands

cubicle: room

lavatories: bathrooms

Perhaps that is the quickest way to die. I feel terribly upset. I couldn't tear myself away while **Miep** told these dreadful stories; and she herself was equally wound up for that matter. Just recently for instance, a poor old crippled **Jewess** was sitting on her doorstep; she had been told to wait there by the Gestapo, who had gone to fetch a car to take her away. The poor old thing was terrified by the guns that were shooting at English planes overhead, and by the glaring beams of the searchlights. But Miep did not dare take her in; no one would undergo such a risk. The Germans strike without the slightest mercy.

Elli too is very quiet: her boy friend has got to go to Germany. She is afraid that the airmen who fly over our homes will drop their bombs, often weighing a million kilos [2.2 million lbs.], on Dirk's head. Jokes such as "he's not likely to get a million" and "it only takes one bomb" are in rather bad taste. Dirk is certainly not the only one who has to go: trainloads of boys leave daily. If they stop at a small station **en route**, sometimes some of them manage to get out unnoticed and escape; perhaps a few manage it. This, however, is not the end of my bad news. Have you ever heard of hostages? That's the latest thing in penalties for **sabotage**. Can you imagine anything so dreadful?

Prominent citizens—innocent people—are thrown into prison to await their fate. If the **saboteur** can't be traced, the Gestapo simply put about five hostages against the wall. Announcements of their deaths appear in the papers frequently. These outrages are described as "fatal accidents." Nice people, the Germans! To think that I was once one of them too! No, Hitler took away our nationality long ago. In fact, Germans and Jews are the greatest enemies in the world.

Thursday, 25 May, 1944

There's something fresh every day. This morning our vegetable man was picked up for having two Jews in his house. It's a great blow to us, not only that those poor Jews are balancing on the edge of an abyss, but it's terrible for the man himself.

The world has turned topsy-turvy, respectable people are being sent off to concentration camps, prisons, and lonely cells, and the dregs that remain govern young and old, rich and poor. One person walks into the trap through the black market, a second through helping the Jews or other people who've had to go "underground"; anyone who isn't a member of the **N.S.B.** doesn't know what may happen to him from one day to another.

This man is a great loss to us too. The girls can't and aren't allowed to haul along our share of potatoes, so the only thing to do is to eat less. I will tell you how we shall do that; it's certainly not going to make

Miep: Dutch woman who helped the Franks

Jewess: Jewish woman

Elli: Dutch woman who helped the Franks

en route: on the way

sabotage: destruction of enemy property

saboteur: one who commits sabotage

N.S.B.: initials of the Dutch Nazi party

things any pleasanter. Mummy says we shall cut out breakfast altogether, have porridge and bread for lunch, and for supper fried potatoes and possibly once or twice per week vegetables or lettuce, nothing more. We're going to be hungry, but anything is better than being discovered.

Thursday, 15 June, 1944

I wonder if it's because I haven't been able to poke my nose outdoors for so long that I've grown so crazy about everything to do with nature? I can perfectly well remember that there was a time when a deep blue sky, the song of the birds, moonlight and flowers could never have kept me **spellbound**. That's changed since I've been here.

spellbound: enchanted

At Whitsun, for instance, when it was so warm, I stayed awake on purpose until half past eleven one evening in order to have a good look at the moon for once by myself. Alas, the sacrifice was all in vain, as the moon gave far too much light and I didn't dare risk opening a window. Another time, some months ago now, I happened to be upstairs one evening when the window was open. I didn't go downstairs until the window had to be shut. The dark, rainy evening, the gale, the scudding clouds held me entirely in their power; it was the first time in a year and a half that I'd seen the night face to face. After that evening my longing to see it again was greater than my fear of burglars, rats, and raids on the house. I went downstairs all by myself and looked outside through the windows in the kitchen and the private office. A lot of people are fond of nature, many sleep outdoors occasionally, and people in prisons and hospitals long for the day when they will be free to enjoy the beauties of nature, but few are so shut away and isolated from that which can be shared alike by rich and poor. It's not imagination on my part when I say that to look up at the sky, the clouds, the moon, and the stars makes me calm and patient. It's a better medicine than either valerian or bromine; Mother Nature makes me humble and prepared to face every blow courageously.

Alas, it has had to be that I am only able—except on a few rare occasions—to look at nature through dirty net curtains hanging before very dusty windows. And it's no pleasure looking through these any longer, because nature is just the one thing that really **must be unadulterated**.

must be unadulterated: experienced directly

Seven weeks after Anne wrote this last entry in her diary, the Nazis discovered her family's secret hiding place. They arrested Anne and her family and sent them to a concentration camp. Only Anne's father survived. Anne Frank was one of 6 million Jews murdered by Nazi Germany in concentration camps during the Holocaust. The Nazis also killed 6 million other people in concentration camps, including Poles, Russians, Czechs, Slavs, and Gypsies. Anne Frank's courage in the face of one of the greatest horrors in world history remains a testament to the human spirit.

Source: Anne Frank, *The Diary of Anne Frank: The Critical Edition*. New York: Bantam Doubleday Dell Publishing Group, Inc., 1989.

Defeating Nazi Germany

Poster, 1942

When Nazi Germany invaded Poland in 1939, World War II broke out in Europe. By the end of 1941, four of the world's strongest nations—the United States, the Soviet Union, Great Britain, and France—had joined forces to fight Germany and the other Axis nations. In 1942 the United States government printed the following poster to help raise money and build support for the war effort. How does this poster show the joint effort being taken by the Allied nations against Germany?

In 1945 the combined efforts of the Allied nations defeated Germany and the other Axis nations. Altogether, more than 55 million men, women, and children died in World War II, making it the most deadly conflict in history. The cooperation of the United States, the Soviet Union, Great Britain, France, and other countries made victory possible.

Source: Charles Goodrum and Helen Dalrymple, *Advertising in America: The First 200 Years.* New York: Harry N. Abrams, Inc., Publishers, 1990.

Never Give Up the Fight

by Winston Churchill and Franklin Roosevelt, 1941

World War II began in September 1939, when German forces invaded Poland. Soon after, the Germans conquered France, and they began bombing Britain. Britain and France were joined by Russia, which was invaded by Germany in the summer of 1941. They were known as the Allies. The United States supported the Allies but had not yet entered the war. Germany, Japan, and their forces were known as the Axis powers. The following are excerpts of speeches made during the war by two world leaders—British Prime Minister Winston Churchill

Winston Churchill, October 29, 1941

Never give in, never give in, never, never, never, never—in nothing, great or small, large or petty—never give in except to convictions of honor and good sense. Never yield to force; never yield to the apparently overwhelming might of the enemy. We stood all alone a year ago, and to many countries it seemed that our account was closed, we were finished....

petty: minor

convictions: firm beliefs

Very different is the mood today. Britain, other nations thought, had drawn a sponge across her slate. But instead our country stood in the gap. There was no flinching and no thought of giving in; and by what seemed almost a miracle to those outside these Islands, though we ourselves never doubted it, we now find ourselves in a position where I say that we can be sure that we have only to persevere to conquer.

Franklin Roosevelt, December 8, 1941

Yesterday, December 7, 1941—a date which will live in infamy—the United States of America was suddenly and deliberately attacked by naval and air forces of the Empire of Japan....

infamy: memory of a wrongdoing

I believe that I interpret the will of the Congress and of the people when I assert that we will not only defend ourselves to the uttermost but will make it very certain that this form of treachery shall never again endanger us.

treachery: betrayal

Hostilities exist. There is no blinking at the fact that our people, our territory, and our interests are in grave danger.

With confidence in our armed forces—with the unbounding determination of our people—we will gain the inevitable triumph—so help us God.

unbounding: limitless

inevitable: certain

The United States entered the war in December 1941, after the Japanese attack on Pearl Harbor, Hawaii, that President Roosevelt refers to in the last excerpt above. The Allies ultimately defeated the Axis powers in August 1945. President Roosevelt did not live long enough to see the end of the war, however. He died in April 1945.

Sources: David Cannadine, ed., *Blood, Toil, Tears and Sweat: The Speeches of Winston Churchill*. Boston: Houghton Mifflin Company, 1989; John Bartlett, ed., *Familiar Quotations*. Boston: Little, Brown & Co., Fifteenth ed., 1980; B.D. Zevin, ed., *Nothing to Fear: The Selected Addresses of Franklin Delano Roosevelt, 1932-1945*. Boston: Houghton Mifflin Co., 1946.

ATTACK ON PEARL HARBOR

from *The New York Times*, 1941

After World War II broke out in 1939, the United States tried to remain at peace. But on December 7, 1941, without any warning, Japan made a surprise attack on a United States naval base in Pearl Harbor, Hawaii. Below is the front page of the New York Times reporting this event the next day. As you read this front page, suppose that it is December 8, 1941, and you have just bought this newspaper. How might you have reacted to the news?

The day after the attack, the United States declared war on Japan. Soon after, Germany declared war on the United States. World War II now became truly a world conflict—a war that affected people all over the world.

When the A-Bomb Fell

by Yoshihiro Kimura, 1951

By the summer of 1945, the United States had been fighting Japan in World War II for more than three and a half years. In an effort to force the Japanese to surrender, the United States dropped an atomic bomb on the Japanese city of Hiroshima (hihr uh SHEE muh) on August 6, 1945. This bomb, the first nuclear weapon ever used in a war, shattered people's lives along with buildings. More than 75,000 people died. Many more thousands were injured or made homeless. One of those injured was a third-grade student named Yoshihiro Kimura. In 1951, six years after the bombing, a Hiroshima professor named Dr. Arata Osada collected the stories of children who were in Hiroshima when the bomb exploded. In the following account Yoshihiro describes that tragic day when the bomb fell. How does he cope with the disaster?

On the morning of August 6th, my father was running a temperature and he didn't get up. My brother . . . was toasting some dried **squid**. After everyone had gone off, I and my father and my mother and my other sister were left. The two of us got ready to go to school.

squid: sea animal

My sister went to the real school and I went to the branch school. . . . My friends and I were talking about the war.

We heard a voice saying, "Air raid alarm."

I hurried home and was playing. This is because I was already used to this sort of thing. Then the alert ended and I went back to school. . . .

Pretty soon we heard a hum and saw a little aeroplane in the sky to the southeast. And this gradually grew larger and came over our heads. I was watching the aeroplane the whole time. I [couldn't] tell whether it [was] a foreign plane or a Japanese plane. Then suddenly a thing like a white parachute came falling. Five or six seconds later everything turned yellow in one instant. It felt the way it does when you get the sunlight straight in your eye. A second or two later, CRASH! There was a tremendous noise. Everything became dark and stones and roof tiles came pouring down on our heads. For a while I was **unconscious**. A whole lot of lumber came piling around my hips and I wanted to protest, "Stop, that hurts!" I **came to** again with the pain. I quickly crawled outside. There were lots of people lying around there; the faces of most of them were **charred**. I got out to the street and just as I heaved a sigh of relief my right hand suddenly began to hurt. When I looked closely at it I found that the skin of my right arm was peeled off from my elbow to my fingers and it was all red. I wanted

unconscious: knocked out
came to: woke up

charred: burned

153

to go home right away and I figured out the direction and started to walk toward the house when I heard a voice call . . . and I turned and looked and it was my sister. Her clothes were torn to rags and her face was so changed that I was amazed.

The two of us started off toward the house together, but the house was flattened and there was no one there. We searched around the neighborhood and then came back and looked and there was Father. Father was pulling off the roof and trying to get something out. But then he seemed to give that up and he came toward us.

When I asked, "Mother?" he said tiredly, "She's dead." . . .

Pretty soon a muddy rain began to fall so we went under the railroad bridge. The railroad bridge was making a **sputtering** noise as it **smoldered**. When the rain stopped it suddenly got cold. . . .

sputtering: hissing
smoldered: burned slowly

I got terribly thirsty so I went to the river to drink. From upstream a great many black and burned **corpses** came floating down the river. I pushed them away and drank the water. At the **margin** of the river there were corpses lying all over the place. Among them were some who weren't dead yet and there were some children who were screaming, "Mother! Mother!" When I saw the corpses I was already so used to it I didn't think anything of it. There were also some people who came **tottering** to the edge of the river and fell in and died just like that. Pretty soon my sister too—was it because of her burns?—fell down on the road. My father carried her and laid her down where our house had been. In the evening my brother came back. . . .

corpses: dead bodies
margin: edge

tottering: wobbling

There are only four left: I and Father and my big brother and the other sister. I didn't have the strength to say another thing. Everybody was in a sort of **daze**. That night I couldn't sleep either. When I got up to go to the bathroom I tried calling, "Mother."

daze: confusion

But Mother wasn't there anymore. When I finally realized she was dead, I can't describe to you the loneliness and sorrow that attacked me. I cried with my whole soul. But no matter how hard I cry, Mother won't come back. . . .

After a while another misfortune came to us. On the 15th of August at about three o'clock my sister finally died. . . . That day the war ended. . . .

The deaths of my kind mother and sisters are all because of that war. I wouldn't hate any special person, blaming him for my mother's death. However, only war alone I *will* hate. I hope that this hateful war will never be repeated.

War is the enemy of everyone. If we can do away with war and if peace comes, I am certain that my mother in heaven will be happy.

Three days after dropping the atomic bomb on Hiroshima, the United States dropped a second atomic bomb on Nagasaki. Six days later Japan surrendered, ending World War II. The people of Hiroshima and Nagasaki have since rebuilt their cities. Each year in August, the Japanese hold ceremonies to honor the atomic bomb victims and urge an end to warfare.

Source: Dr. Arata Osada, ed., *Children of the A-Bomb: The Testament of the Boys and Girls of Hiroshima.* London: Peter Owen Limited, 1963.

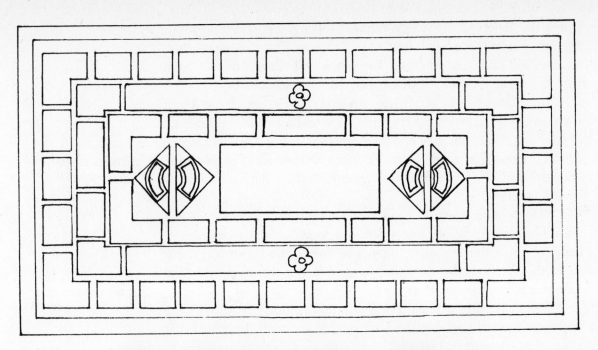

No Tears for Mao

by Niu-Niu, 1995

Mao Zedong became the Communist leader of mainland China in 1949. When he feared that the Chinese people were losing their enthusiasm for Communism, in 1966, he started a policy called the Cultural Revolution. This was a call for the destruction of all non-Communist beliefs by Mao's faithful, young, and often violent supporters, called the Red Guard. Many books and works of art were destroyed. "Intellectuals," who were considered to be dangerous, were sent to work on farms or imprisoned in "reeducation camps," where they were forced to study Communist beliefs. No Tears for Mao is the autobiography of Niu-Niu, a Chinese girl whose parents were beaten and dragged away to a reeducation camp when she was just four years old. What would it be like to live in a culture where only one type of belief was acceptable? What are some of the most important ideas that Niu-Niu's grandmother is trying to explain in this excerpt?

"**A**h, it's true, my poor Niu-Niu, you were not born at a good time. Not only were you not a boy, but on top of that, the Cultural Revolution began ten days after you were born. The Red Guards began to kill the 'intellectuals.' Mao said he was a Red Guard himself; he set a percentage—three to five percent of those who were to be found guilty of '**revisionism.**' They said they were fighting against what they called the four outmoded ways: 'old culture, old customs, old habits, and old ways of thinking.' They even changed the names of the streets. Now each of their heroes has a boulevard named after him. They changed old-fashioned names for places of business—restaurants used to be called things like 'The Best Taste'; florists' shops

revisionism: act of altering the facts

155

were called 'Delicate and **Subtle** Fragrances.' Now they're all called things like 'Triumph of the Revolution.'—all you see in shop windows are large portraits of Mao. It used to be different. There were streamers all over—a kind you don't see any more. All these *dazibaos*—wall posters—what a waste! All that paper, ink and paintbrushes....

Subtle: difficult to detect

"Your parents and their friends decided to write articles and post them in public to present their point of view. That caused them a lot of grief—as if they had touched the rump of the tiger, they had roused the wild beast. Their **subversive** opinions and our family's past were enough to make us criminals and counterrevolutionaries. You know what happened then....

subversive: anti-governmental

"But it's important that you know, Niu-Niu, that your family was always honorable. We've never lied. We were accused of murder, of keeping in touch with relatives who fled abroad and so forth. We thought that they were finished with us after the **Liberation**, but they never give up.

Liberation: end of noncommunist rule

"You're terribly young, Niu-Niu, and I don't know if you understand everything that I've told you, but you must remember that when they torment us this way, when they push your grandfather to the brink, they do it out of **malice**, pure and simple. We've never been criminals. Don't hate us. You must respect your parents as much as they love you. We've always been honest and we've always told the truth...."

malice: evil intentions

My grandmother talked on until the candle burned down. In spite of the late hour, I didn't feel tired at all. I didn't quite understand everything she said, but I remembered all of it. Grandma warned me never to let anyone know what she had told me, or else things would get worse for us.

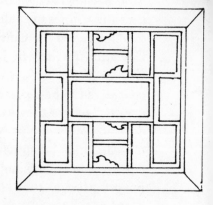

The sun rose at the cry of the rooster and once again the world stirred to life. I felt that I had grown up in one night. From then on, I was warmed by a great hope: I wanted to become an adult so that I could know everything and help my grandparents. I thought I could find a way to bring my parents back. Ten thousand questions whirled around in my head. The first: why did I have to wait to grow up?

The Cultural Revolution brought many more tragic events into Niu-Niu's life, including the murder of her grandfather and her teacher by the Red Guard. Mao Zedong died in 1976, and the Cultural Revolution ended shortly thereafter. When Niu-Niu's parents finally returned home after nine years in prison, she did not even recognize them. Niu-Niu went on to attend university in Beijing, but she was very unhappy there. She never finished school, but she succeeded in getting a passport and left China to find freedom in 1986. She now lives in Paris, where she is an actress and filmmaker. Niu-Niu hopes to return to China someday.

Source: Niu-Niu, *No Tears for Mao: Growing Up in the Cultural Revolution.* Academy Chicago Publishers, 1995.

Charter of the
United Nations

International agreement, 1945

The United Nations was formed immediately after World War II to keep international peace and security, and to cooperate on economic, social, and other problems facing the countries of the world. The Charter of the United Nations, which states its purpose, was written in 1945, at the organization's first gathering in San Francisco. Below is the preamble, or introduction, that sums up the Charter. Do you think the United Nations has lived up to its Charter? What can the United Nations accomplish that would be difficult for individual nations?

WE THE PEOPLES OF THE UNITED NATIONS
DETERMINED

to save succeeding generations from the **scourge** of war, which twice in our lifetime has brought untold sorrow to mankind, and

scourge: destruction

to **reaffirm** faith in fundamental human rights, in the dignity and worth of the human person, in the equal rights of men and women and of nations large and small, and

reaffirm: firmly declare again

to establish conditions under which justice and respect for the obligations arising from treaties and other sources of international law can be maintained, and

to promote social progress and better standards of life in larger freedom,

AND FOR THESE ENDS

to practice tolerance and live together in peace with one another as good neighbors, and

to unite our strength to maintain international peace and security, and

to ensure, by the acceptance of principles and the **institution** of methods, that armed force shall not be used, save in the common interest, and

institution: setting up officially

to employ international **machinery** for the promotion of the economic and social advancement of all peoples,

machinery: methods

HAVE RESOLVED TO COMBINE OUR EFFORTS TO
ACCOMPLISH THESE AIMS.

Accordingly, our respective Governments...do hereby establish an international organization to be known as the United Nations.

Fifty-one countries met in 1945 to form the United Nations. Today, it has 184 members. The United Nations headquarters is in New York City.

Source: Leland M. Goodrich, Edvard Hambro, Anne Patricia Simons, eds., *Charter of the United Nations: Commentary and Documents.* New York: Columbia Univ. Press, 1969.

Attack on the Congo River: One View

by Henry M. Stanley, 1885

During the period of imperialism, which began in the mid-1800s, European powers conquered much of Africa and divided the continent into colonies. During these years Europeans and Africans often failed to understand each other's cultures. The document below and the next document on pages 160–161 give an example of one of these misunderstandings. In 1877 a reporter named Henry Stanley explored the Congo River, known today as the Zaire River, in central Africa. Stanley was an American citizen, but his trip was being paid for by the government of Belgium. At a spot near where the Congo River joins the Lualaba River, Stanley and his traveling party encountered a group called the Basoko. Eight years later Stanley wrote a book describing this encounter. As you read the excerpt below from Stanley's book, notice some of the harsh terms he uses to describe the Basoko. What does Stanley believe the Basoko are trying to do to him? After you read this excerpt, compare Stanley's view of the encounter to the description by Chief Mojimba, a Basoko leader, on pages 160–161.

At 2 P.M., we emerge out of the shelter of the deeply wooded banks [at the place where the Congo River joins the Lualaba River.] As soon as we have fairly entered its waters, we see a great **concourse** of canoes hovering about some islets, which stud the middle of the stream. The canoe-men, standing up, give a loud shout as they **discern** us, and blow their horns louder than ever. We pull briskly on to gain the right bank. . .when, looking up stream, we see a sight that sends the blood tingling through every nerve and fibre of the body. . .a **flotilla** of gigantic canoes bearing down upon us, which both in size and numbers utterly **eclipse** anything encountered **hitherto**! Instead of aiming for the right bank, we form in line, and keep straight down

concourse: crowd

discern: notice

flotilla: fleet
eclipse: surpass
hitherto: before

river, the boat taking position behind. Yet after a moment's reflection, as I note the numbers of the savages, and the daring manner of the pursuit, and the apparent desire of our canoes to abandon the steady **compact** line, I give the order to drop anchor. . . .

compact: closely united

We have sufficient time to take a view of the mighty force bearing down on us, and to count the number of war-vessels, which have been collected from the [Congo-Lualaba River]. There are fifty-four of them! A monster canoe leads the way, with two rows of upstanding paddles, forty men on a side. . . . All the paddles are headed with ivory balls, every head bears a feather crown, every arm shows gleaming white ivory **armlets**. . . .

armlets: bracelets worn high up on the arm

The crashing sound of large drums, a hundred blasts from ivory horns, and a thrilling chant from two thousand human throats, do not tend to soothe our nerves or to increase our confidence. . . . We have no time to pray, or to take [a] sentimental look at the savage world, or even to breathe a sad farewell to it. So many other things have to be done speedily and well.

As the **foremost** canoe comes rushing down, and its **consorts** on either side beating the water into foam. . . I turn to take a last look at our people, and say to them:

foremost: front
consorts: accompanying boats

"Boys, be firm as iron; wait until you see the first spear, and then take good aim. Don't fire all at once. Keep aiming until you are sure of your man. Don't think of running away, for only your guns can save you.". . .

The monster canoe aims straight for my boat, as though it would run us down; but, when within fifty yards [45 m] off, swerves aside and, when nearly opposite, the warriors above the manned **prow** let fly their spears, and on either side there is a noise of rushing bodies. But every sound is soon lost in the ripping, crackling **musketry**. For five minutes we are so absorbed in firing that we take no note of anything else; but at the end of that time we are made aware that the enemy is **reforming** about 200 yards [180 m] above us.

prow: front of a boat

musketry: gunfire

reforming: organizing again

Our blood is up now. It is a murderous world, and we feel for the first time that we hate the filthy, **vulturous ghouls** who inhabit it. We therefore lift our anchors, and pursue them upstream along the right bank, until rounding a point we see their villages. We make straight for the banks, and continue the fight in the village streets and those who have landed, hunt them out into the woods, and there only sound the retreat, having returned the daring cannibals the compliment of a visit.

vulturous: like vultures
ghouls: evil beings

Like many other Europeans of his time, Henry Stanley looked down on Africans. In his encounters with the Basoko people, Stanley believed he understood the situation correctly and was right in attacking. Stanley, however, was not the only one to give a description of this encounter. For a different view, read the next document on pages 160–161.

Source: Henry M. Stanley, *Through the Dark Continent*. New York: Harper and Brothers, 1885.

Attack on the Congo River: Another View

by Mojimba, 1907

In 1907, 30 years after Henry Stanley and the Basoko people encountered each other in what is today the nation of Zaire, Chief Mojimba, a Basoko leader, described the same encounter to a Belgian missionary. As you read Mojimba's account, compare it to Stanley's account that you read on pages 158–159. On what parts do they agree? On what parts do they differ? What do these differences tell you about relationships between Europeans and Africans during the late 1800s?

When we heard that the man with the white flesh was journeying down the Lualaba [River] we were open-mouthed with astonishment. We stood still. All night long the drums announced the strange news—a man with white flesh. That man, we said to ourselves, has a white skin. He must have got that from the river-kingdom. He will be one of our brothers who were drowned in the river. All life comes from the water and in the water, he has found life. Now he is coming back to us, he is coming home. . . .

We will prepare a feast, I ordered, we will go to meet our brother and escort him into the village with rejoicing! We **donned** our ceremonial **garb**. We assembled the great canoes. We listened for the gong which would announce our brother's presence on the Lualaba. Presently the cry was heard: He is approaching. . . . Now he enters the river! Halloh! We swept forward, my canoe leading, the others following with songs of joy and with dancing to meet the first white man our eyes had beheld, and to him honor.

donned: put on
garb: clothing

But as we drew near his canoes there were loud **reports**, *bang! bang!* and **fire-staves** spat bits of iron at us. We were paralyzed with fright; our mouths hung wide open and we could not shut them. Things such as we had never seen, never heard of, never dreamed of—they were the work of evil spirits! Several of my men plunged into the water. . . . What for? Did they fly to safety? No—for others fell down also, in the canoes. Some screamed dreadfully—others were silent—they were dead, and blood flowed from little holes in their bodies. "War! that is war!" I yelled. "Go back!" The canoes sped back to our village with all the strength our spirits could **impart** to our arms.

reports: sounds
fire-staves: guns

impart: give to

That was no brother! That was the worst enemy our country had ever seen.

And still those bangs went on; the long staves spat fire, flying pieces of iron whistled around us, fell into the water with a hissing sound, and our brothers continued to fall. We fled into our village—they came after us. We fled into the forest and flung ourselves on the ground. When we returned that evening, our eyes **beheld** fearful things; our brothers, dead, dying, bleeding, our village **plundered** and burned, and the water full of dead bodies.

beheld: saw
plundered: robbed

The robbers and murderers had disappeared.

Now tell me: has the white man dealt fairly by us? O, do not speak to me of him! You call us wicked men, but you white men are much more wicked! You think, because you have guns you can take away our land and our possessions. You have sickness in your heads, for that is not justice.

The Basokos' ceremonial throwing of spears to greet Henry Stanley in 1877 was actually very similar to the European custom of firing cannons to salute an honored visitor. But as was often the case during the late 1800s, Europeans and Africans failed to understand each other. In the 1900s many Africans began fighting to regain their independence and freedom and to bring an end to colonial rule. To learn more about this movement, read the next two documents on pages 162–167.

Source: Heinrich Schiffers, *The Quest for Africa*. New York: G. P. Putnam's Sons, 1958.

THE MAN WHO SHARED HIS HUT

by Jomo Kenyatta, 1938

In the middle 1800s European powers began dividing up the continent of Africa into colonies by adopting a policy called imperialism. Under imperialism Africans had little control over their land. Europeans set up their own laws and ruled most of the continent. In the 1900s many Africans began fighting to regain their independence. One of the leaders of this fight was Jomo Kenyatta (1897–1978), one of the Kikuyu people, who was born near Nairobi, Kenya. In 1938 Kenyatta wrote Facing Mount Kenya, *a study of the Kikuyu people and culture. In this book, Kenyatta wrote the following tale, a story about the history of imperialism and how European nations had treated Africa. But in this story, called "The Man Who Shared His Hut," no European nations are named. Instead, all the characters except one are animals. As you read this story, try to figure out who and what the different characters represent. How does Kenyatta describe the relationship between Africans and Europeans?*

Once upon a time an elephant made a friendship with a man. One day a heavy thunderstorm broke out, the elephant went to his friend, who had a little hut at the edge of the forest, and said to him: "My dear good man, will you please let me put my trunk inside your hut to keep it out of this **torrential** rain?"

torrential: pouring

The man, seeing what situation his friend was in, replied: "My dear good elephant, my hut is very small, but there is room for your trunk and myself. Please put your trunk in gently."

The elephant thanked his friend, saying: "You have done me a good deed and one day I shall return your kindness."

But what followed? As soon as the elephant put his trunk inside the hut, slowly he pushed his head inside, and finally flung the man out in the rain, and then lay down comfortably inside his friend's hut, saying: "My dear good friend, your skin is harder than mine, and as there is not enough room for both of us, you can afford to remain in the rain while I am protecting my delicate skin from the hailstorm."

The man, seeing what his friend had done to him, started to grumble, the animals in the nearby forest heard the noise and came to see what was the matter. All stood around listening to the heated argument between the man and his friend the elephant.

In this **turmoil** the lion came along roaring, and said in a loud voice: "Don't you all know that I am the King of the Jungle! How dare anyone disturb the peace of my kingdom?"

turmoil: confusion

On hearing this the elephant, who was one of the high ministers in the jungle kingdom, replied in a soothing voice, and said: "My Lord, there is no disturbance of the peace in your kingdom. I have only been having a little discussion with my friend here as to the possession of this little hut which your **lordship** sees me occupying."

lordship: title of respect

The lion, who wanted to have "peace and tranquility" in his kingdom, replied in a noble voice, saying: "I command my ministers to appoint a **Commission of Inquiry** to go thoroughly into this matter and report accordingly." He then turned to the man and said: "You have done well by establishing friendship with my people, especially with the elephant who is one of my honorable ministers of state. Do not grumble any more, your hut is not lost to you. Wait until the sitting of my **Imperial Commission**, and then you will be given plenty of opportunity to state your case. I am sure that you will be pleased with the findings of the Commission."

Commission of Inquiry: panel of investigation

Imperial Commission: government panel

The man was very pleased by these sweet words from the King of the Jungle, and innocently waited for his opportunity, in the belief that, naturally, the hut would be returned to him.

The elephant, obeying the command of his master, got busy with other ministers to appoint the Commission of Inquiry. The following elders of the jungle were appointed to sit on the Commission: (1) Mr. Rhinoceros; (2) Mr. Buffalo; (3) Mr. Alligator; (4) The **Rt. Hon.** Mr. Fox to act as chairman; and (5) Mr. Leopard to act as Secretary to the Commission.

Rt. Hon.: Right Honorable, title of respect

On seeing the **personnel**, the man protested and asked if it was not necessary to include in this Commission a member from his side. But he was told that it was impossible, since no one from his side was well enough educated to understand the **intricacy** of jungle law. Further, that there was nothing to fear, for the members of the Commission were all men of **repute** for their **impartiality** in justice, and as they were gentlemen chosen by God to look after the interests of races less adequately **endowed** with teeth and claws, he might rest assured that

personnel: people appointed

intricacy: complicated matters

repute: honor
impartiality: fairness
endowed: furnished

they would investigate the matter with the greatest care and report impartially.

The Commission sat to take the evidence. The Rt. Hon. Mr. Elephant was first called. He came along with a superior air, brushing his tusks with a **sapling** which Mrs. Elephant had provided, and in an **authoritative** voice said: "Gentlemen of the Jungle, there is no need for me to waste your valuable time in relating a story which I am sure you all know. I have always regarded it as my duty to protect the interests of my friends, and this appears to have caused the misunderstanding between myself and my friend here. He invited me to save his hut from being blown away by a hurricane. As the hurricane had gained access owing to the unoccupied space in the hut, I considered it necessary, in my friend's own interests, to turn the undeveloped space to a more economic use by sitting in it myself; a duty which any of you would undoubtedly have performed with equal readiness in similar circumstances."

After hearing the Rt. Hon. Mr. Elephant's **conclusive** evidence, the Commission called Mr. Hyena and other elders of the jungle, who all supported what Mr. Elephant had said. They then called the man, who began to give his own account of the dispute. But the Commission cut him short, saying: "My good man, please confine yourself to **relevant** issues. We have already heard the circumstances from various **unbiased** sources; all we wish you to tell us is whether the undeveloped space in your hut was occupied by anyone else before Mr. Elephant **assumed** his position?"

The man began to say: "No, but –" But at this point the Commission declared that they had heard sufficient evidence from both sides and retired to consider their decision.

After enjoying a delicious meal at the expense of the Rt. Hon. Mr. Elephant, they reached their verdict, called the man, and declared as follows: "In our opinion this dispute has arisen through a **regrettable** misunderstanding due to the backwardness of your ideas. We consider that Mr. Elephant has fulfilled his sacred duty of protecting your interests. As it is clearly for your good that the space should be put to its most economic use, and as you yourself have not yet reached the stage of **expansion** which would enable you to fill it, we consider it necessary to arrange a compromise to suit both parties. Mr. Elephant shall continue his occupation of your hut, but we give you permission to look for a site where you can build another hut more suited to your needs, and we will see that you are well protected.

The man, having no **alternative**, and fearing that his refusal might expose him to the teeth and claws of members of the Commission, did as they suggested. But no sooner had he built another hut than Mr. Rhinoceros charged in with his horn lowered and ordered the man to quit. A Royal Commission was again appointed to look into the matter, and the same finding was given. This procedure was repeated until Mr. Buffalo, Mr. Leopard, Mr. Hyena and the rest were all accommodated with new huts.

sapling: young tree
authoritative: official

conclusive: convincing

relevant: timely, important
unbiased: fair, open-minded
assumed: took

regrettable: unfortunate

expansion: growth

alternative: other choice

Then the man decided that he must adopt an effective method of protection, since Commissions of Inquiry did not seem to be of any use to him. He sat down and said: "*Ng'enda thi ndeagaga motegi,*" which literally means "there is nothing that treads on the earth that cannot be trapped," or in other words, you can fool people for a time, but not for ever.

Early one morning, when the huts already occupied by the jungle lords were all beginning to decay and fall to pieces, he went out and built a bigger and better hut a little distance away. No sooner had Mr. Rhinoceros seen it than he came rushing in, only to find that Mr. Elephant was already inside, sound asleep. Mr. Leopard next came in at the window, Mr. Lion, Mr. Fox, and Mr. Buffalo entered the doors, while Mr. Hyena howled for a place in the shade and Mr. Alligator basked on the roof.

Presently they all began disputing about their rights of penetration, and from disputing they came to fighting, and while they were all embroiled together the man set the hut on fire and burnt it to the ground, jungle lords and all.

Then he went home, saying: "Peace is costly, but it's worth the expense," and lived happily ever after.

Just like the man in the story, some people in Africa turned to violence to rid their land of European imperialists. Kenya regained its independence from Britain in 1963, and Jomo Kenyatta later served as its president.

Source: Jomo Kenyatta, *Facing Mount Kenya*. London: Martin Secker & Warburg Ltd., 1953.

THE VISION THAT I SEE

by Kwame Nkrumah

During the 1800s European nations divided Africa into colonies and ruled almost the entire continent. In the middle 1900s, however, many Africans began fighting to regain their independence and freedom and to bring an end to this practice, called colonialism. One leader of this fight was Jomo Kenyatta, who wrote the story that appears on pages 162–165. Another major leader in the struggle against imperialism and colonial rule was Kwame Nkrumah (KWAHM ee en KROO muh, 1909–1972), a member of the Nzima people. Nkrumah was born in Nkroful, a village in the British colony called the Gold Coast. Although imprisoned for his beliefs, Nkrumah continued to fight for an end to colonialism. In this speech, delivered in the 1950s, Nkrumah expresses his hopes for the Gold Coast and the rest of Africa. As you read an excerpt from this speech, notice Nkrumah's goals and beliefs. How does Nkrumah use history to support his ideas?

The subject I have chosen to address you on this evening is "The Vision that I See." . . . It is better to be free to manage, or mismanage, your own affairs, than not to be free to mismanage or manage your own affairs. . . .

You know, **Providence** must be at work. I don't want to go back into history because I might be repeating sad memories but imagine the whole question of the slave trade, how Negroes from the West Coast of Africa were all carried over to the United States. And look into Negro history. You see the suffering and **tribulation** these people went through, and yet they survived in the United States of America and the **West Indies**. That's Providence. God Himself came, and, as in the days of Moses and the Israelites, who spent so many hard years in Egypt under all kinds of suffering, what was the result? The day came, yes, when God Himself brought up the man, and that man led them out of Egypt. A greater **exodus** is coming in Africa today, and that exodus will be established when there is a united, free and independent West Africa.

Again I don't want to bore you with history. It is a sad story. Look at the whole country of Africa today. With the possible exception of Liberia, Egypt and Ethiopia, the entire country is divided and sub-divided. . . .

Africa for the Africans! Is this some new concept that has come into being? . . . no! We are bringing into being another Africa for Africans, with a different concept, and that concept is what? A free and independent state in Africa. We want to be able to govern ourselves

providence: God's guidance of human destiny

tribulation: pain

West Indies: Caribbean islands

exodus: mass departure

in this country of ours without outside interference. And we are going to see that it is done.

Ladies and gentlemen, a people without a Government of their own is silly and absurd. Let us therefore **forge ahead** and develop our own countries, politically and economically. We must work for a greater glory and majesty, greater than the civilizations of our **grandsires**, the civilization of Ghana, the civilization of the [Mali] Empire and the civilization of the [Songhai] Empire. Long before the slave trade, long before Imperialistic rivalries in Africa began, civilizations of the Ghana Empire were in existence. And here, you even discover that at one time, at the great University of Timbuktu, Africans **versed** in the science of art and learning were studying their works translated in Greek and Hebrew, and at the same time exchanging professors with the University of Cordova in Spain. These were the brains, and today they come and tell us that we cannot do it. No, give the African a chance and he will show you that he can do it. . . .

And not only that, there have been great Africans, . . . who have distinguished themselves in the **cabinet** and in the field of battle. I need mention only a few: Anthony Amu, a man from the **Gold Coast**, was the first African to graduate with the degree of doctor of philosophy from the University of Wittenberg. Amu became professor of philosophy at the University of Berlin, 1954. He was an African. He came and died in the Gold Coast. That was a brain. . . . And not only that. In the field of battle there is **Toussaint**. Yes, these are the men who have put up the torch of light that we men of today, the youth of Africa, want to learn and **emulate** them, forge ahead, until Africa is **redeemed**, until we are free to manage or mismanage our own affairs in this country.

We believe in the equality of races. We believe in the freedom of the people of all races. We believe in cooperation. In fact it has been one of my **theses** that in this struggle of ours, in this struggle to redeem Africa, we are fighting not against race and colour and creed. We are fighting against a system—a system which degrades and exploits, and wherever we find that system, that system must be **liquidated**. Yes, we believe in peace and cooperation among all countries, but we also **abhor** Colonialism and Imperialism. We abhor man's inhumanity against man. . . .

We must learn to live together. The age of **aristocracy** is gone. God made all of us equal. In the sight of God we are one. We must combine. . . .

forge ahead: move forward

grandsires: male ancestors

versed: educated

cabinet: government

Gold Coast: present-day country of Ghana

Toussaint: Toussaint L'Ouverture, the liberator of Haiti

emulate: equal or surpass

redeemed: freed

theses: beliefs

liquidated: destroyed

abhor: hate

aristocracy: government by a privileged upper class

Four years after delivering this speech, Kwame Nkrumah helped lead his country to independence. On March 6, 1957, the colony of the Gold Coast became the free nation of Ghana. Nkrumah served as president of Ghana from 1960 to 1966 and inspired many other Africans to fight to regain their independence. One by one during the 1950s and 1960s, Africans liberated their nations from European rule.

Source: Bankole Timothy, *Kwame Nkrumah—From Cradle to Grave.* Dorchester, Dorset, Great Britain: The Gavin Press Limited, 1981.

Mountains in Israel

Song about Israel, 1950

Bordered by the Mediterranean Sea on its western coast, the nation of Israel is a land of great beauty. Mountains, valleys, and deserts cover much of the country. How does the Israeli song below describe the geography of this part of the Middle East?

Music by Harry Coopersmith
Words by T.E. Sampter

No pa - la - ces in Is - ra - el, Few ci - ties rich and fine, But

moun - tains rise all 'round the skies, In a long and __ wa - vy line. But

moun - tains rise all 'round the skies In a long and __ wa - vy line.

And there are valleys very deep,
With meadows painted bright,
Like carpets spread, embroidered red
And green and gold and white.
Like carpets spread, embroidered red
And green and gold and white.

Source: Harry Coopersmith, *The Songs We Sing*. New York: The United Synagogue of America, 1950.

Road to Peace

by Yasir Arafat and Yitzhak Rabin, 1993 and 1995

The Israeli and Palestinian people have known a great deal of conflict since the nation of Israel was founded in Palestine in 1948. When Yitzhak Rabin (YIHTS hahk rah BEEN) (1922-1995) became prime minister in 1992, he pledged to work toward peace with the Palestinians. This led to secret meetings in Oslo, Norway, which were successful in achieving a peace agreement which was called the "Declaration of Principles." The first two speeches excerpted below were made at the White House on September 13, 1993, at the signing of the agreement. Yitzhak Rabin and Palestinian leader Yasir Arafat (YAH sur AHR uh fat) (b. 1929) received the 1994 Nobel Peace Prize for their work on the agreement. They signed a second agreement at the White House on September 28, 1995. What views do these leaders seem to have in common?

Speech by Yasir Arafat, September 1993

In the name of God, the most merciful, the passionate, Mr. President, ladies and gentlemen, I would like to express our tremendous appreciation to President Clinton and to his administration for sponsoring this historic event which the entire world has been waiting for.

Mr. President, I am taking this opportunity to assure you and to assure the great American people that we share your values for freedom, justice and human rights…

My people are hoping that this agreement which we are signing today will **usher in** an age of peace, coexistence and equal rights. We are relying on your role, Mr. President, and on the role of all the countries which believe that without peace in the Middle East, peace in the world will not be complete….

Now as we stand on the **threshold** of this new historic era, let me address the people of Israel and their leaders, with whom we are meeting today for the first time, and let me assure them that the difficult decision we reached together was one that required great and exceptional courage.

We will need more courage and **determination** to continue the course of building coexistence and peace between us. This is possible and it will happen with **mutual** determination and with the effort that will be made with all parties on all the tracks to establish the foundations of a just and comprehensive peace….

[P]utting an end to [the Palestinian's] feelings of being wronged and of having suffered an historic injustice is the strongest guarantee to achieve coexistence and openness between our two peoples and future generations. Our two peoples are awaiting today this historic hope, and they want to give peace a real chance….

usher in: bring about

threshold: entranceway

determination: firm purpose

mutual: shared

I thank you, Mr. President. We hope that our meeting will be a new beginning for **fruitful** and effective relations between the American people and the Palestinian people....

Ladies and gentlemen, the battle for peace is the most difficult battle of our lives. It deserves our **utmost** efforts because the land of peace, the land of peace yearns for a just and comprehensive peace. Thank you.

Speech by Yitzhak Rabin, September 1993

President Clinton, the President of the United States, your excellencies, ladies and gentlemen. This signing of the Israeli-Palestinian declaration of principles here today is not so easy, neither for myself as a soldier in Israel's wars, nor for the people of Israel, nor for the Jewish people in the **Diaspora** who are watching us now with great hope mixed with **apprehension**. It is certainly not easy for the families of the victims of the wars, violence, terror, whose pain will never heal, for the many thousands who defended our lives with their own and have even sacrificed their lives for our own. For them, this ceremony has come too late.

Today, on the eve of an opportunity for peace, and perhaps an end to violence and wars, we remember each and every one of them with everlasting love. We have come from Jerusalem, the ancient and eternal capital of the Jewish people. We have come from an **anguished** and grieving land. We have come from a people, a home, a family that has not known a single year, not a single month, in which mothers have not wept for their sons. We have come to try and put an end to the hostilities so that our children, and our children's children, will no longer experience the painful cost of war, violence and terror. We have come to secure their lives and to ease the sorrow and the painful memories of the past, to hope and pray for peace.

Let me say to you, the Palestinians, we are **destined** to live together on the same soil in the same land. We, the soldiers who have returned from battles stained with blood; we who have seen our relatives and friends killed before our eyes; we who have attended their funerals and cannot look into the eyes of their parents; we who have come from a land where parents bury their children: we who have fought against you, the Palestinians, we say to you today in a loud and a clear voice, enough of blood and tears. Enough!...

Today here in Washington at the White House, we will begin a new **reckoning in** the relations between peoples, between parents tired of war, between children who will not know war.... Ladies and gentlemen, the time for peace has come...

In the Jewish tradition, it is customary to conclude our prayers with the word "Amen." With your permission, men of peace, I shall conclude with words taken from the prayer recited by Jews daily. I would ask the entire audience to join me in saying "Amen."

May He who makes peace on High, make peace for us and all Israel. Amen.

fruitful: productive

utmost: greatest

Diaspora: the scattering of Jews to many parts of the world
apprehension: fear

anguished: suffering

destined: fated

reckoning in: evaluation of

Speech by Yasir Arafat, September 1995

It has been two years since we met at the White House to sign the Declaration of Principles, to which we and our Israeli partners have agreed to in Oslo. We meet again today to make new headway in giving hope to this historic process...

Today, standing before you, I tell you with courage and a sense of responsibility that our participation in the great peace process means that we are betting everything on the future....

From this day on we do not want to see any waste of or threat to any innocent Palestinian life or any innocent Israeli life. Enough killing and enough killing of innocent people....

For us to succeed... we are bound to base the emerging Palestinian political system on the principles of liberty, democracy, separation of powers, freedom of expression, and national **initiative**. We are also bound to continue building Palestinian institutions and the Palestinian national economy.

initiative: right of citizens to rule themselves

But this enterprise is still in its early stages and our institutions have yet to mature. The road ahead remains long, indeed.

Speech by Yitzhak Rabin, September 1995

The sight you see—you see before you at this moment was impossible, was unthinkable just two years ago. Only poets dreamt of it. And to our great pain, soldier and civilians went to their death to make this moment possible. Here we stand before you, men who fate and history have sent on a mission of peace to end once and for all 100 years of bloodshed....

Ladies and gentlemen, this week the Jewish people in its thousands of places of **dispersion** has marked a new year, and in their Holy Day prayers, Jews everywhere are saying—May we—I'm translating it to the best of my capability.

dispersion: separation

May we be remembered and **inscribed** before you in the Book of Life and of blessing and peace and prosperity, of deliverance and comfort and opportunity, we and all who **people** the House of Israel, for a good life and peace. These are my wishes to all the Jewish people. These are my wishes to all the citizens of Israel: a good life and a peace. These are also our wishes to our neighbors, to all the world peoples: a good life and peace.

inscribed: written

people: populate

Yitzhak Rabin did not live to see his wish for peace realized. He fell victim to violence on November 4, 1995. Rabin was shot and killed at a peace rally in Tel Aviv by a young Israeli who opposed the peace agreements with the Palestinians. In the words of Yasir Arafat, "the road ahead remains long, indeed."

Sources: Yasir Arafat and Yitzhak Rabin, *Declaration of Principles on Interim Self-Government Arrangements.* Ministry of Foreign Affairs, Government of Israel, 1993; *New York Times*, Sept. 29, 1995.

Poems for Peace

by Tali Shurek and Mahmud Abu Radj, 1974

Peace negotiators, such as the ones you read about on pages 169–171, are not the only people in the Middle East who want peace. Young people living in this region of the world also want to make the Middle East a safer place in which to live. Below are two poems that were written in Israel. The one on the left is by Mahmud Abu Radj, a 12-year-old Arab, and the one on the right is by Tali Shurek, a 13-year-old Jew. How do these two poems use different images to present similar ideas?

When Will It Come, The Day

When will peace take over?
When will it come, the day?
When with armies and bombs will they do away
When all this hostility cease,
A day on which battleships
Will become palaces of leisure and fun
Floating on the seas.

A day on which the steel of guns
Will be melted into pleasure cars;
A day on which generals will begin to raise flowers.

When peace
Will include all the peoples of these neighboring
   lands,
When Ishmael and Israel
Will go hand in hand,
And when every Jew—
The Arab's brother will be.
When will it come, the day?

Mahmud Abu Radj

The Paint-Box

I had a paint-box—
Each color glowing with delight;
I had a paint-box with colors
Warm and cool and bright.
I had no red for wounds and
   blood,
I had no black for an orphaned
   child,
I had no white for the face of
   the dead,
I had no yellow for burning
   sands.
I had orange for joy and life.
I had green for buds and
   blooms,
I had blue for clear bright skies.
I had pink for dreams and rest.
I sat down
and painted
Peace.

Tali Shurek

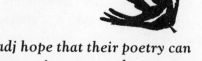

Young people such as Tali Shurek and Mahmud Abu Radj hope that their poetry can help make the world a more peaceful place. If you were to write a poem about peace, what images would you use?

Source: Jacob Zim, *My Shalom My Peace.* Tel Aviv, Israel: American Israel Publishing Co. Ltd., 1974.

Why India Must Be Free

by Mohandas Gandhi, 1930

In the early 1900s many people of India began fighting for the independence of their nation from British colonial rule. The leader of this movement was a lawyer named Mohandas Gandhi (1869–1948). He urged Indians to seek independence through civil disobedience—protest without violence. Gandhi and his followers refused to obey unjust laws. Gandhi wrote the letter on this page to Lord Irwin, the British governor of India, in 1930. How does Gandhi separate his feelings about British rule from his feelings about the British people? What does he believe individuals must do to change the world?

March 2, 1930

Dear Friend,

Before **embarking** on civil disobedience and taking the risk I have dreaded to take all these years, I would **fain** approach you and find a way out.

My personal faith is absolutely clear. I cannot intentionally hurt anything that lives, much less fellow human beings, even though they may do the greatest wrong to me and mine. Whilst, therefore, I hold the British rule to be a curse, I do not intend harm to a single Englishman or to any **legitimate** interest he may have in India.

I must not be misunderstood. Though I hold the British rule in India to be a curse, I do not, therefore, consider Englishmen in general to be worse than any other people on earth. I have the privilege of claiming many Englishmen as dearest friends. Indeed much that I have learnt of the evil of British rule is due to the writings of frank and courageous Englishmen who have not hesitated to tell the **unpalatable** truth about that rule.

And why do I regard the British rule as a curse?

It has **impoverished**... millions by a system of progressive **exploitation** and by a ruinously expensive military and civil administration which the country can never afford.

embarking: setting out

fain: rather

legitimate: rightful

unpalatable: unpleasant

impoverished: made poor

exploitation: misuse

Gandhi's nonviolent campaign succeeded. In 1947 India won its independence from Great Britain.

Source: Martin Green, ed., *Gandhi in India: In His Own Words*. Hanover, NH: University Press of New England, 1987.

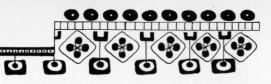

A Woman From Pakistan: SHABANU

by Attiya Inayatullah, 1995

When India gained its independence from Britain in 1947, the Muslim population formed a separate country—Pakistan. In 1971, the new nation divided to form the countries of Pakistan and Bangladesh. Women in these nations have traditionally been denied many of the rights held by men. They are often not allowed to go to school or to take part in business or politics. Marriages are often arranged—young people do not choose their own husbands and wives. Things are changing, however. The following excerpt from a magazine article is about Shabanu, a Pakistani woman who was determined to use her own abilities to make life better for herself and her children. How is Shabanu accomplishing her aims? How might life be better for her children when they become adults?

Shabanu is thirty-eight years old. She comes from a large and **impoverished** family in an area where education for females is regarded as unnecessary or even as a disadvantage. She dropped out of school at eleven, first to look after her brothers and sisters, then to marry a **clansman**. Then her husband deserted her and her four children, and she was forced to borrow from her mother and brothers to make ends meet. She resolved to overcome her dependence and ensure that neither she nor her children would ever be **vulnerable** again.

impoverished: very poor

clansman: member of a group with a common ancestor

vulnerable: easily hurt

She started attending women's group meetings, showing particular interest in sessions devoted to education, **income-generation** and the status of women. Recognizing that she faced problems without formal educational qualifications, she privately prepared for and passed her **matriculation** examination. She also took a training course for birth attendants. She used modern, **hygienic** techniques that benefited the mothers she delivered. Shabanu also participated in a women's festival in which women from all over Pakistan met to share their experience, demonstrate how they were overcoming their problems and participate in rarely available recreational activities.

income-generation: money-earning

matriculation: college enrollment

hygienic: sanitary

When she was appointed as a supervisor in the local women's [program], her income increased and she became able to educate her children. As a supervisor, she motivates other women to take action to improve their lives through education, health, hygiene, family planning and income-generating activities.

Pakistani women now have a strong role model in Prime Minister Benazir Bhutto (BEHN uh zihr BOO toh) (b. 1953). Bhutto is the first woman leader of a modern Muslim nation. She was elected to office in 1988 and again in 1993.

Source: Attiya Inayatullah, "Three Women From Pakistan," *The Unesco Courier*. Paris, France: Unesco, Sept. 1995.

A Bank That Only Lends To The Poor

An interview with Muhammad Yunus, 1995

As you read in Shabanu's story on page 174, women in countries such as Pakistan and Bangladesh are beginning to earn their own incomes and to participate in the economic life of their cultures. Muhammad Yunus, a university professor in Bangladesh, founded the Grameen Bank in 1983. The bank specializes in loaning small amounts of money to poor people who would probably be denied loans by other banks. Most of the bank's customers are women. For what types of projects are the loans often used? Do you think this idea would be successful in other cultures?

■ **What gave you the idea of founding a bank to help the penniless?**

— When Bangladesh became independent in 1971, everyone was **euphoric**. We were convinced our lives would change for the better, but instead things went downhill very fast. In 1974 Bangladesh was hit by a famine. At that time I was teaching economics at Chittagong University, and while I was teaching beautiful economic theories, people were dying. This was very hard to accept, and I started thinking about what I could do to help the poor to rise out of poverty.... So I made up my mind to found by own bank.

euphoric: overjoyed

■ **Today you have 12,000 employees and two million borrowers, 94 per cent of whom are women.**

— Yes, most of our clients are women. It has been a hard struggle to achieve this....

■ **How did you persuade them to borrow from the bank?**

— It wasn't easy. But first one woman took the plunge, then another and another. When one woman succeeds, the others are encouraged. Seeing that it works, the others try their luck.

■ **What kind of projects do they want to finance?**

— Very simple projects such as raising a cow, selling milk, processing rice, weaving baskets or sewing... It is very exciting to see people emerge from poverty. Our aim is to make sure that the two million families that are with us all **cross the poverty line** within the next five years.

cross the poverty line: rise above poverty

The idea behind the Grameen Bank was risky—the bank might have failed if the borrowers could not repay the loans. However, so far, the bank has been an astonishing success. More than a third of their borrowers have already been able to rise above the extreme poverty level. Can you think of any businesses in your community that improve the quality of peoples' lives?

Source: *The Unesco Courier*. Paris, France: Unesco, Sept. 1995.

Tank, the Water Buffalo

by Huynh Quang Nhuong, 1982

Huynh Quang Nhuong (hwin kwahng nyahng) was born in Mytho, a small village in the central highlands of Vietnam. His village consisted of 50 houses made of bamboo frames and covered with coconut leaves. The village was bordered on one side by a dense forest and on the other by a river. Beyond the river lay endless rows of rice fields and a chain of high mountains. Wild animals were a part of everyday life in Mytho. In the following story Huynh describes his childhood and a very special water buffalo named Tank. In what ways is Tank important to Huynh, his family, and his neighbors?

My family had land on which we grew rice. During July to January, the rainy season, the rice field was flooded, and only water buffaloes could be used to till the soil.

We owned three water buffaloes, one male and two females. One day our male died of old age. My father decided to look for the ideal water buffalo to replace him: a bull that was both a hard worker and a good fighter. Fighting ability was important because tigers raided the herd near the edge of the jungle. Buffaloes born and raised among mountain tribes had the reputation of being excellent fighters, but they were often too fierce, violent, and impatient to handle. On the other hand, buffaloes born and raised in the lowlands were patient and obedient, but they did not make good fighters, for they lived in an area where fierce **predators** did not exist. Neither type of buffalo would meet my father's needs.

However, it was possible to have the ideal buffalo if a young bull had a fierce father from the mountains and a patient mother from the lowlands. This unusual mixture occurred if a fierce mountain bull wandered down to the lowlands and met a female which would bear its offspring. The owner of the female might not know that he had a mixed-blood calf until the calf grew older and the thickness of its coat indicated the mountain origin of its father. So sometimes a farmer who had more buffaloes than he needed would unwittingly sell a valuable mixed-blood calf.

My father, by a combination of luck and patience, discovered a mixed-blood buffalo at the ranch of a buffalo merchant in a town far below the river and bought it at a good price.

I was six years old when my father brought the new calf home. He let me give the young buffalo food and water, and sometimes he allowed me to pat its shoulders. But he told me never to approach it when I was alone, for calves were unpredictable. Although they usually obeyed everybody taller than they were, they did not obey small children and sometimes might hurt them.

I listened to my father, but I trusted our calf. I knew he and I would become great friends.

Our calf grew into a handsome and powerful buffalo. He not only became the head of our small herd, but also became the head of all the herds in our **hamlet** after many ferocious and successful fights with the other males. We named him "Tank," because when he hit another male during a fight, he struck as heavily as a tank.

One day a young bull from a nearby hamlet trespassed on Tank's territory and challenged his authority. Tank roared a few times to warn the intruder, but the other buffalo was determined to fight. When we heard Tank's roars we knew that there was trouble in the field. Everyone in the hamlet rushed to a hill to watch the fight. We could not prevent it, so we stayed on high ground to protect ourselves; for a defeated buffalo would often run to humans to be rescued and, in its panic, trample them.

Tank left his herd and faced the **arrogant** intruder. The other buffaloes stopped eating and waited. Suddenly the two bulls charged and ran into each other head on. I heard a mighty thud. Both buffaloes fell back. My heart was pounding. It was the first time any of us had ever seen Tank fall back. Tank was the pride of the hamlet, and we would be very ashamed if he lost the fight; or worse, if Tank were killed, some of our female buffaloes might follow the victorious bull home to the other hamlet, and it would be very hard to bring them back.

The two buffaloes recovered from the powerful collision and ran at each other again. This time they locked horns and tried to twist and break each other's necks. Next, each pushed the other and tried to overturn him. At first the intruder **sustained** Tank's push very well. But then, little by little, he began to lose ground. Tank pushed him farther and farther backward. Unfortunately for the other buffalo, who had fought quite well so far, there was a deep trench behind him. When his two hind legs fell into the trench, the animal was helpless. Tank's sharpened horns hit first his neck, then his shoulders; but unlike other

predators: animals that eat other animals

hamlet: small village

arrogant: proud

sustained: withstood

buffaloes, this one did not call for help.

My father felt sorry for the bull, and he asked my cousin, whom Tank loved the best, to try to stop Tank from killing him. My cousin rushed to Tank's side and called his name. Tank, furious because he was hurt himself, nevertheless listened to my cousin and let him lead him away. The defeated intruder was rescued from the trench and set free, and we never saw or heard from him again.

Tank became so famous that people from far away brought females to breed with him. Buffalo thieves also considered him a prize. One day it rained very hard and Tank did not come home. The next morning we went to look for him. We asked a friend who had a hound dog to help us. My father, my cousin and I, and a few well-armed friends followed the hound and found Tank near a river crossing about fifteen kilometers [9 m] from home, tied to the root of a tree.

When we untied Tank, he was very happy and licked everybody who had come to rescue him. But we were puzzled. There was blood scattered all around, but Tank himself was unharmed. And why, if thieves had taken Tank so far away from our home, had they finally left him there?

Weeks later these questions were answered. At a local wedding we heard a drunken man tell the story of how he had been hurt by Tank during his attempt to steal him. First, he and two **accomplices** had spent many days observing the clothes and mannerisms of my cousin, who took care of Tank and his herd. Then, helped by the pouring rain, which prevented Tank from seeing him clearly, and wearing the same clothes and whistling the same song my cousin did, he approached Tank in the field. When he was close enough he seized the rope that passed through the buffalo's nose. Tank was helpless. If he resisted, the rope would hurt his sensitive nose badly. With the help of his two accomplices, the thief led Tank away. When they reached the river crossing, he loosened the rope so Tank could drink some water. But instead of drinking, Tank hit him with his horns, gashing the man's leg from his knee to the upper thigh. Since the man could not walk, the other thieves had to carry him and leave Tank behind. They knew that we would soon be on their trail with a hound dog. But before they left, they managed to tie Tank's rope to the root of a tree so the angered buffalo couldn't attack them again.

When the thief finished his story, one of the wedding guests asked him why he had not killed Tank, since Tank had hurt him so badly. The thief answered that to kill a buffalo, under any circumstances, would bring bad luck. Besides, he admired Tank too much to kill him. He said that if they had succeeded in stealing Tank, they would have been able to sell him for ten times the price of any ordinary buffalo. Then he added that sometimes he still came to our hamlet just to have a look at the magnificent bull. No other bull was intelligent enough to fool him, a man of many years' experience as a buffalo thief. When asked if he would attempt to steal Tank again, he said no, because this time he would be risking his life for sure. He was right. My father had

accomplices: partners in wrongdoing

removed the rope passing through Tank's nose, just in case anyone tried to steal Tank again.

To our surprise, we learned we did not need the rope to command Tank. He continued to till the soil and guard the herd. We commanded Tank orally now. He quickly learned the meaning of "Left," "Right," and "Stop," and did exactly what my cousin wanted while working in the field. When my cousin put crops on his back and said, "Go," he would walk straight home by himself. And at home after we had unloaded the crops and said, "Go," he would return to the field.

Other buffaloes might be able to do the same job, but not as well as Tank. Most of them could not resist the green grass that bordered the path leading home. When they lingered to eat, they would be late for their tasks. Or sometimes on their way to the field they would see a female buffalo and would stay around and forget everything. But Tank was so exact about his work that one day an angry housewife said she wished that her husband would be as dependable as Tank.

My cousin also trained Tank to fight jungle cats. He made a stuffed tiger with straw and old linen, and **simulated** a tiger attack from different angles. He taught Tank to roll over, for without this trick a buffalo was helpless if a tiger or a panther jumped on its back. But a well-trained buffalo could make a tiger jump away by rolling over, or crush it under its weight. And every morning, my cousin attached a razor-sharp knife to each of Tank's horns before he let him go to the pasture on the edge of the jungle.

simulated: pretended to make

One afternoon all the buffaloes began roaring. Everyone rushed toward the pasture. Hunters blew their hunting horns, and hunting dogs raced out of houses to follow their masters. When we reached the pasture we saw all the adult buffaloes forming a circle to protect their young, and Tank apart from them, fighting with a huge tiger. As we approached, the tiger quit the fight and limped back into the jungle. We examined Tank and found blood on his horns. There was blood scattered all around the ground too, but it was the tiger that had been badly hurt, not Tank. Tank had only a few scratches on his neck.

After this tangle with the tiger, Tank never had to till the soil again. Other inhabitants of the hamlet told my father that if his two other buffaloes were not enough to till the land he owned, they would send theirs to help. Tank's only responsibility now was to guard the hamlet's herd during the dry season.

Huynh Quang Nhuong has written many stories describing his childhood in Vietnam. You can read some of these in his book The Land I Lost. *Huynh graduated from Saigon University and was later drafted into the South Vietnamese army. He was paralyzed by a bullet during the Vietnam War, and in 1969 he came to live in the United States. For a description of life in Vietnam during the Vietnam War, read the next document on pages 180–182.*

Source: Huynh Quang Nhuong, *The Land I Lost: Adventures of a Boy in Vietnam*. New York: J. B. Lippincott Junior Books, 1982.

The War Years in Vietnam

by Le Ly Hayslip, 1989

As the story on pages 176–179 showed, Vietnam is a beautiful land of forests, rice fields, rivers, and mountains. Long, bitter wars, however, have scarred the land and the lives of its people during much of this century. The longest conflict, between North Vietnam and South Vietnam, lasted from the 1950s until 1975. For many of those years, the United States fought in this war on the side of South Vietnam. Le Ly Hayslip was only 12 years old when American soldiers first entered her small village in Vietnam. Because opposing armies competed in the countryside for people's loyalties, Le Ly Hayslip found herself both tortured by the South Vietnamese and sentenced to death by the North Vietnamese. In the excerpt below from her book When Heaven and Earth Changed Places, *Le Ly Hayslip recalls her wartime experiences. What lessons do you think she learned from her father?*

Once, when I was the only child at home, my mother went to [the city of] Da Nang to visit Uncle Nhu, and my father had to take care of me. I woke up from my nap in the empty house and cried for my mother. My father came in from the yard and reassured me, but I was still cranky and continued crying. Finally, he gave me a rice cookie to shut me up. Needless to say, this was a tactic my mother never used.

The next afternoon I woke up and although I was not feeling cranky, I thought a rice cookie might be nice. I cried a fake cry and my father came running in.

"What's this?" he asked, making a worried face. "Little Bay Ly doesn't want a cookie?"

I was confused again.

"Look under your pillow," he said with a smile.

I twisted around and saw that, while I was sleeping, he had placed a rice cookie under my pillow. We both laughed and he picked me up like a sack of rice and carried me outside while I gobbled the cookie.

In the yard, he plunked me down under a tree and told me some stories. After that, he got some scraps of wood and showed me how to make things: a doorstep for my mother and a toy duck for me. . . . My father showed me the mystery of hammers and explained the customs of our people.

His knowledge of the Vietnamese went back to the Chinese Wars in ancient times. I learned how one of my distant ancestors, a woman named Phung Thi Chinh, led Vietnamese fighters against the **Han.** In one battle, even though she was pregnant and surrounded by Chinese, she delivered the baby, tied it to her back, and cut her way to safety wielding a sword in each hand. I was amazed at this warrior's bravery and impressed that I was her **descendant.** Even more, I was amazed and impressed by my father's pride in her accomplishments . . . and his belief that I was worthy of her example. . . .

Han: an ancient Chinese dynasty

descendant: relative

Never again did I cry after my nap. Phung Thi women were too strong for that. Besides, I was my father's daughter and we had many things to do together. . . .

The next day, I took some water out to him in the fields. My mother was due home any time and I used every opportunity to step outside and watch for her. My father stopped working, drank gratefully, then took my hand and led me to the top of a nearby hill. It had a good view of the village and the land beyond it, almost to the ocean. I thought he was going to show me my mother coming back, but he had something else in mind.

He said, "Bay Ly, you see all this here? This is the Vietnam we have been talking about. You understand that a country is more than a lot of dirt, rivers, and forests, don't you?"

I said, "Yes, I understand." After all, we had learned in school that one's country is as sacred as a father's grave.

"Good. You know, some of these lands are battlefields where your brothers and cousins are fighting. They may never come back. Even your sisters have all left home in search of a better life. You are the only one left in my house. If the enemy comes back, you must be both a daughter and a son. I told you how the Chinese used to rule our land. People in this village had to risk their lives diving in the ocean just to find pearls for the Chinese emperor's gown. They had to risk tigers and snakes in the jungle just to find herbs for his table. Their payment for this hardship was a bowl of rice and another day of life. That is why. . . Phung Thi Chinh fought so hard to expel the Chinese. When the French came, it was the same old story. Your mother and I were taken to Da Nang to build a runway for their airplanes. We labored from sunup to sundown and well after dark. . . . Our reward was a bowl of rice and another day of life. Freedom is never a gift, Bay Ly. It must be won and won again. Do you understand?"

I said that I did. . . .

"Hey." He poked me in the ribs. "Are you getting hungry for lunch?"

"No. I want to learn how to take care of the farm. What happens if the soldiers come back? What did you and Mother do when the soldiers came?"

My father squatted on the dusty hilltop and wiped the sweat from his forehead. "The first thing I did was to tell myself that it was my duty to survive—to take care of my family and my farm. That is a tricky job in wartime. It's as hard as being a soldier.... You may remember the night I sent you and your brothers and sisters away with your mother to Da Nang."

"You didn't go with us!" My voice still held the horror of the night I thought I had lost my father.

"Right! I stayed near the village—right on this hill—to keep an eye on the enemy and on our house. If they really wanted to destroy the village, I would save some of our things so that we could start over. Sure enough, that was their plan.

"The real problem was to keep things safe and avoid being captured. Their patrols were everywhere. Sometimes I went so deep in the forest that I worried about getting lost, but all I had to do was follow the smoke from the burning huts and I could find my way back.

"Once, I was trapped between two patrols that had camped on both sides of a river. I had to wait in the water for two days before one of them moved on. When I got out, my skin was **shriveled** like an old melon. I was so cold I could hardly move. From the waist down, my body was black with **leeches**. But it was worth all the pain. When your mother came back, we still had some furniture and tools to cultivate the earth. Many people lost everything. Yes, we were very lucky."

shriveled: wrinkled

leeches: worms that suck blood

My father put his arms around me. "My brother Huong—your uncle Huong—had three sons and four daughters. Of his four daughters, only one is still alive. Of his three sons, two went north to **Hanoi** and one went south to **Saigon**. Huong's house is very empty."...

My father drew me out to arm's length and looked me squarely in the eye. "Now, Bay Ly, do you understand what your job is?"

I squared my shoulders and put on a soldier's face. "My job is to **avenge** my family. To protect my farm by killing the enemy. I must become a woman warrior like Phung Thi Chinh!"

My father laughed and pulled me close. "No, little peach blossom. Your job is to stay alive—to keep an eye on things and keep the village safe.... Most of all, it is to live in peace and tend the shrine of our **ancestors**. Do these things well, Bay Ly, and you will be worth more than any soldier who ever took up a sword."

Hanoi: the capital of North Vietnam at the time

Saigon: the capital of South Vietnam at the time

avenge: seek revenge for

ancestors: family members who lived long ago

Le Ly Hayslip survived the Vietnam War and fled to the United States with her children in 1970. Five years later the war finally ended with the victory of the North Vietnamese. Le Ly Hayslip returned to her homeland in 1986 and had a reunion with her mother and other family members. She now lives in California, where she founded the East Meets West Foundation, a charitable relief and world peace group.

Source: Le Ly Hayslip with Jay Wurts, *When Heaven and Earth Changed Places*. New York: Doubleday, 1989.

Tết Trung
Vietnamese Song

Each year the Southeast Asian country of Vietnam celebrates a festival of the full moon called the Mid-Autumn Festival. This festival takes place in the eighth lunar month—around the middle of September. People gather outside with their friends and relatives to admire the moon. They eat "mooncakes," which are sweet, round cakes filled with fruit and nuts. Children go out into the streets, dancing and singing and carrying lighted lanterns. "Tết Trung" is one of the songs they sing. Notice the different kinds of lanterns mentioned in the song. What songs are part of your culture's annual celebrations?

Vietnamese Song
Collected and Transcribed by
Kathy B. Sorensen
English Words by MMH

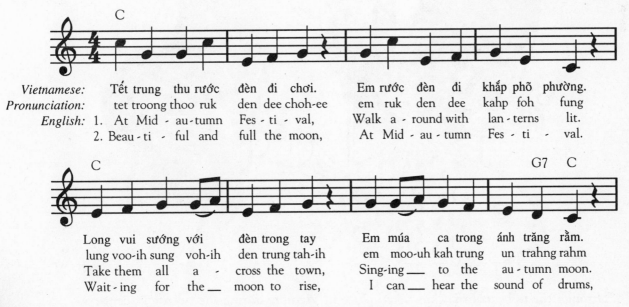

Vietnamese: Tết trung thu rước đèn đi chơi. Em rước đèn đi khắp phõ phường.
Pronunciation: tet troong thoo ruk den dee choh-ee em ruk den dee kahp foh fung
English: 1. At Mid - au - tumn Fes - ti - val, Walk a - round with lan - terns lit.
2. Beau - ti - ful and full the moon, At Mid - au - tumn Fes - ti - val.

Long vui sướng với đèn trong tay Em múa ca trong ánh trăng rằm.
lung voo-ih sung voh-ih den trung tah-ih em moo-uh kah trung un trahng rahm
Take them all a - cross the town, Sing-ing ___ to the au - tumn moon.
Wait - ing for the ___ moon to rise, I can ___ hear the sound of drums,

Đèn ông sao với đèn cá chám.
den ung sah-oo voh-ih den kah chahm
Lan-terns all in dif-fer-ent shapes,
Tung yin yin kak tung yin yin,

Đèn thiên nga với đèn bướm bướm,
den tee-en ngah voh-ih den bum bum
Lan-tern an-gel, lan-tern dream,
Tung yin yin kak tung yin yin.

em rước đèn này đèn cung trăng.
em ruk den nah-ih den koong trahng
Lan-tern fish, or lan-tern star,
I can hear the sound of drums,

Đèn xanh lơ với đèn tím tím.
den sun luh voh-ih den tihm tihm
Lan-tern swan or but-ter-fly.
Tung yin yin kak tung yin yin,

Đèn xanh lam với đèn trắng trắng,
den sun lahm voh-ih den trahng trahng
Take my lan-tern to the sky;
Tung yin yin kak tung yin yin.

trong ánh đèn rực rỡ muôn màu.
trong un den ruk ru moon mah-oo
Take my lan-tern to the moon.
Wel-come, la-dy in the moon!

Through the upheaval that has taken place in Vietnam during the twentieth century, cultural traditions such as the Mid-Autumn Festival have survived. Songs like "Tết Trung" help link Vietnam's past and future.

Source: Kathy B. Sorensen, collector and transcriber, *Share the Music, Grade 5.* New York: Macmillan/McGraw-Hill, 1995.

184

New Year's Address

by Václav Havel, 1990

In November 1989 thousands of people jammed the streets in Czechoslovakia's capital city of Prague (PRAHG) to protest communism and Soviet control of their government. Unlike earlier protests in Czechoslovakia that had been crushed, this time the communist government was forced to resign. In December 1989 Czechoslovakia held its first free elections since 1946 and chose Václav Havel (VAH tslav HAH vul) as president. A leading playwright, Havel had been imprisoned several times for speaking out against the communist government. On January 1, 1990, Havel gave his first major speech as president of Czechoslovakia. As you read an excerpt of his speech, notice how Havel outlines the differences between past governments and the new one. What challenges facing Czechoslovakia does he describe? According to Havel, what are the responsibilities of people in a democracy?

My dear fellow citizens,

For forty years you heard from my **predecessors** on this day different **variations** of the same theme: how our country flourished, how many million tons of steel we produced, how happy we all were, how we trusted our government, and what bright **perspectives** were unfolding in front of us.

I assume you did not propose me for this office so that I, too, would lie to you.

Our country is not flourishing. The enormous creative and spiritual potential of our nations is not being used sensibly. Entire branches of industry are producing goods which are of no interest to anyone, while we are lacking the things we need. A state which calls itself a workers' state **humiliates** and **exploits** workers. Our **obsolete** economy is wasting the little energy we have available. A country that once could be proud of the educational level of its citizens spends so little on education that it ranks today as seventy-second in the world. We have polluted our soil, our rivers and forests, **bequeathed** to

predecessors: past rulers

variations: versions

perspectives: scenes

humiliates: insults
exploits: mistreats
obsolete: outdated

bequeathed: handed down

us by our ancestors, and we have today the most **contaminated** environment in Europe. . . .

contaminated: polluted

But all this is still not the main problem. The worst thing is that we live in a contaminated moral environment. We fell morally ill because we became used to saying something different from what we thought. We learned not to believe in anything, to ignore each other, to care only about ourselves. . . .

We cannot blame the previous rulers for everything, not only because it would be untrue but also because it could **blunt** the duty that each of us faces today, namely, the **obligation** to act independently, freely, reasonably, and quickly. Let us not be mistaken: the best government in the world, the best parliament and the best president, cannot achieve much on their own. And it would also be wrong to expect a general **remedy** from them only. Freedom and democracy include participation and therefore responsibility from us all. . . .

blunt: make less clear
obligation: duty

remedy: cure

We had to pay, however, for our present freedom. Many citizens perished in jails in the **fifties,** many were executed, thousands of human lives were destroyed, hundreds of thousands of talented people were forced to leave the country. Those who defended the honor of our nations during the Second World War, those who rebelled against **totalitarian** rule, and those who simply managed to remain themselves and think freely, were all **persecuted.** We should not forget any of those who paid for our present freedom in one way or another. . . .

fifties: 1950s

totalitarian: absolute
persecuted: treated badly

Our country, if that is what we want, can now permanently **radiate** love, understanding, the power of spirit and ideas. . . .

radiate: send out

Let us try in a new time and in a new way to restore this concept of politics. Let us teach ourselves and others that politics should be an expression of a desire to contribute to the happiness of the community rather than of a need to cheat. . .the community. . . .

There are free elections and an election campaign ahead of us. Let us not allow this struggle to dirty the so far clean face of our gentle revolution. . . .

You may ask what kind of a republic I dream of. Let me reply: I dream of a republic independent, free, and democratic, of a republic economically prosperous and yet socially just, in short, of a humane republic which serves the individual and which therefore holds the hope that the individual will serve it in turn. Of a republic of well-rounded people, because without such it is impossible to solve any of our problems, human, economic, ecological, social, or political. . . .

People, your government has returned to you!

Czechoslovakia was one of several countries in Eastern Europe to overthrow its communist government and free itself from the control of the Soviet Union in 1989 and 1990. The most remarkable political change of all, however, was the collapse of the Soviet Union in 1991. For a description of this event, read the next document on pages 187–188.

Source: Václav Havel, *Open Letters: Selected Writings 1965–1990.* New York: Alfred A. Knopf, 1991.

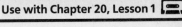

Speech Before the
United Nations

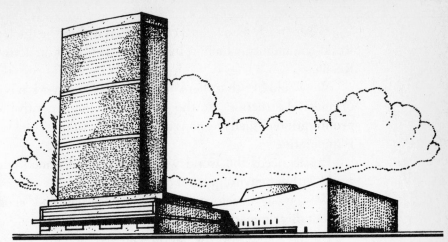

by Boris Yeltsin, 1994

After World War II tensions grew between the United States and the Soviet Union, developing into what became known as the Cold War. Although there was no actual violence, the two nations were hostile to each other. Both countries lived under the threat of war, particularly a nuclear war. Each built up stockpiles of nuclear weapons big enough to destroy the world many times over. With the fall of communism and the breakup of the Soviet Union in the early 1990s, relations between the former Soviet Union and the United States have greatly improved. Russian President Boris Yeltsin made the speech excerpted below before the United Nations General Assembly on September 26, 1994. How do you think the world should handle the problem of nuclear weapons? Do you think it is possible for the nations of the world to live together in peace?

Ladies and Gentlemen! The United Nations Organization approaches its 50th anniversary. With it the whole world becomes 50 years older.

What is this world like nowadays? Has it become better or wiser? And what matters, what will the present generation leave behind to their successors?

There is no state, no people **indifferent to** these issues. And here in the United Nations we have to find answers to them.

indifferent to:
    uninterested in

This is particularly important for Russia. We are trying to understand what world we want to live in, and exactly what world to build; we'll spare no effort.

The new Russia was born in 1991 as a democratic state. This was witnessed by the entire world.

For several years already we have been engaged in **exclusive** large-scale and laborious work. It boils down to removing the legacy of totalitarianism and Cold war.

exclusive: single

Freedom came to Russia. The people got basic civil rights which had been denied to them.

The profound economic reform is in progress in Russia. A free market economy is being put into effect. Thus, each of our new success stories reinforces Russian democracy....

Russia undergoes changes, regains her identity, but by all means remains a great power.

We are ready for an equal cooperation within the framework of the world community, which in its turn would accept an active and open Russia.

We would like that there be no nuclear or other kinds of weapons of mass destruction in the world. Efficient control over **non-proliferation** of such weapons and its production-related technologies is **imperative**.

Russia needs the world without wars and armed conflicts, the world without environmental **calamities**.

We favour development of the international economic ties without **discrimination**.

Russia stands for the world capable of combating terrorism, **narcobusiness** and other types of international crime.

To make such titanic changes possible, efforts by all the United Nations will be required....

And, naturally, one can not do without new relations between the two major nuclear powers. I am convinced that the entire world has a vital stake in the establishment of strategic partnership between Russia and the United States...

For the sake of those living and those who have not been born yet, we must preserve peace and secure stability on our planet. Mankind should finally feel it to be its home which is friendly and reliable.

Our civilization has always been and will continue to be varied. It is precisely in the variety of cultures, traditions and values that the possibility of its development is basically found.

At this time we have reached a stage when different interests and aspirations of people can be realized only through cooperation between them....

U.N. is a child of the world. Fifty years ago when the World War was in progress, it became completely clear that the future of mankind belongs to the **realm** of cooperation and tolerance rather than aggression and hatred.

Cooperation and tolerance are inseparable from the coming century.

This is the most important condition to provide for a worthy future to our planet.

This is a unique chance that the human race has.

I believe that the United Nations will take up a joint responsibility and will not be allowed to miss it.

I believe that the glorious dream of the world, where all peoples and States can find a decent place to live, will finally come true....

non-proliferation: non-production

imperative: absolutely necessary

calamities: disasters

discrimination: unfair difference in treatment

narcobusiness: drug trade

U.N.: United Nations

realm: kingdom

Boris Yeltsin (b. 1931) became the President of Russia in 1991. Along with Mikhail Gorbachev, he helped oversee the breakup of the Soviet Union. Yeltsin also led the Russian government through the difficult and continuing struggle to change from a government-controlled economy to an economy based on free enterprise.

Source: Boris Yeltsin, "Peace Keeping Burden in the Former Soviet Union Lies Upon the Russian Federation," *Vital Speeches of the Day* (Vol. LXI, No. 1, Oct. 15, 1994).

Long Walk To Freedom

by Nelson Mandela, 1994

In 1948 South Africa established a system of laws that enforced racial segregation known as apartheid. Nelson Mandela (b. 1918) is a black South African lawyer who led opposition to apartheid. In 1964 he was imprisoned for his opposition and was not released until 1990. Following are three excerpts from Mandela's autobiography. The first two tell of the hardships Mandela and other political prisoners faced. These hardships included forced labor under inhumane conditions and the denial of rights. Even reading a newspaper was forbidden. In the third excerpt Mandela reflects on his experiences after being released from prison. In the years following his imprisonment, Mandela continued working to tear down apartheid with the help of South African President F.W. DeKlerk. In the final excerpt Mandela says, "the truth is that we are not yet free." Why does he say that?

After arriving in the morning, we would fetch our picks, shovels, hammers, and wheelbarrows from a zinc shed at the top of the quarry. Then we would **array** ourselves along the quarry face, usually in groups of three or four. **Warders** with automatic weapons stood on raised platforms watching us. Unarmed warders walked among us, urging us to work harder. "*Gaan aan! Gaan aan!*" (Go on! Go on!), they would shout, as if we were oxen.

array: arrange
Warders: guards

By eleven, when the sun was high in the sky, we would begin to flag. By that time, I would already be drenched in sweat. The warders would then drive us even harder. "*Nee, man! Kom aan! Kom aan!*" (No, man! Come on! Come on!), they would shout. Just before noon, when we would break for lunch, we would pile the lime into wheelbarrows and cart it over to the truck, which would take it away....

Worse than the heat at the quarry was the light. Our backs were protected from the sun by our shirts, but the sun's rays would be reflected into our eyes by the lime itself. The glare hurt our eyes and, along with the dust, made it difficult to see. Our eyes teared and our faces became fixed in a permanent squint. It would take a long time after each day's work for our eyes to adjust to the **diminished** light.

diminished: decreased

After our first few days at the quarry, we made an official request for sunglasses. The authorities refused. This was not unexpected, for we were then not even permitted reading glasses. I had previously pointed out to the commanding officer that it did not make sense to permit us to read books but not permit us glasses to read them with.

During the following weeks and months, we requested sunglasses again and again. But it was to take us almost three years before we were allowed to have them, and that was only after a sympathetic physician agreed that the glasses were necessary to preserve our eyesight. Even then, we had to purchase the glasses ourselves.

For us, such struggles—for sunglasses, long trousers, study privileges, equalized food—were **corollaries to** the struggle we waged outside prison. The campaign to improve conditions in prison was part of the apartheid struggle. It was, in that sense, all the same; we fought injustice wherever we found it, no matter how large, or how small, and we fought injustice to preserve our own humanity....

corollaries to: natural results of

When I noticed the newspaper lying on the bench, I quickly left my cell, walked to the end of the corridor, looked in both directions, and then plucked the newspaper off the bench and slipped it into my shirt. Normally, I would have hidden the newspaper somewhere in my cell and taken it out only after bedtime. But like a child who eats his sweet before his main course, I was so eager for news that I opened the paper in my cell immediately.

I don't know how long I was reading; I was so **engrossed** in the paper that I did not hear any footsteps. Suddenly, an officer and two other warders appeared and I did not even have time to slide the paper under my bed. I was caught black-and-white-handed, so to speak. "Mandela," the officer said, "we are charging you for possession of **contraband**, and you will pay for this." The two warders then began a thorough search of my cell to see if they could turn up anything else.

engrossed: interested

contraband: smuggled goods

Within a day or two a **magistrate** was brought in from Cape Town and I was taken to the room at headquarters that was used as the island's court. In this instance, the authorities were willing to call in an outside magistrate because they knew they had an open-and-shut case. I offered no defense, and was sentenced to three days in isolation and **deprivation of** meals....

The isolation cells were in our same complex, but in another wing. Although just across the courtyard, they felt enormously distant. In isolation, one was deprived of company, exercise, and even food: one received only rice water three times a day for three days. (Rice water is simply water in which rice has been boiled.) By comparison, our normal ration of **pap** seemed like a feast.

The first day in isolation was always the most painful. One grows accustomed to eating regularly and the body is not used to being deprived. I found that by the second day I had more or less adjusted to the absence of food, and the third passed without much craving at all.

magistrate: government officer

deprivation of: no

pap: ground up food

Such deprivation was not uncommon among Africans in everyday life. I myself had gone without food for days at a time in my early years in Johannesburg.

As I have already mentioned, I found solitary confinement the most forbidding aspect of prison life. There is no end and no beginning; there is only one's own mind, which can begin to play tricks. Was that a dream or did it really happen? One begins to question everything. Did I make the right decision, was my sacrifice worth it? In solitary, there is no distraction from these haunting questions.

But the human body has an enormous capacity for adjusting to trying circumstances. I have found that one can bear the unbearable if one can keep one's spirits strong even when one's body is being tested. Strong **convictions** are the secret of surviving deprivation; your spirit can be full even when your stomach is empty....

convictions: beliefs

It was during those long and lonely years that my hunger for the freedom of my own people became a hunger for the freedom of all people, white and black. I knew as well as I knew anything that the **oppressor** must be liberated just as surely as the oppressed. A man who takes away another man's freedom is a prisoner of hatred, he is locked behind the bars of prejudice and narrow-mindedness. I am not truly free if I am taking away someone else's freedom, just as surely as I am not free when my freedom is taken from me. The oppressed and the oppressor alike are robbed of their humanity.

oppressor: one who controls with force

When I walked out of prison, that was my mission, to liberate the oppressed and the oppressor both. Some say that has now been achieved. But I know that that is not the case. The truth is that we are not yet free; we have merely achieved the freedom to be free, the right not to be oppressed. We have not taken the final step of our journey, but the first step on a longer and even more difficult road. For to be free is not merely to cast off one's chains, but to live in a way that respects and **enhances** the freedom of others. The true test of our devotion to freedom is just beginning.

enhances: improves the quality of

I have walked that long road to freedom. I have tried not to **falter**; I have made missteps along the way. But I have discovered the secret that after climbing a great hill, one only finds that there are many more hills to climb. I have taken a moment here to rest, to steal a view of the glorious **vista** that surrounds me, to look back on the distance I have come. But I can rest only for a moment, for with freedom comes responsibilities, and I dare not **linger**, for my long walk is not yet ended.

falter: hesitate

vista: view

linger: delay

Nelson Mandela and F.W. DeKlerk shared the 1993 Nobel Peace Prize for their work in ending apartheid. In 1994, black South Africans were allowed to vote in nationwide elections for the first time. Nelson Mandela was elected president of South Africa.

Source: Nelson Mandela, *Long Walk to Freedom: The Autobiography of Nelson Mandela*. Boston: Little, Brown and Co., 1994.

Why the Tortoise's Shell Is Not Smooth

by Chinua Achebe, 1958

Legends are stories that try to explain how things happen, or why things are as they are. Author Chinua Achebe (CHI noo weh a CHEH beh) developed an appreciation for the art of storytelling from his older sister when they were growing up. Achebe retold the following Nigerian legend, "Why the Tortoise's Shell Is Not Smooth," in his 1958 novel, Things Fall Apart. The novel is about a person who is torn between preserving traditional Nigerian culture, and choosing to adopt Western customs. The legend itself is part of Achebe's traditional culture. Can you think of any legends from other cultures?

Low voices, broken now and again by singing, reached Okonkwo [oh KOHN kwoh] from his wives' huts as each woman and her children told folk stories. Ekwefi [eh KWEH fee] and her daughter, Ezinma [eh ZEEN mah], sat on a mat on the floor. It was Ekwefi's turn to tell a story.

"Once upon a time," she began, "all the birds were invited to a feast in the sky. They were very happy and began to prepare themselves for the great day. They painted their bodies with red **cam** wood and drew beautiful patterns on them with dye.

cam: African tree

"Tortoise saw all these preparations and soon discovered what it all meant. Nothing that happened in the world of the animals ever escaped his notice; he was full of cunning. As soon as he heard of the great feast in the sky his throat began to itch at the very thought. There was a **famine** in those days and Tortoise had not eaten a good meal for two moons. His body rattled like a piece of dry stick in his empty shell. So he began to plan how he would go to the sky."

famine: scarcity of food

"But he had no wings," said Ezinma.

"Be patient," replied her mother. "That is the story. Tortoise had no wings, but he went to the birds and asked to be allowed to go with them.

" 'We know you too well,' said the birds when they heard him. 'You are full of cunning and you are ungrateful. If we allow you to come with us you will soon begin your mischief.'

" 'You do not know me,' said Tortoise. 'I am a changed man. I have learned that a man who makes trouble for others is also making it for himself.'

"Tortoise had a sweet tongue, and within a short time all the birds agreed that he was a changed man, and they each gave him a feather, with which he made two wings.

"At last the great day came and Tortoise was the first to arrive at the meeting place. When all the birds had gathered together, they set off in a body. Tortoise was very happy as he flew among the birds, and he was soon chosen as the man to speak for the party because he was a great **orator**.

orator: speaker

" 'There is one important thing which we must not forget,' he said as they flew on their way, 'When people are invited to a great feast like this, they take new names for the occasion. Our hosts in the sky will expect us to honor this age-old custom.'

"None of the birds had heard of this custom but they knew that Tortoise, in spite of his failings in other directions, was a widely traveled man who knew the customs of different peoples. And so they each took a new name. When they had all taken, Tortoise also took one. He was to be called *All of you*.

"At last the party arrived in the sky and their hosts were very happy to see them. Tortoise stood up in his many-colored **plumage** and thanked them for their invitation. His speech was so **eloquent** that all the birds were glad they had brought him, and nodded their heads in approval of all he said. Their hosts took him as the king of the birds, especially as he looked somewhat different from the others.

plumage: feathers
eloquent: well-spoken

"After kola nuts had been presented and eaten, the people of the sky set before their guests the most **delectable** dishes Tortoise had ever seen or dreamed of. The soup was brought out hot from the fire and in the very pot in which it had been cooked. It was full of meat and fish: Tortoise began to sniff aloud. There was pounded yam and also yam **pottage** cooked with palm oil and fresh fish. There were also pots of palm wine. When everything had been set before the guests, one of the people of the sky came forward and tasted a little from each pot. He then invited the birds to eat. But Tortoise jumped to his feet and asked: 'For whom have you prepared this feast?'

delectable: delicious

pottage: soup

" 'For all of you,' replied the man.

"Tortoise turned to the birds and said: 'You remember that my name is *All of you*. The custom here is to serve the spokesman first and the others later. They will serve you when I have eaten.'

"He began to eat and the birds grumbled angrily. The people of the sky thought it must be their custom to leave all the food for their king. And so Tortoise ate the best part of the food and then drank two pots of palm wine, so that he was full of food and drink and his body grew fat enough to fill out his shell.

"The birds gathered round to eat what was left and to peck at the bones he had thrown all about the floor. Some of them were too angry to eat. They chose to fly home on an empty stomach. But before they left, each took back the feather he had lent to Tortoise. And there he stood in his hard shell full of food and wine but without any wings to fly home. He asked the birds to take a message for his wife, but they all refused. In the end Parrot, who had felt more angry than the others, suddenly changed his mind and agreed to take the message.

" 'Tell my wife,' said Tortoise, 'to bring out all the soft things in my house and cover the **compound** with them so that I can jump down from the sky without very great danger.'

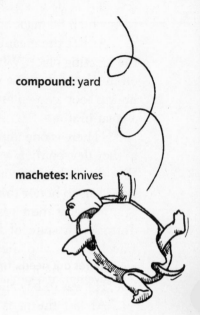

compound: yard

machetes: knives

"Parrot promised to deliver the message, and then flew away. But when he reached Tortoise's house he told his wife to bring out all the hard things in the house. And so she brought out her husband's hoes, **machetes**, spears, guns, and even his cannon. Tortoise looked down from the sky and saw his wife bringing things out, but it was too far to see what they were. When all seemed ready he let himself go. He fell and fell and fell until he began to fear that he would never stop falling. And then like the sound of his cannon he crashed on the compound."

"Did he die?" asked Ezinma.

"No," replied Ekwefi. "His shell broke into pieces. But there was a great medicine man in the neighborhood. Tortoise's wife sent for him and he gathered all the bits of shell and stuck them together. That is why Tortoise's shell is not smooth."

Chinua Achebe (b. 1930) is a member of the Ibo people of Nigeria. As a young man, his friends called him "Dictionary," because of his extensive knowledge of English. Achebe was Nigeria's first world-famous writer. In addition to writing, Achebe has also been a university professor and radio broadcaster.

Source: *Discovering Literature*. Mission Hills, CA: Glencoe/McGraw-Hill, 1991.

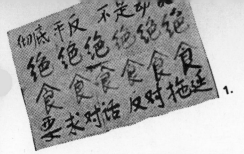

Massacre at Tiananmen Square

Signs of Protest, 1989

In May 1989 thousands of students began gathering at Tiananmen Square, one of the largest open spaces in Beijing, the capital of China. These students were protesting against the oppressive communist government. Each day more and more students gathered in the square and were soon joined by workers, journalists, and others. Within two weeks the number of people demonstrating in Tiananmen Square reached 1 million. Demonstrations were held in more than 80 cities across China in support of the students. What did these protesters want? On this page are pictures showing signs carried during the demonstration in Tiananmen Square. Look at these signs and then read their English translations. How do the signs express the demand of the protesters?

1. This is a completely peaceful demonstration. This is not an act of violence. We object to the way the government ignores our needs. Until the government negotiates new terms with us as we requested, we shall fast.

2. Liberty or Death.

3. In One Voice the Citizens of Beijing Support University Students.

4. We Want to Speak but Can't.

5. Down with the Corrupt Officials.

The Chinese government opposed the demands of the protesters and ordered the demonstration to end. The protesters refused. On June 4, 1989, the government sent in tanks and troops to break up the demonstration. In the massacre that followed, hundreds of people were killed and more than 100,000 were arrested. Many of those who were arrested remain in jail to this day. The courage of the protesters who challenged their oppressive government remains an inspiration to millions of Chinese people today.

195

Japanese School Days

by Christopher and Barbara Mori, 1990

One important part of any culture is its educational system. Christopher Mori and his mother Barbara had an opportunity to learn a great deal about Japanese schooling. In 1983 the Moris moved from Hawaii to Ohara, Japan, a small farming community near Kyoto. Christopher attended Ohara Elementary School from the fourth to the sixth grade. In the following selection Christopher describes what it was like to go to school in Japan. How is Ohara Elementary different from your school?

The Japanese school year is divided into three parts. I entered school in the second part of the fourth grade and attended until the end of the first part of sixth grade. I had the same teacher and classmates the whole time. Students usually stay with the same group and teacher all the way through school, so they get to know one another well. On the first day, I was harassed for being *gaijin* (GĪ zhin), or a foreigner, but I put a stop to that fast.

As I was born in Japan and am also a Japanese citizen, I did not have too much trouble speaking Japanese, but I had a lot of catching up to do with reading and writing the Japanese characters. The hardest things to adjust to, though, were the different school schedule and the social rules.

Because I was attending a public elementary school, I did not have to put on a uniform when I got up in the morning, but most students in Japan wear them. Every school day I met other students from my district, and we all walked to school together. The older children were expected to take care of the younger ones. The first thing I did at school was to change my outdoor shoes for indoor ones, as everyone does in Japan.

Lessons began at 9:00 A.M. and ended at 3:00 P.M. We also had classes from 9:00 A.M. to noon on Saturdays. We studied Japanese language, math, history and social studies, art, physical education, music, and science. In science, we were ahead of what I was learning back in Hawaii. We learned about electronic circuits as well as animals and plants. In the fifth and sixth grades, we had home economics, in which both boys and girls learned to cook and sew....

Each class had 24 to 30 students divided into groups of four or five, called *han*. Each han chose a leader, called a *hancho*, and was responsible for certain class needs. My han took care of the class pets in the fourth grade and the class newspaper in the fifth and sixth grades....

196

We had lunch in our classrooms at our desks. Two han were responsible for bringing the food from the kitchen and serving it. This duty, called *toban*, was rotated weekly.... After lunch, the students on toban had to clean up and return the utensils to the kitchen. Then we had a break outdoors in the school yard. One day a week we had to play with the members of the han, and one day a week we had to play with the members of the class. The other days we could play with anyone. We did not get much chance to meet kids from other classes, though....

When school was over, we all went straight home unless we were on an intramural sports team—soccer for boys and volleyball for girls. We could not stop at stores except to buy school supplies, and we could not visit friends until after we had gone home. I did not like these restrictions. We had homework every day. Many of my classmates also had chores to do when they got home.

There were also some special school activities in which all grades participated. In the spring, we planted rice and sweet potatoes, which we harvested in the fall. In the summer, fifth- and sixth-graders made Japanese pickles because Ohara is famous for its pickles. When they were ready to be eaten, we had them with our lunch. In the autumn, we had Sports Day. In the winter, the fifth-and sixth-graders went skiing, and the school had a *mochi*-making festival. Mochi are pounded rice cakes served as special New Year's food. We made the mochi from the rice we planted.

On Sports Day, the school was divided into four teams—red, yellow, white, and blue—that competed to win a school banner. We spent the month before preparing for it. We had to learn eurhythmics, warm-up exercises set to music, which are like a dance routine. Each grade had certain competition events to prepare. In the fourth grade, we ran relay races, and in the fifth and sixth grades, we had a mock battle where students rode on the shoulders of other students and tried to bring down opposing teams and capture the cap of the king.... There were many different competitions throughout the day. At the end of the day, the points were totaled and the winning team received the banner.

As an American student, I found it difficult to adjust to some of the school rules and routine, but I enjoyed the special activities such as planting rice and making mochi. I made many good friends and especially liked my teacher, who tried to understand my problems as an American in a Japanese school. At Ohara Elementary School, I learned not only how Japanese work together but also the fun of trying different things.

Christopher Mori was born in Japan, and spent half of his childhood there and half in the United States. He graduated from high school in California. Barbara Mori is a professor of sociology at California Polytechnic University in San Luis Obispo. She is currently doing research in China.

Source: *Faces: The Magazine About People* (Vol. 6, No.7). Peterborough, NH: Cobblestone Publishing, 1990.

Ode to an Artichoke by Pablo Neruda, 1958

Pablo Neruda is widely considered Chile's greatest poet. In the following poem about an artichoke, a vegetable with coarse leaves, Neruda describes how it is grown and then sold at the marketplace. How does Neruda use the character of the artichoke to write about peace?

La alcachofa	The soft-hearted	
de tierno corazoń	artichoke	
se vistió de guerrero,	put on armor,	
erecta, construyó	stood at attention, raised	
una pequeña cúpula,	a small **turret**	**turret:** little tower
se mantuvo	and kept itself	
impermeable	watertight	
bajo	under	
sus escamas	its scales.	
a su lado	Beside it,	
los vegetales locos	the **fertile** plants	**fertile:** growing
se encresparon	tangled,	
se hicieron	turned into	
zarcillos, espadañas,	**tendrils**, cattails,	**tendrils:** stems
bulbos commovodores,	moving bulbs.	
en el subsuelo	In the **subsoil**	**subsoil:** dirt below
durmió la zanahoría	the red-whiskered	
de bigotes rojos,	carrot slept,	
la viña	the grapevine	
resecó los sarmientos	**parched** the shoots	**parched:** dried
por donde sube el vino,	that wine climbs up,	
la col	the cabbage	
se dedicó	busied itself	
a probarse faldas,	with trying on skirts,	
el orégano	the **marjoram**	**marjoram:** a spice
a perfumar el mundo,	with making the world smell sweet,	
y la dulce	and the gentle	
alcachofa	artichoke	
allí en el huerto,	in the kitchen garden,	
vestida de guerrero,	equipped like a soldier,	
bruñida	**burnished**	**burnished:** polished
como una granada,	like a grenade,	
orgullosa;	was full of itself.	
y un día	And one day,	
una con otra	packed with others,	
en grandes cestos	in big willow	
de mimbre, caminó	baskets, it marched	
por el mercado	through the market	
a realizar su sueño:	to act out its dream—	

la milicia.
En hileras
nunca fue tan marcial
como en la feria,
los hombres
entre las legumbres
con sus camisas blancas
eran
mariscales
de las alcachofas,
las filas apretadas,
las voces de comando,
y la detonación
de una caja que cae;
pero
entonces
viene
María
con su cesto,
escoge
una alcachofa,
no le teme,
la examina, la observa
contra la luz
como si fuera un huevo,
la compra,
la confunde en su bolsa
con un par de zapatos,
con un repollo y una
botella
de vinagre
hasta
que entrando a la cocina
la sumerge en la olla.
Así termina
en paz
esta carrera
del vegetal armado
que se llama alcachofa,
luego
escama por escama,
desvestimos
la delicia
y comemos
la pacífica pasta
de su corazón verde.

the **militia**.
It was never as **martial**
in rows
as at the fair.
Among the vegetables,
men in white shirts
were
the artichokes'
marshals,
closed ranks,
commands,
the explosion
of a falling crate;
but
then
Maria
shows up
with her basket,
fearlessly
chooses
an artichoke,
studies it, squints at it
against the light
like an egg,
buys it,
dumps it into her bag
with a pair of shoes,
a white cabbage and
a bottle
of vinegar
till
she enters the kitchen
and drowns it
in the pot.
And so
this armored vegetable
men call an artichoke
ends its career
in peace.
Later,
scale by scale,
we strip
this delight
and dine on
the peaceful **pulp**
of its green heart.

militia: army
martial: warlike

marshals: officers

pulp: soft, juicy part

In recognition of his achievements, Neruda was awarded the Nobel Prize for Literature in 1971. His works have had a continuing influence on poetry throughout the world.

Source: Pablo Neruda, *Odas Elementales*. Buenos Aires: Editorial Losada, S.A., 1958. English translation by Cheli Durán, *The Yellow Canary Whose Eye Is So Black*. New York: Macmillan Publishing Co., Inc., 1977.

A TALE OF DISAPPEARANCE

by Alicia Partnoy, 1986

Throughout its history Argentina has been ruled many times by military governments. When the Argentine military seized control of power in 1976, violence in the country increased dramatically. In the next four years, the military kidnapped and tortured many Argentines. Alicia Partnoy was one of these desaparecidos— *"disappeared ones." Born in 1955, Alicia Partnoy was a college student at the time of her arrest in 1976. While in prison, she fought back by smuggling stories about her ordeal to the outside world. From her account of imprisonment and torture, what role do you think writers can play when governments take away people's rights? Read Partnoy's account to learn of her struggle and of what has become of her.*

After the Argentine military seized power in 1976, attending school became **hazardous**. I had to pass between two soldiers who were sitting with machine guns at the entrance of the building. A highly ranked officer would request my I.D., check it against a list of "wanted" activists and search my belongings. I did not know when my name was going to appear on that list. [Out of fear,] I stopped going to classes. But the **coup** triggered my rage, and I decided to become more **militant**. That decision meant risking my life. My daughter, Ruth, was nine months old. My answer to my own fears was that I had to work for a better society for the sake of my child's future. For almost a year I did so. I **clandestinely** reproduced and distributed information on the economic situation, the workers' strikes, and the [government's] **repression**.

I learned about "disappearance": the kidnapping of an individual followed by torture and secret detention, which meant that the military denied the fact that the prisoner was in their hands. I did not know that very soon I would become a disappeared person.

hazardous: dangerous

coup: military overthrow

militant: aggressive, determined

clandestinely: secretly

repression: unjust use of force

On January 12, 1977, at noon, I was **detained** by uniformed Army **personnel** at my home, Canadá Street 240, Apt. 2, Bahía Blanca; minutes later the same military personnel detained my husband at his place of work. I was taken to the headquarters of the 5th Army Corps and from there to a concentration camp, which the military **ironically** named the Little School (*La Escuelita*). We had no knowledge of the fate of Ruth, our daughter. From that moment on, for the next five months, my husband and I became two more names on the endless list of disappeared people.

The old house of the Little School was located . . . near a railroad; one could hear trains, the shots fired at the army command's firing range, and the mooing of cows. I stepped off the Army truck, handcuffed and blindfolded. . . .

In the Little School there were two rooms where an average of fifteen prisoners remained **prone**, our hands bound. The floors were wood, the walls yellowing with high windows and dark green shutters and Colonial wrought iron bars. Separating these rooms was a tiled hall where the presence of a guard insured that we neither moved nor spoke. At the end of the hall were the guards' room, a kitchen and a bathroom. A door opened on the patio, where the "torture room," **latrine** and water tank were located. There was also a trailer where the guards slept; and later they added one or two trailers for more "disappeared" people.

When it rained, the water streamed into the rooms and soaked us. When the temperature fell below zero, we were covered with only dirty blankets; when the heat was unbearable, we were obligated to **blanket** even our heads. We were forced to remain silent and prone, often **immobile** or face down for many hours, our eyes blindfolded and our wrists tightly bound.

Lunch was at 1:00 P.M. and dinner at 7:00 P.M.; we went without food for eighteen **consecutive** hours daily. We were constantly hungry. I lost 20 pounds [7kg], going down to 95 pounds [43 kg]. . . . Added to the **meager** food, the lack of sugar or fruits, was the constant state of stress that made our bodies **consume** calories rapidly. We ate our meals blindfolded, sitting on the bed, plate in lap. When we had soup or watery stew, the blows were constant because the guards insisted that we keep our plates straight. When we were thirsty, we asked for water, receiving only threats or blows in response. For talking, we were punished with blows from a **billy jack**, punches, or removal of our mattresses. The atmosphere of violence was constant. The guards put guns to our heads or mouths and pretended to pull the trigger.

On April 25, after three and a half months, the guards told me they were taking me "to see how the radishes grow"—a **euphemism** for death and burial. Instead, I was transferred from the Little School to another place where I remained disappeared for fifty-two more days. The living conditions were better: no blindfold, no blows, better food, a clean cell, daily showers. The **isolation** was complete and the risk of being killed

detained: held
personnel: employees

ironically: with unintended humor

prone: lying face down

latrine: toilet

blanket: cover

immobile: not moving

consecutive: in a row

meager: skimpy
consume: use up

billy jack: club

euphemism: mild expression replacing a harsh one

isolation: separation from others

201

the same. By June 1977, my family was informed of my **whereabouts**. I "reappeared" but remained a political prisoner for two and a half more years. I could see my daughter [who was being cared for by relatives], and I knew that my husband had also survived.

whereabouts: location

I never discovered why the military had spared my life. My parents, who knocked at every [government official's] door looking for me, might have knocked at the correct door. Yet it is also true that some of the most **influential** people in the country were not able to rescue their own children. My degree of involvement was not the reason for my luck either. People who participated less in politics did not survive. We were **hostages** and, as such, our lives were disposed of according to the needs of our captors.

influential: powerful

hostages: prisoners

While I was imprisoned, no charges were brought against me. Like the majority of the 7,000 political prisoners, I was held **indefinitely** and considered to be a threat to national security. It is estimated that over 30,000 people "disappeared" to detention centers like the Little School. Among them were over 400 children who were either kidnapped with their parents or. . .born in captivity. All but a few of the disappeared still remain unaccounted for.

indefinitely: without time limit

Human rights groups launched an international campaign denouncing the repression in Argentina. One of these was the Mothers of Plaza de Mayo movement, an organization of mothers of disappeared people that demanded answers from the government on the whereabouts of their children. These women soon became targets of repression, and several members disappeared.

Domestic and international pressure forced the **junta** to free a number of political prisoners. In 1979, after the Organization of American States sent a fact-finding mission to Argentina, I was released and forced to leave the country. [United States] President [Jimmy] Carter's human rights policy had also helped. Since some of us were granted U.S. visas and refugee status, the junta knew the United States wanted the release of prisoners.

junta: military leaders

By Christmas 1979, I was taken directly from jail to the airport, where I was reunited with my daughter. Some hours later we flew to the United States. My husband had come two months before.

A short time after my arrival, I started to work on behalf of the remaining prisoners and the disappeared ones. I soon learned more about the widespread use of disappearance as a tool for repression in Latin America. As a survivor, I felt my duty was to help those suffering injustice.

After Alicia Partnoy was released, she continued to work for the freedom of other disappeared ones. In 1982 her testimony before a special Argentine panel led to the conviction of several military officials responsible for the disappearances. In recent years Argentina has become a democracy, and many Argentines are working to ensure that people's rights are never taken away again.

Source: Alicia Partnoy, *The Little School*. Pittsburgh: Cleis Press, 1986.

De Lanterna na Mão

Brazilian Folk Song

Nations of the Americas are becoming more and more interdependent. They have always relied on each other to trade products that they need and want. Today, however, they are working together in new ways. They face challenges such as saving the Amazon rainforests and eliminating the drug trade. This cooperation and friendship has brought about positive results. "De Lanterna na Mão" is a folksong from the South American country of Brazil. It is about searching for a personal friendship. Does the person who wrote the song have success in finding a friend? How can personal friends cooperate to solve problems?

Brazilian Folk Song
English Version by MMH

Portuguese:	E - u	pro - cu - rei, _____		de lan - ter - na na
Pronunciation:	e oo	proh koo rayee _____		lahn tayr nah nah
English:	I ___	search for you _____		with a lan_tern in my

mão, _____	pro - cu - rei, pro - cu - rei,	e a - chei vo -
mau _____	proh koo rayih proh koo rayih	ih ah shayih vaw
hand. _____	Search-ing here, search-ing there	and at last I

1.

ce	pa - ra o	meu cor - a - ção. _____	E - u	pro - cu -
say	pah rah	meooo koh rah sau _____	e oo	proh koo
find	you, and	you are my friend. _____	I ___	look for

203

"De Lanterna na Mão" is sung in Portugese, Brazil's official language. Brazil was ruled
by Portugal from the 1500s until it gained independence in 1822.

Source: *Share the Music,* Grade 6. New York: Macmillan/McGraw-Hill, 1995.

INDEX BY *Category*

ACKNOWLEDGMENTS

(continued from copyright page)

Excerpts from ROYAL COMMENTARIES OF THE INCAS AND GENERAL HISTORY OF PERU, Part One. Translated by Harold V. Livermore. ©1966 University of Texas Press, Austin, TX.

"The Legacy of Columbus", printed in THE COBBLESTONE MAGAZINE Jan. 1992 Vol. 13 by Sarah Elder Hale. ©1992 Cobblestone Publishing, Inc., NH.

"Progress in Industry" from POORS MANUAL OF RAILROADS, 1887 advertisement for E.S. Greeley & Co., Manufacturers, Importers and Dealers in Railway and Telegraph Supplies (TPB). Reprinted by permission of General Research Division, The New York Public Library, Astor, Lenox and Tilden Foundations.

Excerpt from CLARA'S DIARY: AN AMERICAN GIRL IN MEIJI JAPAN by Clara A.N. Whitney, edited by M. William Steele and Tamiko Ichimata. ©1978 in Japan. Kodansha International Ltd., NY.

Excerpt from THE ENDLESS STEPPE: GROWING UP IN SIBERIA by Esther Hautzig. ©1968 Esther Hautzig. Thomas Y. Crowell Company, NY.

Excerpt from FAMILIAR QUOTATIONS by John Bartlett. ©1980 Little, Brown and Company.

Excerpt from NO TEARS FOR MAO: GROWING UP IN THE CULTURAL REVOLUTION by Niu-Niu; translated by Enne and Peter Amman. ©1989 Robert Laffont, S.A. Paris. Academy Chicago Publishers, 1995.

Excerpt from CHARTER OF THE UNITED NATIONS: COMMENTARY AND DOCUMENTS by Leland M. Goodrich, Edvard Hambro and Anne Patricia Simons. ©1969 Columbia University Press, NY.

"A Woman from Pakistan: Shabanu" from THREE WOMEN FROM PAK-ISTAN by Attiya Inayatullah, an article in THE UNESCO COURIER. © September 1995 by The United Nations Educational, Scientific and Cultural Organization, France.

"Têt Trung". Kathy B. Sorensen, English words by Macmillan/McGraw-Hill. ©1991 Kathy B. Sorensen. Macmillan/McGraw-Hill.

Excerpt from LONG WALK TO FREEDOM by Nelson Mandela. ©1994 Nelson Rolihlahla Mandela. Little, Brown and Company, NY.

"Why the Tortoise's Shell Is Not Smooth" by Chinua Achebe from DIS-COVERING LITERATURE. ©1959 Reprinted by permission of Astor-Honor, Inc., NY.

Excerpt from "Japanese School Days" printed in FACES MAGAZINE by Christopher and Barbara Mori. ©1990 Cobblestone Publishing Inc., NH.

DE LANTERNA NA MÃO. ©1995 SHARE THE MUSIC, Book 6, Macmillan/McGraw-Hill School Publishing Co., NY.

"Observations of a 14th Century Traveler" from AFRICAN CIVILIZATION REVISITED by Basil Davidson. Copyright © 1991 Basil Davidson. Africa World Press, NJ.

"Ode to an Artichoke" by Pablo Neruda from THE YELLOW CANARY WHOSE EYE IS SO BLACK edited and translated by Cheli Duran. Copyright © 1977 by Cheli Duran Ryan. Used with permission of Macmillan Publishing Company. "Oda a la alcachofa" from ODAS ELEMEN-TALES by Pablo Neruda. C Editorial Losada, S.A. 1958. Agencia Literaria Carmen Balcells, S.A.

"A Tale of Disapearance" from TALES OF DISAPPEARANCE & SURVIVAL IN ARGENTINA by Alicia Partnoy. Copyright ©1986 by Alicia Partnoy. All rights reserved. Cleis Press.

"The Sayings of Confucius" from SOURCES OF CHINESE TRADITION I by William Theodore de Bary. Copyright ©1965 Columbia University Press, New York.

"From Mouse to Bat" from THE BIRD WHO CLEANS THE WORLD by Victor Montejo. Copyright ©1991 by Wallace Kaufman. All rights reserved. Curbstone Press.

"The War Years in Vietnam" from WHEN HEAVEN AND EARTH CHANGED PLACES by Le Ly Hayslip. Copyright ©1989 by Le Ly Hayslip and Charles Jay Wurts. Doubleday, a division of Bantam Doubleday Dell Publishing Group, Inc.

Excerpt from THE DIARY OF ANNE FRANK: THE CRITICAL EDITION by Anne Frank. Copyright ©1986 by Anne Frank-Fonds, Basle/Switzerland. Doubleday, a division of Bantam Doubleday Dell Publishing Group, Inc.

"The Vision that I See" from Ch. 10 "Nkrumah the Orator" from KWAME NKRUMAH: FROM CRADLE TO GRAVE by Bankole Timothy. Copyright ©1981 by Bankole Timothy. Gavin Press Limited.

Excerpt from JONATHAN DOWN UNDER by Patricia Beatty. Copyright © 1982 by Patricia Beatty. William Morrow and Company, New York 1982.

"Labouring With the Hoe" from OLD BUSH SONGS AND RHYMES OF COLONIAL TIMES from the collection of A. B. Paterson by Douglas Stewart and Nancy Keesing. Copyright © 1957 by Angus & Robertson LTD. Reprinted 1964 by Halstead Press, Sydney.

"Tank, The Water Buffalo" from THE LAND I LOST by Huynh Quang Nhuong. Text Copyright ©1982 by Huynh Quang Nhuong. Illustrations Copyright ©1982 by VoDinH Mai. HarperCollins Publishers.

Excerpt from "Mahabharata" from POEMS FROM INDIA selected by Daisy Aldan. Copyright ©1969 by Daisy Aldan. Published by Thomas Y. Crowell Company.

Excerpt from ALL QUIET ON THE WESTERN FRONT by Erich Maria Remarque. "Im Wesen Nichts Neues" Copyright ©1928 by Ullstein A.G.; Copyright renewed ©1956 by Erich Maria Remarque. "All Quiet on the Western Front" Copyright ©1929, 1930 by Little, Brown and Company; Copyright renewed ©1957, 1958 by Erich Maria Remarque.

Excerpt from JI-NONGO-NONGO MEANS RIDDLES by Verna Aardema. Text Copyright ©1978 by Verna Aardema. Four Wind Press.

"The Aeneid" from THE AENEID FOR BOYS AND GIRLS retold by Alfred J. Church. Copyright ©1962 by Macmillan Publishing Company.

"The Splendors of Hangzhou" from CHINESE CIVILIZATION AND SOCI-ETY by Patricia Buckley Ebrey. Copyright ©1981 by The Free Press.

"The Iliad" from THE CHILDREN'S HOMER: THE ADVENTURES OF ODYSSEUS AND THE TALE OF TROY by Padraic Colum. Copyright ©1918 by Macmillan Publishing Company, Copyright renewed ©1946 by Padraic Colum and Willy Pogany.

"Kokoom" (The Origan of the moon) from A FOLKLORE SAMPLER FROM THE MARITIMES edited by Herbert Halpert. Copyright ©1982 by Memorial University of Newfoundland, Department of Folklore, Canadian Studies, Mount Allison University.

"When the A-Bomb Fell" from CHILDREN OF THE A-BOMB edited by Dr. Arata Osada. Copyright ©1959 and 1963 by Dr. Arata Osada, Peter Owen Publishers, London.

"Test of a Friendship" from THE DANCING PALM TREE AND OTHER NIGERIAN FOLKTALES by Barbara Walker. Text Copyright ©1968 by Barbara Walker. Published by Texas Tech University Press, 1990,

"Oodgeroo (Paperbark Tree)" from DREAMTIME ABORIGINAL STORIES by Oodgeroo Noonuccal. Copyright © 1972 by Oodgeroo Noonuccal. Lothrop, Lee & Shepard Books, New York.

"Sur le Pont d'Avignon" from AROUND THE WORLD IN SONG by Dorothy Gordon. Copyright ©1930, 1932 by E.P. Dutton & Co., Inc. Penguin USA.

"The Story of the Flood" from THE EPIC OF GILGAMESH translated by N.K. Sanders. Copyright ©1960, 1964, 1972 N.K. Sanders. Penguin Books Ltd.

"Praying at the Western Wall" from GAVRIEL AND JEMAL by Brent Ashabranner. Copyright ©1984 by Brent Ashabranner. G.P. Putnam's Sons.

"Fighting for Freedom" from THIS GILDED AFRICAN: TOUSSAINT L'OUVERTURE by Wenda Parkinson. Copyright ©1979 by Wenda Parkinson. Quarter Books Ltd.

Excerpt from EASTER ISLAND: The Mystery Solved by Thor Heyerdahl. Copyright ©1989 by Thor Heyerdahl. Random House, Inc.

"New Year's Address" from OPEN LETTERS: SELECTED WRITINGS 1963-1990 by Vàclav Havel. Copyright ©1991, by A.G. Grain. Preface/transtlation Copyright ©1985, 1988, 1991, by Paul Wilson. Alfred A. Knopf, Inc.

Excerpt from THE TALE OF GENJI by Murasaki Shikibu, translated by Edward Seidensticker. Copyright ©1975 by Edward Seidensticker. Alfred A. Knopf, Inc.

"The Man Who Shared His Hut" from FACING MOUNT KENYA by Jomo Kenyatta. First published 1938 by Martin Secker and Warburg Ltd. R.I.B. Library, Reed Book Services, Rushden, England.

Excerpt from "The Ringdove" in KALILA WA DIMNA: FABLES FROM A FOURTEENTH CENTURY ARABIC MANUSCRIPT, by Esin Atil. Published by Smithsonian Press, Copyright ©1981 by Smithsonian Institution.

"A Queen's Promise" from "Obelisk Inscriptions" in ANCIENT EGYPTIAN LITERATURE, THREE VOLUMES translated by Miriam Lichtheim. Copyright ©1973-1980 Regents of the University of California. University of California Press.

"The Lakota and Nature" from LAND OF THE SPOTTED EAGLE by Luther Standing Bear. Copyright ©1933 by Luther Standing Bear, re-newal Copyright ©1960 by May Jones. University of Nebraska Press.

"Why India Must Be Free" from GANDHI IN INDIA In His Own Words edited by Martin Green. Copyright ©1987 by the Navajivan Trust. University Press of New England.

"The Glory of the Incas" from THE INCAS OF PEDRA DE CIEZA DE LEÓN edited by Victor Wolfgang von Hagen. Copyright ©1959 by the University of Oklahoma Press. University of Oklahoma Press.

"Notebooks from the Renaissance" FROM SELECTIONS FROM THE NOTEBOOKS OF LEONARDO DA VINCI edited with commentaries by Irma A. Richter. Copyright © 1952 by Oxford University Press.

"Working in the Mines" from VICTORIAN WOMEN: A Documentary Account Of Women's Lives In Nineteenth-Century England, France, And The United States edited by Erma Olafson Hellerstein, Leslie Parker Hume and Karen M. Offen. Copyright ©1981 by the Board of Trustees of the Leland Stanford, Junior University.

"Fall Rain Fall Rain" by Joseph Shabalala. Courtesy of Full Keel Music Company o/b/o Gallo Music Publishers.

"Mountains in Israel" Music by H. Coopersmith; Words by T.E. Sampter. from THE SONGS WE SING, selected and edited by Harry Coopersmith. Copyright ©1950 by The United Synagogue of America. Published by The United Synagogue Commission of Jewish Education.

"Saving the Rainforest" from p. 193 from THE FATE OF THE FOREST Developers, Destroyers and Defenders of the Amazon by Susanna Hecht and Alexander Cockburn. Copyright ©1989 by Susanna Hecht and Alexander Cockburn. First published by Verso, 1989.

"A Pilgrimage to Mecca" from WE LIVE IN SAUDI ARABIA by Abdul Latif Al Hoad. Copyright ©1982 Published by Wayland (Publishers) Ltd.

"Life of a Hindu Priest" from WE LIVE IN INDIA by Veenu Sandal. Copyright ©1981 Published by Wayland (Publishers) Ltd.

"Becoming a Buddhist Master" from WE LIVE IN MALAYSIA AND SINGAPORE by Jessie Wee. Copyright ©1984 Published by Wayland (Publishers) Ltd.

"A Craftsman in Bethlehem" from WE LIVE IN ISRAEL by Gemma Levine. Copyright ©1981 by Wayland (Publishers) Ltd.

"Poems for Peace" from MY SHALOM MY PEACE Paintings and Poems by Jewish and Arab Children. First published in Hebrew under the title Hashalom Sheli ©1974 by the American Israel Publishing Co., Ltd. and Sonol. Israel Ltd. English translation Copyright ©1975 by Sabra Books, Tel Aviv.

"Letter from Jamaica" from SELECTED WRITINGS OF BOLIVAR com-piled by Vicente Lecuaa, edited by Harold A. Bierck, Jr., translated by Lewis Bertrand. Volume One 1810-1822. Second edition published by the Bolivarian Society of Venezuela. Published by The Colonial Press Inc.

"This Scepter'd Isle from Richard II" from THE ANNOTATED SHAKE-SPEARE edited by A.L. Rowse.

"A Bank that Lends Only to the Poor" an interview with Muhammad Yunnus from THE UNESCO COURIER. © September 1995 by The United Nations Educational, Scientific and Cultural Organization, France.

CREDITS

TEACHING Strategies

Teachers share a common goal—to help their students become successful learners who can understand, remember, and apply important knowledge and skills. This important goal is best supported when students are offered a variety of ways in which to learn.

The Social Studies Anthology offers you the rich and varied tools that you need to help your students learn. It includes such diverse sources as diaries, poems, songs, stories, legends, and posters — all of which draw students into the sights and sounds of the places and times they are studying.

You may invite students to explore the Anthology selections in many unique ways— rewriting documents in another genre, dramatizing the selection, creating posters or collages, or writing original poems, stories, and songs. We have provided a strategy for teaching each selection in the Anthology. But these strategies, of course, are only suggestions. You should feel free to teach the selections in any way that you feel is best suited for your own classroom.

A Cassette accompanies the Social Studies Anthology and provides additional support in teaching the documents. Sometimes the recordings reproduce the voices of the people who wrote the selections. A Cassette logo lets you know which selections have been recorded.

SEEING EARTH FROM SPACE
by Patricia Lauber, 1990
Pages 2–3

Use with Chapter 1, Lesson 1

Objectives

- ☐ *Recognize how perspectives change when viewing Earth from space.*
- ☐ *Identify problems common to all cultures on Earth.*
- ☐ *Write a proposal about working together for the good of all on Earth.*

Writing a Proposal

After students have read the selection, have them think about what Earth looks like from space. (From space the planet seems small and fragile, boundaries are blurred, and effects of pollution are noticeable.) *What are problems that all cultures on Earth face?* (Environmental problems are common to all inhabitants of Earth, regardless of political or religious differences—loss of tropical forests is causing land erosion, oil slicks pollute the oceans, and so on.) Then ask students to consider how one's perspective might be changed by viewing Earth from space. (Responses will vary but should touch on the idea of the small size of Earth and that all people share the same environment.)

Have students write a proposal about working together to preserve the beautiful natural features of the planet. You may wish to have partners work together on the proposals. Proposals should take into account environmental problems all over the world. Encourage students to share their proposals with the class.

EASTER ISLAND
by Thor Heyerdahl, 1989
Pages 4–7

Use with Chapter 2, Lesson 2

Objectives

- ☐ *Investigate Thor Heyerdahl's theory of the technology that produced the statues of Easter Island.*
- ☐ *Recognize how archaeologists uncover facts about the past.*
- ☐ *Create a mural illustrating the carving and moving of a statue.*

Creating a Mural

Before students begin reading, explain that the selection tells how anthropologist Thor Heyerdahl investigated a puzzling history mystery on Easter Island that he could not easily explain. By searching for clues, just as archaeologists do, he discovered a possible solution to the mystery.

As students read the selection, encourage them to picture the scenes that Thor Heyerdahl describes. Tell students that they are going to create a mural, or wall-sized illustration, that illustrates the process of making and moving the *moai*. Divide the class into five groups and assign each a different step in the process—the opening ceremony, the tools and process of carving, the singing and feasting before moving the *moai*, the "walking" of the *moai*, and the setting up of the *moai* in its resting place. Have each group meet to discuss how to illustrate its step of the process and make up a list of pictorial elements that illustrate it. You may wish to borrow a copy of *Easter Island* by Thor Heyerdahl from the library for students to use as a visual reference.

Spread a long length of butcher paper on the floor of the classroom. Assign each group a portion of the paper and have them draw or paint their scenes on it to create an Easter Island mural. Display the completed mural on a wall of the classroom.

OLD STONE AGE CAVE PAINTINGS

about 18,000 B.C.
Page 8

Use with Chapter 3, Legacy

Objectives

- [ ] *Recognize the archaeological significance of the Stone Age cave paintings.*
- [ ] *Understand how archaeologists use such discoveries to learn about the people who lived during a particular time.*
- [ ] *Write a description of the cave paintings.*

Background Information

The discovery of Old Stone Age cave paintings throughout southwestern Europe has enriched our understanding of the life and culture of the peoples of this time. The paintings show bison, mammoths, woolly rhinoceroses, panthers, owls, and even hyenas. Archaeologists are unsure why the paintings were made. However, they do know that the paintings are rich in detail, indicating the artists' understanding of symbolism. This points to the ability to think in complex ways.

Writing a Description

After students have had a chance to look at the cave painting, ask them to discuss what they see. Then encourage students to discuss what such paintings reveal about the people who drew them. (The people had developed tools and skills for drawing and painting; they thought it was important to represent a part of their lives and preserve it in some way through art.) *Why was the discovery so important?* (It helps us to further understand life in the Old Stone Age.)

Have students write a description of the cave painting. Encourage students to share their descriptions with the class.

FIRST FRUITS OF THE FIELD

Kabyle Legend, Retold by Anne Pellowski, 1990
Pages 9–10

Use with Chapter 3, Lesson 2

Objectives

- [ ] *Recognize the characteristics that make this story a legend.*
- [ ] *Appreciate the significance of agriculture in the course of human history.*
- [ ] *Write a description of early farming.*

Writing a Description

After students have read the selection, discuss with them what they know about legends. Point out that a **legend** is a story that explains how something came to be, often something in nature. In every culture legends are passed down from generation to generation, by word of mouth or by writing. This particular legend is from North Africa. Ask students what event this legend explains. (how people came to grow their own food) *What is the growing of plants and the raising of animals called?* (agriculture) Then ask students what character in the legend explained how to grow plants and animals. (an ant) *What did the First Parents need to know about in terms of growing crops.* (They needed to know about the importance of water for growing crops and for cooking the food that was raised.)

Have students write descriptions of early farming. Encourage them to conduct further research about farming during ancient times using encyclopedias and other reference sources. Students can share their descriptions with the class.

THE ROSETTA STONE
Egyptian Decree, 196 B.C.
Pages 12–13

Use with Chapter 4, Lesson 2

Objectives

☐ *Understand how the Rosetta Stone enabled scholars to decipher Egyptian hieroglyphics.*

☐ *Write and read hieroglyphic writing.*

Background Information

The Rosetta Stone was discovered in 1799 by French soldiers. They were part of an army commanded by Napoleon Bonaparte that had invaded Egypt the year before. Soldiers were digging trenches near the town of Rosetta when they dug up a large black stone covered with three kinds of writing. Scholars read the Greek inscription easily and were able to use it to decipher the demotic and hieroglyphic inscriptions on the stone.

Writing and Reading Hieroglyphic Writing

Ask students if any of them have worked with rebus puzzles. If possible, demonstrate a sample of rebus writing for the class. Tell students that rebus writing is somewhat similar to hieroglyphic writing. Like a rebus symbol, a hieroglyphic sign can sometimes represent an object whose name is part of a larger word that means something different. Hieroglyphic signs can also stand for ideas. For example, a picture of a man carrying something could mean "carrying." Some hieroglyphic signs help explain other signs. For instance, a sign shaped like an eye might indicate that another sign nearby has to do with seeing. Have students look at the pictures of hieroglyphic writing and identify signs that look like people or familiar objects such as birds.

After students have read the selection, have them use the symbols that are explained in the selection to write one or two hieroglyphic sentences on a piece of paper—for example, "Strength gave him victory." Then have them exchange papers with a classmate and try to read each other's sentence(s).

A QUEEN'S PROMISE
by Hatshepsut, 1500 B.C.
Page 14

Use with Chapter 4, Lesson 3

Objectives

☐ *Recognize what Hatshepsut claimed gave her the right to rule Egypt.*

☐ *Identify what Hatshepsut considered to be her achievements.*

☐ *Write an obituary for Hatshepsut.*

Rewriting in Another Genre

After students have read the selection, help them to understand who Hatshepsut was. Point out to them that she was one of Egypt's few female pharaohs. Ask students: *What did Hatshepsut claim made her the ruler of Egypt?* (Students should understand that Hatshepsut claimed to hold power as a grant from the gods of Egypt.) *What did she think was her major accomplishment?* (to have been the absolute ruler of Egypt as well as all foreign lands) *What did Hatshepsut seem to be most concerned about?* (how history would remember her) Students should understand that although the carvings on Hatshepsut's obelisk seem to reveal an enormous amount of vanity and personal pride, ancient monarchs often recorded similar sentiments on official monuments.

Provide students with current newspaper obituaries and with encyclopedia information about Hatshepsut. Encourage students to study the obituaries to see the kinds of information they contain and then have them write an obituary for Hatshepsut in the same style. Have volunteers share their obituaries with the class.

217

A VISIT FROM AN ANCIENT PHARAOH

by Carolyn Clark, 1996
Pages 15–21

Use with Chapter 4, Lesson 3

Objectives

- ☐ *Recognize the contributions made by Hatshepsut, the most powerful female pharaoh of Egypt.*
- ☐ *Identify the role archaeologists play in helping us to understand the past.*
- ☐ *Perform a play.*

Performing a Play

After students have read the play, discuss with them some of the things they learned about Hatshepsut's reign. (She believed in cooperation rather than in warfare; she instituted trade relations with other countries so that Egypt could get some of the goods that it needed; she is often portrayed as a sphinx or a man in monuments; and so on.) Ask students why a woman was allowed to be pharaoh. (Her father had been the pharaoh, and her stepson was too young to rule when her father died.) *What occurred during Hatshepsut's reign?* (Egypt entered a phase of cooperation with other nations, rather than seeking to conquer them.) Encourage students to discuss the role that archaeologists play in helping us to understand the past. *What do archaeologists do? What do their findings tell us?* (Archaeologists dig for artifacts in geographical areas that were inhabited by ancient civilizations; artifacts, such as pottery, utensils, and bones, tell us about how people in the past lived, what they valued, and so on.)

Have students perform the play for another class. Students can read the play, using a Readers Theater approach, or actually memorize the lines. Remind students that in Readers Theater they do not move about but try to read with expression. You may wish to have two casts so that more students can participate.

THE EPIC OF GILGAMESH

Sumerian Epic, 3000–2000 B.C.
Page 22

Use with Chapter 5, Lesson 2

Objectives

- ☐ *Explore the world's oldest epic.*
- ☐ *Illustrate an epic.*

Background Information

The Epic of Gilgamesh is named for a legendary king of the Sumerian city of Uruk, who may have lived in about 2700 B.C. Uruk, which is referred to as Erech in the Bible, was located on the Euphrates River near the modern city of Warka, Iraq. *The Epic of Gilgamesh* was preserved by many later Mesopotamian peoples who added to and modified the story. The story of the flood was probably added to *The Epic of Gilgamesh* by a later people. No one knows for certain when this occurred, but it was probably based on an independent tradition of flood stories that were widespread in ancient Mesopotamia.

Illustrating an Epic

After students have read the selection, discuss the background information with them. Ask students: *What is the overall tone of this story?* (Students may suggest that it is an emotional and tragic story since human beings are "turned to clay," or destroyed, although the narrator survives.)

Have students create illustrations of different portions of the story that reflect its dramatic tone. Explain to students that, according to the epic, the deck of the boat was a 120-cubit-long square and took up an acre. (A cubit is the distance from fingertip to elbow.) There were six decks below the main one, and the boat held all of the narrator's large household as well as "the beast of the field, both wild and tame." Students may wish to look up Sumerian art in the encyclopedia or the library to get an idea of what Sumerian clothes were like. Have students display their work around the classroom.

A FATHER'S COMPLAINT
by a Sumerian scribe, about 1700 B.C.
Page 23

Use with Chapter 5, Lesson 2

Objectives

❑ *Recognize the selection as a primary source.*

❑ *Identify the importance of primary sources to our understanding of history.*

❑ *Write a response to the selection.*

Writing a Response

After students have read the selection, discuss why the father was so disappointed in his son. Ask how students think the father viewed his profession. (The father thought that being a scribe was important work because at that time few people could write; he was disappointed in his son because the custom of the time was for sons to follow the work of their fathers.) Then point out to students that this letter is a **primary source**, that is, it was written by someone who actually lived during the period described. Encourage students to discuss why primary sources are valuable to our understanding of history. (They give a first-person account of historical events and times.)

Have students write a response to the father's letter. In their responses students can state whether they agree or disagree with the father's disappointment in his son. Whichever side the students take, they should support their opinions with reasons.

PRAYING AT THE WESTERN WALL
by Brent Ashabranner, 1984
Pages 24–25

Use with Chapter 5, Lesson 3

Objectives

❑ *Identify religious traditions.*

❑ *Recognize how religious traditions can bind people together.*

❑ *Write a report about a Jewish tradition.*

Writing a Report

After students read the selection, ask them to discuss the traditions of Judaism that are described in the selection. (praying at the Western Wall, bar mitzvah, tefillin, mezuzah, songs on Shabbat or Passover) *How do such traditions bind families together?* (Point out how bonds grow from our shared traditions.)

Then have students work in small groups to research a religious tradition that they know about and report to the class. Groups of five can work together to write their reports.

LIFE OF A HINDU PRIEST

by Hardwari Lal, 1984
Pages 26–27

Use with Chapter 6, Lesson 3

Objectives

- ❏ *Recognize religious traditions.*
- ❏ *Identify the religious duties of a Hindu priest.*
- ❏ *Create a log of a Hindu priest's daily duties.*

Creating a Log

Discuss with students how important religion is in the lives of the Hindus of India. Ask students what distinctive features of Hinduism Hardwari Lal describes. (Responses will vary but should mention 330 million deities, large number of idols, and grand ceremonies.) Then ask students to talk about what the daily life of a Hindu priest is like.

Have students research the duties of another religious leader such as a Jewish rabbi, a Catholic priest, or a Protestant minister. Then ask students to write a log or record of one day in the life of a religious leader. After students have completed their logs, encourage them to compare what they wrote.

MAHABHARATA

Ancient Hindu Epic, about 400 B.C.
Page 28 🔲

Use with Chapter 6, Lesson 3

Objectives

- ❏ *Identify some elements of the Hindu ethical outlook as described in the Mahabharata.*
- ❏ *Create posters that illustrate these ideas.*

Creating Posters

Have the class listen to the audio cassette and then read the stanzas aloud. Ask students: *What kinds of behavior do the first four stanzas urge people to practice?* (enjoyment, forbearance, and patience) Discuss with the class how these precepts suggest accepting what happens without anxiety or anger. Ask students: *How do the last four stanzas suggest more active behavior?* Help students to see that these stanzas urge people to try to change things, too—to try to correct bad things by countering them with good actions.

Ask students if they know of similar ideas from other religions. For example, Roman Catholic St. Francis of Assisi created a prayer for peace, part of which goes: "Where there is hatred, let me sow love; where there is injury, pardon; where there is doubt, faith; where there is despair, hope; where there is darkness, light; and where there is sadness, joy."

Divide the class into small groups and have each group create a poster to illustrate how good actions can counter bad ones. Students may wish to include related sayings from other religions on their posters. Combine the posters in a display for the classroom bulletin board.

WHERE THE MIND IS WITHOUT FEAR

by Rabindranath Tagore, 1910
Page 29

Use with Chapter 6, Lesson 3

Objectives

- ☐ *Identify how the poet uses language to convey his message of peace.*
- ☐ *Write a poem about peaceful solutions.*

Writing a Poem

After students have listened to the cassette and read the poem, invite volunteers to read the poem aloud to the class. Then discuss with students the poet's message. *What is his hope for his country? How will a "mind without fear" help his country achieve its goals?* (He hopes that his country will find peace and tranquillity amidst its diversity; peace and tranquillity in a country of diverse religious and political beliefs is best achieved when fears about differences have been laid to rest.)

Have students write a poem about the benefits of peaceful solutions. Students may wish to write about a current world situation or a more personal situation. You may wish to brainstorm ideas with the whole class and write students' suggestions on the chalkboard so that they can refer to them as they write.

BECOMING A BUDDHIST MASTER

by Sek Bao Shi, 1985
Pages 30–31

Use with Chapter 6, Lesson 4

Objectives

- ☐ *Recognize religious traditions.*
- ☐ *Identify the process through which a person becomes a Buddhist master.*
- ☐ *Write a story about the life of a Buddhist master based on the selection.*

Writing a Story

After students have read the selection, ask them to discuss why they think so much discipline is involved in becoming a Buddhist master. (Such a disciplined life enables the person who is seeking to become a master to be more open to Buddha's teachings.) Then ask students to talk about why the Buddhists in the temple are vegetarians. (They do not believe in harming any living creature.)

Have students write a story about Sek Bao Shi or a leader from another religion with which they are familiar. Students may also be interested in conducting research to add details to their stories.

O MAGNIFICENT AND MANY
from the Shih Ching, about 1100–600 B.C.
Page 32 📼

Use with Chapter 7, Lesson 2

Objectives

- ☐ *Recognize how the poet uses language to describe the celebration of a great leader.*
- ☐ *Rewrite the poem as a news story.*

Background Information

Like poetry from other cultures, Chinese poetry uses many forms, meters, and styles. However, it is different from Western poetry in several ways. First, Chinese poetry has a 3,000-year history, making it a more ancient tradition than Western poetry. Second, Chinese poetry has always been closely tied to music. Most poems were written to be chanted, not just read aloud. Third, tone and pitch, rather than stressed and unstressed syllables, are the basis for the rhythmic quality of Chinese verse. Finally, Chinese poetry tends to be more concise because of the frequent omission of the subject in a sentence.

Rewriting in Another Genre

After students have listened to the cassette and read the poem, have volunteers read the poem aloud to the class. Encourage students to discuss what the poem is describing. (A celebration honoring ancestors and the descendent of the founder of the Shang dynasty.) *What part do music and dance play in the ceremony? What musical instruments are mentioned?* (The celebration includes formal dances and music played on tambourines, drums, flutes, chimes, and bells.)

Have students imagine that they are covering the celebration for the local newspaper. Then have them write a feature article about the celebration. In their articles students should include what the occasion was, who was there, what food was served, what entertainment was provided, and so on.

The SAYINGS OF CONFUCIUS
by Confucius, about 500 B.C.
Page 33

Use with Chapter 7, Lesson 4

Objectives

- ☐ *Identify major Confucian teachings.*
- ☐ *Compare Confucius's ideas with other Asian beliefs.*

Comparing Beliefs

After students have read the sayings, discuss the meaning of each of them. Ask students: *Which of these sayings do we know as "the Golden Rule"?* (reciprocity) *What is Confucius's attitude toward learning? What examples can you find of this?* (The second, third, fourth, and sixth sayings show that Confucius thought learning was very important.) *How might you summarize his views on learning?* (perhaps that truth and knowledge were essential to living life properly)

Expand the scope of the discussion by asking students: *Do any of Confucius's ideas remind you of ideas you have already met in your study of Asian beliefs? What similarities can you find?* (Encourage students to reexamine selections on Hinduism and Buddhism to find common ideas such as a belief in simplicity, truth, self-knowledge, and self-improvement.) Have students write a paragraph describing ways that some of these ideas might be applied. Encourage volunteers to share their paragraphs with the class.

A LETTER FROM A HAN EMPEROR

by Emperor Wen Ti, about 160 B.C.
Page 34

Use with Chapter 7, Lesson 4

Objectives

- ☐ *Recognize that historically many world leaders have worked for peaceful solutions.*
- ☐ *Identify the diversity that existed in China in ancient times.*
- ☐ *Write a letter to the emperor.*

Writing a Letter

After students have read the selection, discuss why the letter was significant. (It was written by the emperor of China, who was urging the people of the northern steppes and the people of the House of Han to live together in peace.) Ask students to describe how the people to the north of the wall were different from the people south of the wall. (The people to the north were hunters who used bow and arrows to hunt their food, while the people south of the wall were engaged in agriculture and the manufacture of cloth.)

Have students write a letter to the emperor from the captain of the people of the northern steppes. How will he reply to the emperor of China? You may wish to brainstorm ideas with the whole class before they write their letters.

THE ILIAD

by Homer, about the 8th century B.C.
Pages 36–38

Use with Chapter 8, Lesson 2

Objectives

- ☐ *Recognize the excerpt from Homer's The Iliad as a part of a classic work of ancient Greek literature.*
- ☐ *Identify recurring themes in Greek mythology that appear in the selection.*
- ☐ *Construct a fuller account of Achilles' role in The Iliad.*

Building Knowledge

Indicate to students that they are going to read an excerpt from one of the oldest and most famous examples of European literature—Homer's *The Iliad*. Help them get a sense of just how long ago it was written—over 2,500 years ago. Then have them read the excerpt. After they have finished, discuss the idea that Greek mythology focuses on mortal heroes, gods and goddesses, and on relations between mortals and gods. Ask students: *Who is the hero of this tale?* (Achilles) *In what ways was he involved with gods and goddesses? How did they help him?* Help students to see how closely intertwined the lives of mortals and gods were in ancient Greek literature—mortals could even have gods as parents, as Achilles did in Thetis, and gods could intercede for and directly help mortals, just as Thetis and Hephaistos helped Achilles. Help students to recognize the tone of tragedy that is a common feature of Greek mythology.

Point out to the class that there is much more to the Achilles legend than appears in this excerpt. Have them do research to find out how Hector and Achilles met their ends and the origin of the term *Achilles' heel*. Tell students to write their own expanded accounts of the story.

HOW THE CITY OF ATHENS GOT ITS NAME

by Navidad O'Neill, 1996
Pages 39–44

Use with Chapter 8, Lesson 2

Objectives

- ❏ *Recognize that the play offers an explanation of how something came to be as well as providing entertainment.*
- ❏ *Perform a play.*

Performing a Play

After students have read the play, discuss the legend that the play is based on. *What makes this story a legend?* (A legend is a story that explains how something came to be; this play explains how the city of Athens got its name.) Then ask students why there was a disagreement over what to name the city. (Two powerful Greek gods, Athena and Poseidon, wanted to be the protector of the city; the people who believed that wisdom was the greatest of the virtues felt the city should be named for Athena, the goddess of wisdom; other people believed that because the city was by the sea, which provided food, it should be named for Poseidon, the god of the sea.) *How was the problem finally resolved?* (Athena and Poseidon competed by bringing gifts to the people. Poseidon brought water that was salty and Athena brought an olive tree. The people decided that the olive tree was more useful and chose Athena as their protector and namesake for their city.)

Have students perform the play. (Students can either read the play or memorize lines.) You may choose to assign parts or have students volunteer. Once students are satisfied with their reading or performance, they may wish to present it for another class.

THE BIRDS

by Aristophanes, 414 B.C.
Pages 45–46

Use with Chapter 8, Lesson 3

Objectives

- ❏ *Recognize that the play entertains as well as provides information about life in Athens.*
- ❏ *Identify how Aristophanes used satire in his plays.*
- ❏ *Write a review of the play.*

Writing a Review

After students have read the excerpt from *The Birds*, discuss why Aristophanes wrote the play. (to protest Athens's war with Sicily) Then remind students that **satire** is a special form of humor often used to ridicule human vices and follies. Ask students what elements of satire they can find in the play. (choice of birds to represent the perfect Athenians, building a walled city between Heaven and Earth so that the Sicilians cannot get over it) *Are satires still written today? Do playwrights still write plays to protest events?* (Responses will vary, but students should be aware that satire is still used as a literary device and that plays are sometimes written to protest political events.)

Have students write a review of the play as if they had attended a performance. Did it effectively protest the war? Was the humor apparent? You may wish to have partners work together to write their reviews.

FUNERAL SPEECH FOR ATHENIAN HEROES
by Pericles, 431 B.C.
Pages 47–48

Use with Chapter 8, Lesson 3

Objectives

☐ *Identify the characteristics that made Athens a great city-state in the eyes of Pericles.*

☐ *Recognize the contributions Athens made to later civilizations.*

☐ *Write a description of the form of government in the United States.*

Writing a Description

After students have read and listened to the selection, have them discuss the characteristics of Athens that Pericles admired. (democratic government, reward for merit, refined lifestyle, excellent military training, and so on) *What was the role of the Athenian citizen, according to Pericles?* (The Athenian citizen had the responsibility to take part in public affairs and to understand politics.) Then ask students to think about the contributions that Athens made to future civilizations. (the form of government, the idea that an informed citizenry is best)

Have students write a description of the form of government that exists in the United States today. Encourage them to include a comparison between the United States' democracy and Athens's democracy. Students can work in small groups to conduct some research if necessary. Students can share their findings with the class.

AENEID
by Virgil, 19 B.C.
Pages 49–50

Use with Chapter 9, Lesson 3

Objectives

☐ *Sample a classic of ancient Roman literature—Virgil's Aeneid.*

☐ *Draw inferences from the Aeneid about what people valued in ancient Rome.*

☐ *Rewrite an episode from the Aeneid as a news story.*

Rewriting in Another Genre

After students have read the selection, help them to draw inferences about the society it treats. Ask students such questions as: *What does the way that King Acestes greeted Aeneas tell you about the ancient Romans' attitude toward visitors?* (They believed that showing hospitality was important.) *What does Aeneas's remembrance of his father reveal?* (that respect and honor were due to one's ancestors) *What do the games and how they were run tell you about Roman society's values?* (that they highly valued competition, winning, and prizes) *How did their sense of fair play differ from our own?* (They considered Nisus's cheating to be acceptable behavior.) *What does the Aeneid tell us about ancient Roman religious beliefs?* (that the Romans believed in omens, or signs from the gods)

Have students imagine that they are sports reporters sent to cover the games described in the *Aeneid*. Have them describe the events in the form of a news story for the sports pages. If possible, have newspaper clippings of sports stories available for students to use as models.

THE ERUPTION OF MOUNT VESUVIUS

by Pliny the Younger, A.D. 79
Page 51

Use with Chapter 9, Lesson 3

Objectives

- ☐ *Recognize the effect of natural disasters on ancient civilizations.*
- ☐ *Identify the significance of primary sources to the study of history.*
- ☐ *Write a news report about the eruption.*

Writing a News Report

After students have read the selection, discuss what effect the eruption had on the people of Pompeii. (Many lost their lives, and many lost their homes and belongings.) *Why was it difficult for them to escape?* (Although there had been some earth tremors, the people were not alarmed and did not have sufficient warning to make their escape.) Point out that the people were so frightened by this natural phenomenon that they thought the gods had been killed and that the end of the world had come. Remind students that this selection is a primary source, that is, it was written by someone who actually experienced the event. Ask students why primary sources are so valuable to the study of history. (They give us first-hand descriptions of actual events.)

Have students write a news report about the eruption. Remind them to tell *who, what, when, where, why,* and *how* in their reports. You may wish to create a bulletin-board display of students' reports along with some illustrations of Vesuvius.

A CRAFTSMAN IN BETHLEHEM

by Avram Hissan, 1981
Pages 52–53

Use with Chapter 9, Lesson 4

Objectives

- ☐ *Identify religious traditions.*
- ☐ *Understand how religion has shaped the life of Avram Hissan, a Christian who lives in Bethlehem.*
- ☐ *Build knowledge about modern-day Bethlehem.*

Building Knowledge

After students have read the selection, discuss the importance of Bethlehem in the religious traditions of Christians. (According to the New Testament, Bethlehem was the birthplace of Jesus.) Then discuss with students what kinds of crafts Avram Hissan makes. (He creates religious articles from olive wood and mother of pearl for the many tourists and religious pilgrims who come to Bethlehem.)

In the selection Hissan mentions that Muslims, Jews, and Christians have long lived together in Bethlehem. Have students conduct some research about modern-day Bethlehem to find out what the city is like today and the role it plays in the current events of the area. Encourage students to share their findings with the class.

THEODORA'S BRAVERY
by Procopius, about A.D. 550
Page 54

Use with Chapter 9, Lesson 5

Objectives

- ❑ *Recognize the role of a strong woman in the Byzantine empire.*
- ❑ *Identify the decision that resulted from Theodora's advice.*
- ❑ *Write a report about the empire ruled by Justinian and Theodora.*

Writing a Report

After students have read the selection, discuss with them the role Theodora played in reaching a decision about what actions should be taken. (She offered her opinion that they should not flee from their enemies.) *Why do you think the emperor and his court paid attention to her opinion?* (She ruled the empire with Justinian, and she displayed great courage by saying that her husband and the court could flee, but that she would not.) *What effect did Theodora's courage have on the others?* (They, too, were filled with boldness as a result of her courage.) *What was the result of the decision they made?* (They stayed and fought and crushed the rebellion.)

Encourage students to conduct further research about the Byzantine empire ruled by Justinian and Theodora. Students may be interested in finding out more about Theodora or about the Body of Civil Law. Have students share their reports with the class.

A DESCRIPTION OF CONSTANTINOPLE
by Benjamin of Tudela, about 1165
Page 55

Use with Chapter 9, Lesson 5

Objectives

- ❑ *Recognize the importance of the city of Constantinople in the 1100s.*
- ❑ *Appreciate the architecture of Constantinople.*
- ❑ *Write a travel brochure for Constantinople.*

Writing a Travel Brochure

After students have read the selection, discuss with them the characteristics of Constantinople that made it important in the 1100s. (The city was a major center of trade and was famous for its outstanding architecture; it was also a city of great riches.) *What were two of the grandest buildings in Constantinople, according to this traveler?* (St. Sophia, a church, and the Hippodrome, a stadium for circuses and sports as well as Christmas celebrations) Encourage students to discuss what life was like in Constantinople and to compare life there to other less wealthy cities of the time.

Have students write a travel brochure for Constantinople. They can use some information from the selection, but they can also consult reference materials. More information about the church of St. Sophia (or the *Hagia Sophia*) may be found in articles about Istanbul, the present-day name for Constantinople. Encourage students to illustrate their travel brochures and to share them with the class.

PILGRIMAGE TO MECCA
by Samaan bin Jabir Al Nasaib, 1987
Pages 56–57

Use with Chapter 10, Lesson 2

Objectives
- [ ] *Identify religious traditions.*
- [ ] *Recognize the pilgrimage to Mecca as a significant Muslim religious event.*
- [ ] *Write a description of the pilgrimage.*

Writing a Description

After students have read the selection, discuss the "five pillars of Islam" with them. (the pilgrimage; a belief in one god; prayer five times a day; the giving of alms, or aid to the poor; and fasting during the holy month of Ramadan) Point out that the Islamic religion teaches that all Muslims should try to make the pilgrimage to Mecca once in their lifetime. Then have students recount what happens during the pilgrimage and discuss why great physical stamina is required. (Pilgrims often journey long distances to Mecca and once there must engage in rituals such as washing, prayer, walking, and running.)

Have students write a description of what happens once the pilgrims reach Mecca. Students may write their description as a list of events, or they may write a paragraph describing the events. Encourage students to discuss the events in their small groups.

AN ISLAMIC HOSPITAL
by Abd-ul-Wáhid al-Marrakhshí, about 1200
Page 58

Use with Chapter 10, Lesson 3

Objectives
- [ ] *Recognize the contributions made by Islamic civilization in the area of medical care.*
- [ ] *Link the selection to current events by writing an editorial about universal medical care.*

Linking to Current Events

After students have read the selection, encourage them to think about how this hospital was historically significant. *What did the hospital look like? What was provided for the patients? Whom did the hospital serve?* (The hospital was beautifully decorated with sculpture and tree-filled grounds, and the rooms had flowing water; the patients were given a daily ration of food, medicines, and clothing; the hospital served both the rich and the poor.) Point out that the patients who needed money were given some when they left the hospital and that the Prince of Marrakesh visited the patients every Friday. Ask students to compare and contrast this hospital with hospitals of today.

Have students write an editorial supporting or opposing universal medical care today. Tell them to be sure to include reasons to support their viewpoint. Encourage students to share their editorials with the class.

THE RINGDOVE
by Bidpai, about A.D. 300, translated by
Abdallah Ibn al-Muqaffa, about A.D. 750
Pages 59–61

Use with Chapter 10, Lesson 3

Objectives

- ☐ *Interpret the moral of a fable.*
- ☐ *Recognize the benefits of cooperation.*
- ☐ *Create a fable of cooperation.*

Writing Your Own Fable

After students have read the fable, remind them of when it was written—about 1,700 years ago. Explain that *Aesop's Fables*, a collection of Greek fables, was written more than 2,500 years ago. Discuss the point that fables are both ancient and universal in human experience. Ask students: *Why do you suppose the writer of* The Ringdove *chose animals as his characters?* (Help students to see that by giving animals human characteristics, the fable writer was able to conceal human truths in a simple story.) *What is the moral for this fable?* (Encourage the class to come up with morals that reflect the advantages of trust and cooperation.)

Divide the class into small groups and tell each group to make up a fable that has a moral of cooperation. It might be totally fictional or based on personal experience. Have a representative from each group tell the group's fable to the class.

AN HONEST COUNSELLOR
Anonymous, about 1300
Page 62

Use with Chapter 10, Lesson 3

Objectives

- ☐ *Recognize the characteristics that make the selection a parable.*
- ☐ *Retell the lesson of the parable.*
- ☐ *Write a parable that teaches a lesson.*

Writing a Parable

After students have read the selection, point out that it is a **parable.** A parable is a short story that teaches a lesson through an example. Ask students if they know of any other stories that teach a lesson. (Students may mention folktales or fables.) Then ask students to restate the lesson of this parable. (It pays to be honest.) *How did the counsellor show his honesty in this parable?* (He gave his truthful opinion to the caliph that he should not misuse his money by giving too large a gift; then, once he knew that the gift was intended for himself, he recommended that the caliph take back the gift.)

Have students write a parable of their own. Small groups can work together to decide the lesson they wish to teach. Then the group can write one parable that teaches the lesson through an example. Encourage students to share their parables with the class.

SAVING THE RAIN FOREST
by Paiakan, 1988
Page 63

Use with Chapter 11, Lesson 1

Objective

- ❏ *Recognize the view of Paiakan, an Indian of the Amazon rain forest, concerning his home.*
- ❏ *Identify the recommendations for saving the rain forest in the selection.*
- ❏ *Write about the rain forest from a different perspective.*

Rewriting from Another Perspective

Before students read the selection, review with them what they know about the Amazon rain forest—about how and why new settlement threatens it. Discuss the following questions: *Why are settlers coming to the Amazon rain forest?* (to exploit its natural resources) *How are they affecting it?* (They are rapidly destroying the rain forest.) *Who stands to gain from cutting down the Amazon rain forest?* (loggers, miners, ranchers, and farmers) *Who stands to lose?* (everyone, but especially the Indians who live there) Then have them read the selection to gain the perspective of an Indian whose way of life is threatened by new settlement.

Explore the case made by Paiakan. Ask students: *Who is Paiakan?* (a leader of the Kayapó Indians) *Why does he want to save the forest?* (It is his home.) *How does he say it must be done?* (through the cooperation of all the interested groups) Refer the class to the conclusion of the selection, which describes the Brazilian government's action against Paiakan. Ask: *Why do you suppose the government acted as it did?* Tell students to write a statement that might be given by the Brazilian government, explaining its perspective on how rain forest land should be used.

FROM MOUSE TO BAT
Maya Fable, Retold by Victor Montejo, 1991
Pages 64–65

Use with Chapter 11, Lesson 3

Objectives

- ❏ *Interpret the moral of the fable.*
- ❏ *Write a fable with a moral.*

Writing Your Own Fable

Remind the class of the many cultures that have fables that include morals. (for example, *Aesop's Fables*, which were first told among the ancient Greeks) Tell students that they are going to read a fable from another civilization—that of the Maya.

After students have read the fable, help them to identify its theme of discontent with one's condition and explore it with them. Ask students: *Why was Tx'ow discontented? What did he do about it?* (He thought he deserved more than he had; he convinced the other mice that they also deserved more.) *What did his discontent get him?* (the chance for a change, but not necessarily for an improvement in his lot) *What would you say the moral of this fable is?* (Encourage all reasonable answers; possible answers include: Be satisfied with your lot—it could be worse; Don't count your chickens before they are hatched—the change that you are sure will be for the better may be for the worse.) As students suggest different morals, list them on the chalkboard. Then encourage them to suggest other morals with which they are familiar, such as "A stitch in time saves nine" or "Pride goeth before a fall." Finally, have each student choose a moral and write his or her own fable about it.

INCIDENTS OF TRAVEL
by John Lloyd Stephens, 1841
Page 66

Use with Chapter 11, Lesson 3

Objectives

- ❑ *Recognize some of the characteristics of Maya culture.*
- ❑ *Identify the role archaeologists play in preserving history and culture.*
- ❑ *Write a report about the Maya.*

Writing a Report

After students have read the selection, discuss what they learned about Maya culture from it. (Responses will vary but should mention that the Maya lived in cities with big temples, pyramids, and other buildings made from stone; they also created large monuments, covered with hieroglyphics.) Then ask students to describe how Stephens felt when he uncovered these ruins. (He was overwhelmed by their beauty.) *What role did he play in preserving this culture?* (By making this discovery, he assured that the civilization would not be lost.) Encourage students to discuss the importance of discoveries that other archaeologists have made.

Have students conduct further research on the Maya civilization. They may use their textbook, the encyclopedia, or other reference books. Students may wish to include illustrations in their reports and share their findings with the class.

SUR LE PONT D'AVIGNON
Traditional French Song, 13th century
Page 68

Use with Chapter 12, Lesson 2

Objectives

- ❑ *Listen to a traditional French song.*
- ❑ *Perform the song as a class.*

Performing a Song

Play the cassette of the song for students while they read the lyrics in French and English. (The cassette includes an additional verse of the song.) Help students to identify the four kinds of people mentioned in the song: beau gallants (handsome and fashionable young men), fine ladies, grave abbés (dignified churchmen), and brave soldiers.

Have students create their own rendition of the song—singing and moving to it. Divide the class into five groups. Have one group practice singing "Sur le Pont d'Avignon." Assign each of the other groups one of the four kinds of people that are mentioned in the song and have them devise movements that reflect how those people might move and dance on the bridge. Encourage them to use their imaginations and to feel free to exaggerate. Give the groups time to rehearse and then perform together, with the singers singing the song and the dancers performing their movements during the stanza that relates to their characters.

TALE OF KING ARTHUR
Retold by Sir James Knowles, 1923
Pages 69–72

Use with Chapter 12, Lesson 2

Objectives

☐ *Sample a well-known legend handed down from medieval times.*

☐ *Learn about medieval customs as described in the legend.*

☐ *Dramatize the legend of King Arthur.*

Background Information

The first stories about King Arthur probably involved a fifth-century Celtic warrior chief who fought against invading Saxon tribes. These early legends were very different from those we are familiar with today and included exploits such as leading an attack on the Celtic underworld. The legend of King Arthur began to resemble its modern form around the twelfth century, when it became mixed with other legends about British history and the search for a magical grail. This selection is from a twentieth-century retelling of the legend, which includes most of the elements with which we are familiar today.

Dramatizing the Legend

Introduce the legend by naming King Arthur and asking what students know about him. Then propose that they dramatize the legend of King Arthur, based on this selection. Divide the class into groups—one to create the script, another the props, another the scenery, another to be the narrators and actors (and, if time and materials are available, another to create costumes). You will need a director, too, perhaps yourself. Then have students read the selection, keeping in mind what their parts in dramatizing it will be.

Although the legend does not take place at a particular point in medieval history, encourage students to fix an approximate date and do some research about medieval customs. When the class has pulled its dramatization together and rehearsed it, invite another class in for the performance or present it at an assembly.

A CONTRACT BETWEEN A VASSAL AND A LORD
Contract from the 7th Century
Page 73

Use with Chapter 12, Lesson 2

Objectives

☐ *Explore the nature of a contract from the Middle Ages.*

☐ *Recognize the relationship that existed between lord and vassal.*

☐ *Write a contract.*

Writing Your Own Contract

First discuss with the class what a contract is—a binding agreement between parties in which each promises the other something. Then have students take turns reading this contract aloud. Have students pause as they encounter any difficult terms. Have them identify what each party to the contract pledges the other and what he expects in return. Ask students: *What does the vassal get from the lord?* (food, clothing, protection) *What does the lord get from the vassal?* (service)

Have students work in pairs to write a contract between a student and a teacher. Tell them to include what a teacher expects from a student and what a student expects from his or her teacher.

NOTEBOOKS FROM THE RENAISSANCE
by Leonardo da Vinci, about 1482–1519
Pages 74–76

Use with Chapter 12, Lesson 4

Objectives

- ☐ _Recognize Leonardo da Vinci as one of the world's best-known artists._
- ☐ _Appreciate how da Vinci made broad knowledge the basis for his art and ideas._
- ☐ _Create a da Vinci collage._

Creating a Collage

Explain to the class that da Vinci is called a "Renaissance man," that is, a person who knows a great deal about a wide variety of subjects. Da Vinci was therefore exemplary of the burst of learning that took place during the Renaissance. Encourage students to examine his accomplishments as treated in the Anthology and discuss each one. Ask students: _What areas of knowledge did da Vinci obviously explore deeply?_ (art, anatomy, the laws of motion, and other physical laws) Help students to see how he used his knowledge to bring reality and movement to his art and to create far-seeing inventions.

Divide the class into groups and tell each group to create a collage presenting a cross section of da Vinci's work. Encourage students to find further examples of his work in the library and to either reproduce them or draw copies of them. Then have the groups use their selections to make collages for classroom display.

THIS SCEPTER'D ISLE
from _Richard II_ by William Shakespeare, 1597
Page 77 🔊

Use with Chapter 12, Legacy

Objectives

- ☐ _Identify Shakespeare as one of the most famous writers in the English language._
- ☐ _Recognize the love for England as expressed in the speech from the play Richard II._
- ☐ _Write a speech in praise of the United States._

Writing Your Own Speech

Have students follow along in their books while they listen to the cassette of the speech. Point out to the class that these lines of a speech from _Richard II_ are among the most famous in English literature. You may wish to discuss the meaning of passages like "this seat of Mars" (meaning that England is strong in war). Work on a choral reading of the speech with the class, stressing expressiveness and emotion. Remind students that the way the actor speaks the words on the recording helps express their meaning. Help students to recognize the beauty of the words and how they reflect the character's love of England.

Discuss with the class how the speech describes England. After students have identified the praise that Shakespeare lavishes on England—its natural beauties, its strength, its happy people—tell students to think about their own country. Ask students: _What lines would you write to praise it?_ Encourage students to write a speech that a character in a play might make to describe our country. Have volunteers share their speeches with the class.

FALL RAIN, FALL RAIN

by Ladysmith Black Mambazo, 1987
Page 78 🖭

Use with Chapter 13, Lesson 1

Objectives

☐ *Interpret a modern African song.*

☐ *Understand how a song can celebrate the climate and geography of a region.*

☐ *Write song lyrics about nature.*

Writing Your Own Song Lyrics

Have students listen to the cassette and follow the lyrics in their Anthologies. Point out to the class that Ladysmith, the hometown of Ladysmith Black Mambazo, is in a mountainous region of abundant rainfall. Ask students: *What does the songwriter seem to think about the rain?* (The songwriter seems to love it, although some lines say, "Don't disturb me, beautiful rain" and "Oh come, never come.") *What else does the song describe?* (the sun going down over the mountains, birds singing on trees at night, dreaming of the sun)

Point out to students that songs can celebrate many things, including the geography or climate of a region. Then have students write the words to a song about the geography or climate of their area. Have volunteers read their lyrics to the class.

THE KINGDOM OF KUSH

Ancient Artifacts and Accounts, 450 B.C.–A.D. 77
Pages 79–81

Use with Chapter 13, Lesson 2

Objectives

☐ *Explore ancient Greek and Roman writings about Kush society.*

☐ *Trace a route from Kush to India.*

Tracing a Route

Before students read the selection, distribute copies of an outline map that shows northeastern Africa and southwestern Asia. Point out the area that was once Kush on a wall map—the area surrounding the Nile River from the border of modern Egypt and Sudan to where it forks into the Blue and White Nile rivers. Point out the locations of the cities mentioned in the parts of the selection by Herodotus and Strabo and have students mark and label them on their outline maps. Syene was near the site of the modern city of Aswan, Egypt. Meroë was on the Nile River, about 150 miles north of modern Khartoum, Sudan. Myos Hormos was on the African side of the Red Sea where it divides into the Gulf of Suez and the Gulf of Aqaba, about 50 miles north of the modern city of Bur Safajah, Egypt. Also remind students that the Nile flows south to north, so traveling up the Nile means traveling south.

After students have read the selection, encourage them to offer evidence that Kush was a highly advanced civilization. (Kush had organized religion, trade with far-off lands like India, a written language, and a sophisticated artistic tradition.) Have students turn to their outline maps and, using information from Strabo's account, trace the route that Kushite traders might have followed to India. (from Meroë north on the Nile, overland from the point where the Nile forms a loop north of Syene to Myos Hormos, by boat south on the Red Sea into the Gulf of Aden, and east to India)

OBSERVATIONS OF A 14TH-CENTURY TRAVELER
by Ibn Battutah, 1352–1353
Pages 82–83

Use with Chapter 13, Lesson 3

Objectives

☐ *Interpret Ibn Battutah's observations about the government of Mali.*

☐ *Identify the values Ibn Battutah points out that are honored by Mali society.*

☐ *Write a character sketch.*

Writing a Character Sketch

After students have read the selection, encourage them to discuss their impressions of Mali's government. (rule by a powerful emperor, well-organized and well-policed political subdivisions, well-protected borders)

Ask students: *What were some of the values of the people who lived under this government?* (Help students identify such values as a strong belief in justice, a respect for life and property, and an intense respect for religion.) Then have students write a paragraph creating a character sketch of a Malian woman, man, or child. These paragraphs should reflect the moral code by which that person lives as well as provide basic facts about the person's life. Encourage students to share their sketches with the class.

THE EMPIRE OF MALI
by Al Omari, 1336
Page 84

Use with Chapter 13, Lesson 3

Objectives

☐ *Identify aspects of court life in the empire of Mali.*

☐ *Create a graphic illustrating the scene within the royal palace.*

Creating a Graphic

After students have read the selection, discuss with them what court life was like in Mali during the rule of Mansa Musa. (The court life was very rich and luxurious; the sultan sat on an ornate throne and was surrounded by many people who were there to serve him.) *What kind of clothing did the sultan wear?* (large trousers made of a special cloth) *What was the significance of the ever-present executioner?* (Responses will vary but should include the idea that justice was swift and that the sultan probably wished everyone to be aware of his power.)

Have students work in small groups to create an illustration of the scene described in the selection. As an alternative, students may want to create a floor plan of the court. Encourage students to share their illustrations with the class.

TEST OF FRIENDSHIP
Yoruba Tale, Retold by Barbara Walker, 1968
Pages 85–86

Use with Chapter 13, Legacy

Objectives

☐ *Identify the moral of this Yoruba tale—that conflict can occur even when both sides are in the right.*

☐ *Create a Story Theater performance of the folktale.*

Using Story Theater

To help students explore the conflict and moral in this tale, have them act it out in Story Theater. In Story Theater some students perform all of the actions silently, while others tell the story, and still others deliver all of the spoken lines.

After students have read and discussed the story, either assign roles or call for volunteers—three students to play the parts of the wise neighbor, Omoteji, and Olaleye; three others to deliver their lines; and several narrators to describe their actions. Other students may create costumes and props. If possible, students making the costumes should conduct research into the traditional clothes of the Yoruba.

Oral readers should take time to rehearse their lines and to work on their interpretation and expression. Actors should develop their movements while listening to the oral readers. The narrators and speaking actors should try to pace their different parts so that the miming actors do not have to rush through some parts and stall during others. Then have students perform the folktale, combining the oral reading and mimed action.

After the performance, discuss it with the class. Ask students questions such as the following to help them evaluate the story: *What ideas came across most vividly? Did playacting the conflict make it more understandable? How clearly did the moral of the tale come across?*

JI-NONGO-NONGO
African Riddles Collected by Verna Aardema, 1978
Pages 87–88

Use with Chapter 13, Legacy

Objectives

☐ *Sample African riddles.*

☐ *Draw inferences from riddles.*

☐ *Write a riddle.*

Writing Your Own Riddle

As you go through these riddles with the class, help students to see that the love for riddles is universal—not only do people all over Africa tell them, but so do people on every other continent. Ask students: *What is the subject matter of most of these riddles? What does this tell you about the people who make them up?* Help students to see that many of the riddles deal with nature—animals, plants and trees, landforms—which reflects a closeness to nature.

Have students make up their own riddles about nature or other subjects. If possible, have some books of riddles available for more examples. Have each student pose one for the class.

THE EPIC OF LIYONGO

A Swahili Epic, 1600–1800
Pages 89–92 🔲

Use with Chapter 13, Lesson 4

Objectives

☐ *Recognize that the epic is a poetic form that tells the story of a great hero.*

☐ *Identify qualities that make people heroes.*

☐ *Write an epic about a hero.*

Writing an Epic

Have students follow along in their books as they listen to the selection. Call on volunteers to read it aloud. You may wish to assign readers to each of the stanzas. Then ask students to discuss the story that the poem tells. *What sort of man do you think Liyongo is? What details from the poem support your opinion of him?* (He appears to be very clever for having suggested the dance in the prison, which gave his mother a chance to help him escape; he also appears to be very brave because he does not let fear get the better of him.) Then point out to students that this poem is an epic. An **epic** is a long narrative poem that recounts the deeds of an historic or legendary hero. Ask students if they know of any other epics. (for example, *The Iliad* or the *Odyssey*) Then ask students to discuss what qualities epic heroes tend to have. (Responses will vary but could include bravery, cleverness, popularity, honorableness, wisdom.)

Have students write an epic about someone they consider a hero. Students may wish to work in small groups to write their epics. After the small group brainstorms, each member can write one or two stanzas. Encourage the small groups to share their epics with the class.

THE HOCA

Two Turkish Tales, Retold by
Barbara K. Walker, 1988, 1990
Pages 93–95

Use with Chapter 14, Lesson 2

Objectives

☐ *Recognize the anecdote as a form of humor common to many cultures.*

☐ *Identify the Hoca as a recurring character in these Turkish tales.*

☐ *Write an anecdote about a lovable character.*

Writing an Anecdote

After students have read the selections, discuss with them the sort of character the Hoca is. (He is lovable but gets into trouble frequently; he likes to have the last word.) *Why is the Hoca the main character in many Turkish tales?* (Responses will vary but should get at the idea that many cultures have recurring characters in their tales and stories; for example, Coyote is a recurring character in many Native American tales.) Point out to students that a short humorous story about situations that characters sometimes find themselves in is called an **anecdote.** Anecdotes are common to all cultures. Then ask students how the Hoca got the last word in each of the anecdotes. (In the first, he got back at his friends by heating the dinner with one candle, and in the second he gave an excellent explanation for riding backward on the donkey.)

Have students write an anecdote of their own. First have students brainstorm about some funny things that have happened to them or to someone they know. Then ask students to write a short anecdote about the incident.

THE SPLENDORS OF HANGZHOU

by an Unknown Chinese Traveler, 1235
Pages 96–98

Use with Chapter 14, Lesson 5

Objectives

- ☐ *Recognize the richness and variety of a Chinese city over 700 years ago.*
- ☐ *Create illustrations that show its wonders.*

Creating Illustrations

As students read this selection, encourage them to try to picture the scenes that they are reading about. When they have read the selection, ask them if the scenes described remind them of any places they know today. (perhaps malls or street fairs or kinds of entertainment they have seen, like circuses featuring acrobatic acts)

Divide the class into five groups. Assign to each group one of the parts of the selection—Markets, Commercial Establishments, Entertainment Centers, Boats, and Specialty Stores. Have each group create a poster-sized illustration of the sights described by the unknown author. Encourage students to do art research so as to depict the citizens and city of Hangzhou of the 1200s as authentically as possible. Students should divide the responsibilities for planning, researching, and drawing the different goods, places, and people to be seen in Hangzhou.

THE TRAVELS OF MARCO POLO

by Marco Polo, 1298
Pages 99–101

Use with Chapter 14, Lesson 5

Objectives

- ☐ *Recognize the contribution Marco Polo made to our understanding of the areas of Asia through which he traveled during the 1200s.*
- ☐ *Identify some customs, traditions, and characteristics of life in China, Japan, and India at the time of Marco Polo's travels.*
- ☐ *Write a report about Marco Polo.*

Background Information

Marco Polo was an Italian merchant who left Venice in 1271 and traveled in Asia for almost 25 years. For part of that time, Marco Polo lived with the Kublai Khan, the leader of China, who sent him to look after important business in distant parts of the Chinese empire. Polo learned the language and customs of China and wrote a book about his travels throughout Asia when he returned to Venice in 1295.

Writing a Report

After students have read the selection, discuss with them some of the things that Marco Polo observed on his travels. (the feast for the Great Khan, the resources and architecture of Japan, pearl harvesting in India) *Why was the Great Khan interested in conquering Japan?* (The country was rich in gold, and the Great Khan wanted its wealth.) Then ask students why they think Marco Polo's travels were so important. (He made Europeans aware of a part of the world that was previously unknown to them.)

Have students conduct further research and write a report on Marco Polo and his travels. Encourage them to share their findings with the class.

THE TALE OF GENJI
by Murasaki Shikibu, early 1000s
Pages 102–103

Use with Chapter 14, Lesson 6

Objectives
- ☐ *Sample part of a Japanese novel of 1,000 years ago.*
- ☐ *Perform the tale in Readers Theater.*

Using Readers Theater

This tale lends itself well to the technique of Readers Theater, in which students take the roles of characters and read their lines with expression. They do not mime the action but convey it with their oral interpretation.

Turning this tale into a reading script calls for appointing a director (you may want to act as director), naming one or more narrators, and casting the different roles (Genji, several of his retainers, and fisherfolk). You may want to change some of the paragraphs describing what Genji is doing to lines that he speaks himself. For example, you might want to change "Genji thought he could see…" to "I thought I could see… "or "Genji offered prayers…", to "I offered prayers…"

Following the performance, hold a discussion of the tale among the performers and the audience. Encourage both groups to speculate about the meaning of the events in the selection. For example, ask students: *What could have been the reason for the dangerous storm?* (Perhaps the king of the sea sent the storm to show his displeasure with Genji for ignoring a summons.) *What do you think Genji might have done next?* Use questions such as these to explore the values and attitudes of the Japanese nobility of the early eleventh century.

2–RABBIT, 7–WIND
Retold by Toni De Gerez, 1971
Pages 104–105 🔲

Use with Chapter 15, Lesson 2

Objectives
- ☐ *Recognize how the poet describes the characteristics of people respected by the Aztec culture.*
- ☐ *Illustrate the poem.*

Illustrating a Poem

This poem was intended to be read as either a single poem or as four separate poems. After students have listened to and read the complete selection call on volunteers to read the poem aloud. Then ask students why the poet believes that the Toltec were wise. (because they conversed with their own hearts) Encourage students to talk about the three types of occupations that are discussed in the poem and what qualities the people in these roles must possess. (painters, storytellers, doctors; the painter paints god into things, the storyteller says things boldly and with joy, the doctor knows herbs, stones, trees, and roots.) *What does the poet think of the true artist, storyteller, and doctor?* (The poet admires the wisdom and skill of the artist, the boldness, joy, and language of the storyteller, and the knowledge and resourcefulness of the doctor.) *What does the poem tell you about Aztec culture?* (It was one that appreciated highly developed skills and talents; the people felt closely tied to their predecessors, the Toltec.)

Have students illustrate one portion of the poem. You may wish to have partners work together on the illustrations. Once students have finished their illustrations, they can place them on a bulletin board along with a copy of the poem.

THE GLORY OF THE INCAS
by Pedro de Cieza de León, 1553
Pages 106–108

Use with Chapter 15, Lesson 3

Objectives

- ☐ *Appreciate the accomplishments of the Incas.*
- ☐ *Determine the credibility of a source.*

Determining the Credibility of a Source

After students have read the document, discuss with them the document's author, his era of history, and the circumstances under which the document was written. Once the author of the source has been identified (Cieza de León, an observant young Spanish soldier traveling the Inca empire at its height), ask students how reliable an account this represents of what life among the Incas was really like. Students should think about whether the source was well informed about the topic (the author was actually there at the time; he was obviously very interested and carefully recorded what he saw) and whether he had anything to gain by inaccurately recording his observations (students may point out that people sometimes exaggerate to make stories seem more interesting). Finally, students should try to check what Cieza de León reported against what they already know about the Incas.

Discuss with students Cieza de León's point of view toward the people he studied. Ask students: *What did he admire about them? What information in the document supports his viewpoint?* Help students to identify and understand the positive qualities of Inca society—its strong work ethic and devotion to craftsmanship, its high level of organization (illustrated by the census and the storehouses), and its humanity in taking care of the unfortunate.

THE LAKOTA AND NATURE
by Luther Standing Bear, 1933
Pages 109–110

Use with Chapter 15, Lesson 4

Objectives

- ☐ *Recognize the Lakota's deep attachment to the earth.*
- ☐ *Understand the author's principle of reverence for all life.*
- ☐ *Write a poem expressing a personal relationship with nature.*

Writing a Poem

After students have read the selection, discuss its major ideas with them. Ask students: *Why do the Lakota want to stay in close contact with the earth?* (It is sacred to them; they believe their strength and well-being flow from it.) *What relationship do the Lakota believe they have with other living things?* (They are all kin, created by the same Creator and equal in importance.) *Why do the Lakota think that this relationship is crucial to being a good human being?* (It makes people kinder to all living things, including other humans.)

Have students make a list of their thoughts about nature, the earth, and living things. Tell them to write a poem on their own in which they express their viewpoint about nature. Encourage volunteers to read their poems to the class.

KOKOOM
Cree Tale, Retold by Garry Gregory
J. Ladouceur, 1982
Page 111

Use with Chapter 15, Lesson 4

Objectives

- ☐ *Understand that folktales provide clues to a people's traditions and beliefs.*
- ☐ *Recognize that folktales sometimes seek to explain natural events.*
- ☐ *Write a folktale that explains something in nature.*

Writing Your Own Folktale

After students have read the selection, discuss with them what folktales are and how they kept ancient beliefs and traditions alive long before there was writing. Point out to the class that folktales sometimes explain how a natural phenomenon came to be. Ask students: *According to the story, how did the moon come into being? Who was responsible for this happening? What did the moon do for the Cree?* Use these and other questions to help students understand the fear of the dark that many people feel and the desire for protection that the Cree fulfilled in this folktale by turning the moon into the beloved old grandmother Kokoom. Discuss the relationship between this transformation and the Cree's real love of the moon.

Encourage students to discuss the Cree children in the story who feared the darkness of night. Ask students: *What were they afraid of? How did they feel about the moon, or Kokoom, coming out to protect them?* Tell students to write a folktale of their own that tells a story about how some natural feature or phenomenon might have come to be. The story may be about anything in the natural world that students can think of. Because many folktales, like *Kokoom*, are set in a mythical time when the world was different from today, students should not hesitate to have impossible things happen in their story. For example, there might have been no sun or moon, or perhaps animals could talk. Have volunteers read their folktales to the class.

SUGAR MAPLING
by Jacqueline Sletto, 1992
Pages 112–113

Use with Chapter 15, Lesson 4

Objectives

- ☐ *Recognize that traditions are part of the history of a culture.*
- ☐ *Compare and contrast sugar mapling today with how it was done by early Ojibwa.*
- ☐ *Describe a community tradition.*

Writing a Description

After students have read the selection, discuss the history of sugar mapling. (Long before Europeans came to the area, woodland peoples such as the Ojibwa engaged in sugar mapling; today Lisa Erle, an Ojibwa, continues the tradition with her family.) Then encourage students to discuss the process that Lisa Erle uses. (Four-inch-long tubes are inserted into the trees to draw sap into containers at the ends of the tubes.) *What do the family do to the sap once they have collected it?* (They boil it over an open fire to boil away the water.) *What products can the family make from the sap?* (maple syrup, sugar, sweets) Have students discuss how the process differed during the time of the early Ojibwa. (They slashed the maple trees and inserted a wooden chip, reed, or piece of bark into the slash to divert the sap into birch bark containers. The boiling process was laborious because they did not have iron kettles but had to heat the sap by dropping in heated rocks.) *How was the process the same?* (The entire family participated in the collecting and boiling of the sap.)

Have students write a description of a tradition in their community. Encourage students to discuss what happens and who participates in the tradition. You may wish to brainstorm with the whole class before students write their descriptions.

LONELINESS SONG
by an Unknown Navajo Woman, 1864
Page 114 📼

Use with Chapter 15, Lesson 4

Objectives

☐ *Recognize that the song communicates loneliness as well as the Navajo's search for beauty in all aspects of life.*

☐ *Write a poem about an aspect of life or nature that is beautiful.*

Writing a Poem

After students have read the lyrics to the song, play the song for them on the cassette or on a piano if you have access to one. Invite students to sing along. Discuss with students why a "beautiful path" is important. ("Beautiful path" probably refers to one's path through life; the song is asking for a beautiful life.) Ask students if they can find any clues that the song was partly inspired by "The Long Walk" of the Navajo people. (The song was written just after "The Long Walk"; the song is about walking; the mood of the phrase "alone in my loneliness" is melancholy.)

Have students write a poem that describes an aspect of life or nature that is beautiful to them. You may wish to brainstorm with the whole class before students write their poems. You can record ideas on the chalkboard so that they may refer to them as they write. Encourage students to share their poems with the class.

CAPTAIN COOK'S JOURNAL
by James Cook, 1770
Pages 116–117

Use with Chapter 16, Lesson 2

Objectives

☐ *Recognize the contribution that Cook's explorations made to an understanding of the Aboriginal culture.*

☐ *Write an account of the meeting of two cultures from the Aborigines' perspective.*

Rewriting from Another Perspective

After students have read the selection, discuss what Cook's exploration of Australia meant to Great Britain. (He claimed eastern Australia for Great Britain in 1770.) Then ask students to discuss Cook's viewpoint of the Aborigines. *How does Cook describe them?* (Students should note his physical description and his comments on their character and their practices concerning food and shelter.) *What does Cook think about their way of life?* (He seems to be impressed by their simplicity in living, their equality, and their lack of materialism.) Students may conclude that Cook admires the Aborigines and perhaps envies them their happiness.

When students have constructed a picture of Cook's view of Aboriginal society, encourage them to imagine what the Aborigines might have thought of Cook. *What do you suppose the Aborigines would consider important enough to mention? How might they have interpreted objects and behavior that were similar to those they already knew? What about things with which they were totally unfamiliar?* Students should think about what might have been comprehensible about the behavior and equipment of British sailors and what could be confusingly foreign. For example, Cook's crew and the Aborigines would have both understood boats, cutting tools, and food. On the other hand the Aborigines seem to have had no use for or appreciation of cloth. Encourage students to write a short speech that one Aborigine might make to another concerning the British explorers. Encourage volunteers to share their speeches with the class.

BATTLE OF TENOCHTITLÁN
by Aztec Historians, 1521
Pages 118–119

Use with Chapter 16, Lesson 3

Objectives

❑ *Interpret an Aztec pictograph.*

❑ *Create a pictograph of an event.*

Creating Your Own Pictograph

Have students turn to the pictograph on page 119 but have them temporarily cover the explanation that accompanies it. First discuss what a pictograph is and how it uses drawings, many of them symbols, rather than words. Encourage students to speculate about what the figures in this pictograph show. After they have made their own interpretation, have them uncover and read the explanation. Ask students: *Whose version of the battle of Tenochtitlán is this?* (the Aztec version) *How does the pictograph show dates? Locations? Different groups of people?* Use such questions to explore and identify the various symbols that are used.

After the discussion tell each student to choose another event in the history of Latin America and to draw a pictograph that describes it. Encourage them to think in terms of drawn symbols rather than illustrations or written words. Have students exchange pictographs and try to interpret the pictographs drawn by their classmates.

ROYAL COMMENTARIES OF THE INCAS
by Garcilaso de la Vega, El Inca, 1612
Page 120

Use with Chapter 16, Lesson 3

Objectives

❑ *Recognize the value of primary sources to the understanding of history.*

❑ *Identify some of the things the Spanish introduced to the existing culture of Peru.*

❑ *Write a diary entry from the point of view of an Inca.*

Exploring Perspectives

After students have read the selection, discuss the value of primary sources to the study of history. *What is a primary source?* (It is something that was written or recorded during the period being studied.) *Why are primary sources valuable?* (They give a firsthand account of actual events by someone who was there.) Then ask students to discuss what things this Inca writer mentions that were not part of his culture before the arrival of the Spanish. (horses, beasts of burden, sheep, goats, hunting and lap dogs, wheat, wine, oil, and Spanish fruits and vegetables) *What does the author think of the things the Spanish brought with them?* (Responses will vary but could include the idea that the author says the Indians had been getting along without them before the arrival of the Spanish; students may also say that the items and ideas were useful and a source of amazement to the Indians as well.)

Have students write a diary entry from the point of view of an Inca who is experiencing the changes brought about by the arrival of the Spanish. Encourage students to share their reflections with the class.

TEARS OF THE INDIANS
by Bartolomé de Las Casas, 1542
Pages 121–122

Use with Chapter 16, Lesson 3

Objectives

- ☐ *Explain the selection's description of the Spanish treatment of the Indians.*
- ☐ *Understand how Las Casas tried to end cruelty toward the Indians.*
- ☐ *Write an interview with Las Casas.*

Rewriting in Another Genre

After students have read Bartolomé de Las Casas's indictment of early Spanish rule in Latin America, explore with the class the accusations that he makes. Ask students: *How does he say the Spanish have mistreated the Indians? What effects has this had on them?* (By making war against and enslaving the Indians, the Spanish had killed large numbers and forced the survivors to live under often intolerable conditions.) Ask students: *How would you say that Las Casas's view of the Indians was different from that of many other Spaniards?* (Las Casas saw them as human souls to be saved; many others treated them as beasts of burden.) *Whom is Las Casas trying to reach with his words?* (fellow Spaniards, especially those with the power to end the cruel treatment of the Indians) *How convincing do you think his arguments are?* (He backs up some of his statements with numbers and he uses very strong language.)

Following this discussion, tell students to act as though they are reporters sent to interview Las Casas about his cause. Have students pair up to write question-and-answer interviews, providing both questions and the possible replies of Las Casas. (For example: *Q:* What can be done to improve the treatment of Indians? *Las Casas:* The Spanish government should impose rules to enforce humane treatment.) Ask pairs of volunteers to take turns reading their interviews to the class, with one person playing the part of the reporter and the other providing Las Casas's answers.

THE LEGACY OF COLUMBUS
by Sarah Elder Hale, 1992
Page 123

Use with Chapter 16, Lesson 3

Objectives

- ☐ *Recognize the various points of view concerning the legacy of Columbus.*
- ☐ *Identify how the voyage of Columbus changed the world.*
- ☐ *Write a speech for Columbus Day.*

Writing a Speech

After students have read the selection, encourage them to discuss the main idea. *What point does the author make?* (There are differing points of view about what the voyage of Columbus meant to the world—the mingling of the cultures created an exchange that brought about today's cultural diversity; native cultures suffered under Spanish colonialism.) *How did the voyage affect the course of history?* (Europeans came to the Americas in the wake of the voyages and settled the land; the native peoples were displaced as a result of the exploration and settlement.) *Why are cultural exchanges important to history?* (We would not be able to further our understanding of the world around us, and without exchange, cultures would become isolated and stagnant.)

Have students write a speech for Columbus Day. Encourage students to express their point of view in the speech. Have students present their speeches to the class.

CAPTURED!
by Olaudah Equiano, 1789
Pages 124–125

Use with Chapter 16, Lesson 4

Objectives

- ☐ *Identify the horrors of enslavement as described by Olaudah Equiano.*
- ☐ *Empathize with Equiano's experience.*
- ☐ *Write an editorial criticizing the slave trade.*

Writing an Editorial

After students have read the selection, encourage them to discuss their reactions to it. Have them think about the fright of young children who were kidnapped and taken away from their families to be sold into slavery. Explain to the class that the harmful effects of the slave trade did not end with the separation of young children from their families. Tell students that, like millions of other people who were kidnapped from Africa, young Olaudah Equiano and his sister suffered a long, dangerous ocean voyage in the cramped hold of a ship. Most of those who survived such voyages faced lifetimes of overwork and harsh treatment as well as repeated forced separations from loved ones.

Have students suppose that they are the editors of an antislavery newspaper who are writing an editorial criticizing the slave trade and calling for its end. Explain to students that editorials are newspaper articles that give the opinion of the newspaper's editors about some issue. Students should research the effects of this trade both on people who were sold into slavery and on African society. Have students share their editorials with the class.

JONATHAN DOWN UNDER
by Patricia Beatty, 1982
Pages 126–129

LABOURING WITH THE HOE
by Frank Macnamara, early 1820s
Page 130

Use with Chapter 16, Lesson 5

Objectives

- ☐ *Understand how early English and American settlers might have experienced Australia.*
- ☐ *Recognize the contribution made by convicts to the growth of Australia.*
- ☐ *Write a scene in order to examine how people in very different circumstances might be able to understand one another.*

Writing a Scene from a Story

After students have read the selections, discuss both selection's main character. Point out that many of Australia's first settlers came freely in the pursuit of fortune while others were brought there as convicts against their will. In the first story, Jonathan is coming to Australia with his father to look for gold. In *Labouring With the Hoe*, the speaker was convicted by "England's hostile crown" and sent to work hard hours in "slavery's fettered bound." Discuss how the two characters' different situations might make them feel about Australia and each other.

Ask students to imagine what might happen if the character of Jonathan were to meet the convict who wrote "Labouring With the Hoe." Perhaps the convict had become free by this time. Would the two characters get along? Have students write a scene in which the two characters encounter each other.

OODGEROO (PAPERBARK TREE)
by Oodgeroo Noonuccal, 1972
Pages 131–132

Use with Chapter 16, Lesson 5

Objectives

❏ *Identify and discuss the symbols used in this story.*

❏ *Recognize that stories are often used to explain how things came to be.*

❏ *Create storyboards using pictures and captions to tell the tale in two ways.*

Creating a Storyboard

Tell the students that as they read the story they should picture the scenes. After they have read the selection, discuss the imagery and symbols used. Talk about what some of these symbols might mean. What could paperbark represent? (writing paper) Charred sticks? (writing utensils such as pencils, also remnants of the old stories and traditions of her ancestors)

Divide the students into groups to draw storyboards, or a sequence of pictures to help tell the story, and have them write captions in their own words. Have half of them do storyboards that show the actual things that are mentioned in the story. (paperbark trees, charred sticks) Have the other half do storyboards that show what these actual images might represent. (writing paper, pencils) Discuss some of the ways that using symbols and images might make a story more interesting. What might this story explain about the life of Oodgeroo? (how she became a writer)

FIGHTING FOR FREEDOM
by Toussaint L'Ouverture, 1795
Page 133 🎧

Use with Chapter 17, Lesson 2

Objectives

❏ *Describe what Toussaint L'Ouverture stated as goals for his land and people.*

❏ *Link conditions in Haiti today with those 200 years ago.*

Background Information

Explain to students that at the time Toussaint L'Ouverture gave the speech they are about to hear, the people of Haiti had already won their freedom from slavery in 1793. Then Toussaint and other formerly enslaved Haitians joined their former enemy France in fighting the English and Spanish, who still permitted slavery, and the Emigrés, who were French but opposed the French government. Later the Haitian people fought against France again when it tried to regain control of Haiti.

Linking to Today

After students have heard the selection on the cassette, ask them what Toussaint L'Ouverture wanted and why. (the expulsion of all enemies so that the people of Haiti could have liberty and justice) Ask students if this reminds them of any similar events from history. Help them to see the parallels with the revolt against Britain by the 13 colonies in the Revolutionary War. Also point out more recent demands for liberty by the peoples of Eastern Europe, the Soviet Union, and China. Help students see that the desire for freedom is in all human beings.

Help students to determine how successful the people of Haiti have been in preserving their liberty. Have students research the current situation in Haiti——if possible, provide students with recent news clippings. Have students write a letter addressed to Toussaint L'Ouverture telling him which of his hopes have come true and which have not.

LETTER FROM JAMAICA
by Simón Bolívar, 1815
Pages 134–135

Use with Chapter 17, Lesson 2

Objectives

☐ *Identify the reasons that Bolívar wanted independence for Spain's American colonies.*

☐ *Recognize the role of hyperbole in Bolívar's impassioned plea.*

☐ *Write an interview with Simón Bolívar.*

Writing an Interview

After students have read the selection, point out that although Bolívar writes in letter form, his words seem more appropriate to dramatic speech. Write the word *hyperbole* on the chalkboard and tell students that it is a word from literature that refers to exaggeration made for dramatic effect. Encourage students to look through the selection again to find the reasons that Bolívar gives for overthrowing Spain and note his use of hyperbole. (for example, sufferings at the hands of "that unnatural step-mother"; the Spanish military attack on Venezuela made out of "insatiable ... thirst for blood and crimes"; comparison to "those first monsters who wiped out America's ... [earliest people]")

As students identify Bolívar's reasons, write them on the chalkboard. Then have students act as journalists from a country outside Latin America. Have pairs of students write interviews with Simon Bolívar in which the questioner tries to find out what Bolívar's specific ideas and criticisms of the Spanish government are. Students should keep in mind that Bolívar was a very daring and passionate man whose answers might be as full of hyperbole as his letters. Have volunteers act out their interviews for the class.

WORKING IN THE MINES
by Ann Eggley and Elizabeth Eggley, 1842
Pages 136–137

Use with Chapter 17, Lesson 3

Objectives

☐ *Identify children's working conditions during the Industrial Revolution as described in the selection.*

☐ *Identify the Eggleys' description of the effects of such conditions.*

☐ *Compare working conditions then and now.*

Linking to Today

As students read this selection, tell them to visualize what is being described and to think what it would be like to work in similar conditions. After they have finished reading, encourage volunteers to share their first impressions. Ask students: *What do you think about Ann's and Elizabeth's lives? What aspects of their lives do you think would be the hardest to endure? Why?* Help students to empathize with the backbreaking, long hours at work, the tiredness, the dirty conditions, and the lack of opportunity for education.

List the conditions that students identify on the chalkboard. Encourage students to compare these conditions with what they know about working conditions today. Opposite each condition on the chalkboard, list students' description of that condition as it is experienced today—for example, 12-hour workday/8-hour workday and only after age 16; no education for children/compulsory school attendance until at least age 16, and so on.

PROGRESS IN INDUSTRY
An Advertisement, 1887
Page 138

Use with Chapter 17, Lesson 3

Objectives

- ☐ *Identify the effect of the Industrial Revolution on the economy of the United States.*
- ☐ *Recognize the need for advertising in a growing economy.*
- ☐ *Write an advertisement for the technology of today.*

Linking to Today

After students have examined the advertisement, ask them to discuss why E. S. Greeley and Company probably came into existence. (With the Industrial Revolution came many inventions, including the steam engine for ships and trains and the telegraph; manufacturers were needed to supply parts for these inventions. The economy grew.) Then encourage students to discuss what they know of advertising. *Why did the E. S. Greeley Company need to advertise?* (Responses will vary somewhat but should include the idea that in a growing economy, suppliers of goods need to show consumers how their products are better than those of their competitors.)

Have students write an advertisement for the technology of today. Advertisements could be for a compact disc, a computer, a video recorder, or another technological product of their choice. You may wish to create a bulletin board of students' advertisements.

CLARA'S DIARY
by Clara Whitney, 1875–1887
Pages 139–140

Use with Chapter 17, Lesson 4

Objectives

- ☐ *Identify aspects of Japanese culture in the late nineteenth century as seen through the eyes of a young American girl.*
- ☐ *Write interview questions for Clara about her life in Japan.*

Writing Interview Questions

After students have read the diary entries, discuss some of the observations that Clara made about Japanese culture. *Which events did Clara write about in her diary that showed traditional Japanese culture?* (the Shinto religious ceremony, the celebration of the emperor's birthday, the imperial procession on the day she met the emperor and empress of Japan) *Which events illustrated Japan's modernization?* (the National Exhibition and the opening of the Central Telegraph Office)

Have students work in small groups to come up with interview questions for Clara. Groups should write at least five questions. Then the whole class can decide on the ten best questions and make a plan for finding plausible answers for them. You may wish to have pairs of students take one question and present the interview for their classmates.

ALL QUIET ON THE WESTERN FRONT

by Erich Maria Remarque, 1929
Pages 142–143

Use with Chapter 18, Lesson 1

Objectives

- ☐ *Explore the realities of trench warfare as described in* All Quiet on the Western Front.
- ☐ *Recognize the impact of a major piece of antiwar literature from World War I.*
- ☐ *Write a letter describing trench warfare.*

Rewriting in Another Genre

The American poet Walt Whitman once said, "The real war will never get in the books." However, that was half a century before Erich Maria Remarque wrote *All Quiet on the Western Front*. Tell students that Remarque, who had served in the German Army during World War I, wrote *All Quiet on the Western Front* to describe the horror and futility of war. After students have read this excerpt, help them to understand what a powerful effect Remarque's book had on people of many nations when it came out. Remarque wanted to convince readers that there was nothing noble or glorious about war. Have students discuss how Remarque's book achieved this. (It showed them the horrible side of war.) Ask students: *What adjectives do you think Remarque would use to describe war?* (horrible, frightening, inhuman, and so on) You may wish to point out to the class that Adolf Hitler banned *All Quiet on the Western Front* and hounded Remarque out of Germany because Hitler wanted Germans to embrace war and regard it as glorious.

Tell students to suppose that they are young soldiers in the United States Army during World War I and are experiencing the same kind of trench warfare that Remarque did. Have each student write a letter home, describing a day in the soldier's life. Encourage volunteers to read their letters to the class.

THE ENDLESS STEPPE

by Esther Hautzig, 1968
Pages 144–145

Use with Chapter 18, Lesson 2

Objectives

- ☐ *Recognize the hardships experienced by political prisoners during the Russian Revolution.*
- ☐ *Consider the ways that political prisoners survive adversity.*
- ☐ *Write a report about an aspect of the Russian Revolution.*

Writing a Report

After students have read the selection, discuss what life was like for the Rudomin family in Siberia. (The family was put into a labor camp, where they had to work as dynamiters or truckers; children were responsible for the planting and harvesting of crops.) Point out that during the Russian Revolution and under the government of the Soviet Union, anyone opposed to communism was considered an enemy of the nation. These enemies were exiled to Siberia, a barren and harsh area of Russia, where they were forced to work as slave labor. Then ask students to speculate about how the family coped with their situation. (Responses will vary but could include speculations that the family coped by doing the work assigned to them and bonding together in order to survive.)

Have students conduct some further research to use in a report about the Russian Revolution. Students may wish to concentrate on one aspect of the revolution, such as the first leader of the Soviet Union or the treatment of political prisoners. Encourage students to share their reports with the class.

THE DIARY OF ANNE FRANK
by Anne Frank, 1942–1944
Pages 146–149

Use with Chapter 18, Lesson 3

Objectives

- ☐ *Empathize with the terrible situation confronting Anne Frank and her family.*
- ☐ *Appreciate the power of the ideals that helped the Frank family withstand their ordeal.*
- ☐ *Write diary entries from another perspective.*

Background Information

The Frank family and four others went into hiding in 1942 and stayed there for over two years. When they were discovered by the Nazis in 1944, their captors dumped Anne's diary on the floor with some other papers. It was later found by two of the Franks' Dutch benefactors, who gave it to Anne's father after the end of World War II. The diary became a best-selling book when it was published in 1947 and was later turned into both a play and a movie.

Rewriting from Another Perspective

Have students think about what life was like for Anne Frank and her family as they read the selection. Ask students: *What was the fear that haunted Anne and her family?* (that they might be discovered by the Nazis and sent to a concentration camp to be murdered) Explain to the class that, while in hiding, Anne Frank continued to believe that people were good at heart. Point out to students that Anne's belief in the goodness of people may have been encouraged by the example of the Dutch friends who helped the Franks, despite the risks. Help students understand that these were not fearless people but that they overcame their fear because of their affection for Anne's family and their belief that what the Nazis were doing was wrong.

Have students discuss what the thoughts and feelings of the Franks' Dutch friends might have been. Have them write part of a secret diary that someone helping the Franks stay hidden might have written. Have volunteers share their diary entries with the class.

DEFEATING NAZI GERMANY
Poster, 1942
Page 150

Use with Chapter 18, Lesson 3

Objectives

- ☐ *Identify the swastika as a symbol of Nazi Germany.*
- ☐ *Identify the poster as a means of Allied persuasion during World War II.*
- ☐ *Create a poster.*

Background Information

The swastika is an ancient symbol, the original meaning of which, scholars are unsure. The swastika was later adopted by the Nazis to symbolize their theory of "racial superiority." Following World War II, it was banned in Germany.

Creating Posters

Be sure that students recognize the swastika as the symbol of Nazi Germany. Ask students: *What message does this poster symbolically present?* (Four Allied nations are breaking Nazi Germany apart.) *How are the Allied nations achieving this?* (They are cooperating.) Help students to recognize the role that cooperation is playing in this instance. The poster is trying to persuade all nations to cooperate in order to defeat the Nazi enemy.

Have students create their own posters urging different nations to cooperate in solving a worldwide problem, such as hunger or pollution. Then hang their posters around the classroom.

NEVER GIVE UP THE FIGHT
by Winston Churchill and Franklin Roosevelt, 1941
Page 151 📼

Use with Chapter 18, Lesson 3

Objectives

❏ *Recognize how two world leaders used language to comfort and inspire people in the early years of World War II.*

❏ *Present a speech by Roosevelt or Churchill.*

Presenting a Speech

After students have read the quotations and listened to them on the cassette, point out to them that during World War II both Franklin Roosevelt and Winston Churchill made frequent speeches to the American and British public. *Why did Roosevelt and Churchill make speeches during the war?* (The times were tense, and people of both countries were alarmed; these leaders sought to reassure the public by keeping them informed; they also wanted to bring the people together to face a common enemy.) *What do the words of both leaders have in common?* (They acknowledge the seriousness of the situation and encourage the people to be strong and to have courage.)

Have students find copies of speeches delivered by Churchill and Roosevelt during the war years. Have students practice reading the speeches and then present them to the class. You may wish to tape-record the speeches so that students can listen to them during your study of World War II.

ATTACK ON PEARL HARBOR
from the *New York Times*, 1941
Page 152

WHEN THE A-BOMB FELL
by Yoshihiro Kimura, 1951
Pages 153–154

Use with Chapter 18, Lesson 3

Objectives

❏ *Understand the circumstances which led to Japan's attack on Pearl Harbor during World War II.*

❏ *Recognize the horrors of atomic war as described by Yoshihiro Kimura.*

❏ *Write a haiku that calls for peace.*

Background Information

The 1920s were years of increasing democracy and freedom for Japan. Economic hardship due to worldwide depression helped bring this to an end during the 1930s. Right-wing radicals assassinated government officials and agitated to increase the power of the military. By 1940 the government of Japan was controlled by the military.

Writing a Haiku

After students have read both selections discuss their thoughts about Japan's experience in World War II. Ask students: *Did Japan need to attack the United States to defend itself?* (No, Japan did so for aggressive reasons.) *What were the effects of the dropping of the atomic bomb as experienced by the author?* (buildings collapsed; people were burned; death of family members. The author decided the war is the enemy of everyone.) Explain to students that, because of their terrible experience in World War II, many Japanese remain suspicious of their own military and oppose rebuilding a strong armed force or obtaining nuclear weapons.

Review with the class what a haiku is—an unrhymed poem consisting of 17 syllables, usually in three lines of 5, 7, and 5 syllables each. Have students use this selection and their reactions to it to compose haikus calling for peace. Encourage students to share their haikus with the class.

NO TEARS FOR MAO
by Niu-Niu
Pages 155–156

Use with Chapter 18, Lesson 4

Objectives

❑ *Identify the changes that took place in China during the Cultural Revolution.*

❑ *Create a poster protesting the Cultural Revolution.*

Creating a Poster

After students have read the selection, discuss the events that the grandmother describes. (Intellectuals were killed, street names were changed, names of businesses were changed, pictures of Mao were hung everywhere, and people who disagreed with the new government were punished.) Point out to students that Niu-Niu's parents were sent off to a camp because they protested the new government. Ask students to speculate about why this might have been so and why the events described by the grandmother occurred. (Responses will vary but should include the idea that in a dictatorship or oppressive form of government, all opposition is eliminated and everyone is expected to support the ruler without question.)

Have students conduct further research on the Cultural Revolution of Mao and create posters protesting events of the revolution. Encourage students to present their posters to the class. Discuss the fact that protests such as these would have been severely punished during the Cultural Revolution.

CHARTER OF THE UNITED NATIONS
International Agreement, 1945
Page 157

Use with Chapter 18, Lesson 5

Objectives

❑ *Identify the goals of the United Nations.*

❑ *Write additional goals for a world peace organization.*

Linking to Current Events

After students have read the charter, discuss the goals of the United Nations as expressed in its charter. (practice tolerance, live in peace, maintain international peace and security, promote economic and social advancement of all people) Ask students what kind of organization the United Nations is. (It is an international organization created to preserve peace and agreements of international law and to protect human rights in the world.)

Remind students that the United Nations was created after World War II. Encourage them to think about world events that have occurred since World War II and have them research the role of the United Nations in those events. After discussing their findings, have students write other goals for this international organization. Encourage students to share their goals with the class.

ATTACK ON THE CONGO RIVER: ONE VIEW
by Henry M. Stanley, 1885
Page 158–159

ATTACK ON THE CONGO RIVER: ANOTHER VIEW
by Mojimba, 1907
Pages 160–161

Use with Chapter 19, Lesson 1

Objective

☐ *Identify the cultural misunderstanding that led to a clash between the Basoko and Europeans.*

☐ *Compare two accounts of the same event.*

Comparing Two Accounts

After students have read Stanley's account, have them discuss his reaction to the Basoko people. Ask students: *What made Stanley decide to run away from the Basoko?* (There were many of them, and they came toward Stanley's party in great numbers.) *Why did Stanley think that the Basoko were hostile?* (They made a lot of noise and came armed with spears.)

After students have read Mojimba's description of the battle, ask them: *What did the Basoko expect from the Europeans?* (friendship) *Why did they expect the Europeans to be friendly?* (The Basoko believed that the Europeans were the spirits of drowned kinsfolk.)

Discuss both accounts. Ask students: *On what points do the two accounts agree?* (The Basoko rushed toward Stanley's group in their canoes, Stanley's people opened fire and pursued the survivors.) *Where do they disagree?* (Stanley believed that the Basoko were hostile, whereas Mojimba claimed that his people were friendly.) *How did the expectations of Mojimba differ from those of Stanley?* (Stanley was predisposed to expect an attack; Mojimba expected to meet friends.)

Have students write a report of the battle that takes into account the expectations and perceptions of both groups. Students should try to explain the actions of the two groups in terms of their mistaken beliefs about each other. Have volunteers discuss their reports with the class.

THE MAN WHO SHARED HIS HUT
by Jomo Kenyatta, 1938
Pages 162–165

Use with Chapter 19, Lesson 1

Objectives

☐ *Interpret the symbols and symbolic action in Jomo Kenyatta's story as an allegory.*

☐ *Write an allegory.*

Writing Your Own Allegory

Explain to the class what an **allegory** is—a story in which fictitious characters and actions are used to symbolize real characters and actions. Allegories are also intended to teach a lesson. Tell students that the story they are about to read is an allegory.

After students have read the selection, have them match up the symbolic characters and actions with what they represent. (The hut represents Africa; the man represents the African people; the animals represent the various colonial powers who seized control of Africa.) Ask students: *How did the animals justify taking over the man's hut?* (by claiming that they were doing so in order to help him) *What excuse did they give for not giving the hut back?* (that he was not making good use of it) *What did they say gave them the right to make decisions for him?* (He was too backward or poorly educated to make decisions for himself.) Help students understand that these were the excuses that European countries gave for invading and taking over Africa against the will of the African people during the nineteenth and early twentieth centuries. Explain that, like the elephant in the story, the real reason was that the colonial powers wanted to take Africa's wealth for themselves.

Divide the class into groups and have each group write a brief allegory. Encourage students to think of some current situation, perhaps a news story about a part of Africa, that they might retell in an allegory. Have volunteers present their allegories and ask other students to identify the characters and actions represented in them.

THE VISION THAT I SEE

by Kwame Nkrumah, 1953
Pages 166–167 🔲

Use With Chapter 19, Lesson 1

Objectives

☐ *Identify Kwame Nkrumah's goals for Africans as conveyed in his speech.*

☐ *Create a personal vision for Africa.*

Writing Your Own Speech

Play the speech on the cassette while students follow along in their Anthologies. After students have listened to the speech, help them to identify its main idea. Ask students: *If you had to state the major theme of Nkrumah's vision, what would it be?* (Answers will vary but should touch on the idea of self-determination.) *How does Nkrumah use examples from history to enrich his vision?* (He gives examples of African achievements to show that great things are possible; he also gives examples of people enduring great suffering.) *What does Nkrumah think will help bring about his vision?* (fighting to end colonialism and imperialism in order to bring about equality) List students' responses on the chalkboard and discuss each of the ideas with the class. Ask students if these ideas remind them of the personal visions of any people from other countries.

Have students suppose that they are Africans who want a better life for people in their countries. Ask students what their goal for the future might be. Have students write a short speech expressing their goal. Students may wish to look up an African country of their choosing in the encyclopedia to find detailed historical examples for their speeches. Encourage volunteers to share their speeches with the class.

MOUNTAINS IN ISRAEL

Israeli Song, 1950
Page 168 🔲

Use with Chapter 19, Lesson 2

Objectives

☐ *Interpret an Israeli folk song.*

☐ *Illustrate the landscape the Israeli folk song describes.*

Illustrating a Folk Song

Have students picture the landscapes being described as they read the words to the song and listen to the cassette. If possible, try to have some travel magazines that show the countryside of Israel. Ask students: *What could the lines that mention colors like "carpets spread, embroidered red" and the other colors stand for?* (growing things, soil, rocks, or sand)

Point out to students that this folk song is like a painting in words—"a long and wavy line" for mountains and a multicolored "carpet" for valley meadows. Have students create their own illustrations of the song based on the impressions it conveys. Display the illustrations around the classroom.

ROAD TO PEACE
**by Yasir Arafat and Yitzhak Rabin,
1993 and 1995
Pages 169–171** 🔲

Use with Chapter 19, Lesson 2

Objectives

- ☐ *Recognize how two world leaders addressed their hopes for peace in the Middle East.*
- ☐ *Understand past conflicts between Israel and Palestine.*
- ☐ *Write an editorial presenting a point of view about the issue of peace in the Middle East.*

Writing an Editorial

After students have read and heard the speeches, discuss the points of view expressed by each leader. (Both leaders are happy that the two countries have reached an agreement; Rabin seems especially mindful of past hostilities in his speeches; both leaders know that the road to peace will take exceptional courage and perseverance.) Point out that these speeches were made in September 1993 and September 1995. Ask students what significant event has occurred since then. (Rabin was assassinated by one of his countrymen who opposed the peace agreement with Palestine.)

Have students conduct further research into the Palestinian/Israeli conflicts over land in the Middle East. Based on their findings, encourage students to write an editorial about one of the issues that emerged. For example, students could support Israeli claims, Palestinian claims, or a compromise position. Suggest that students share their editorials with the class.

POEMS FOR PEACE
**by Mahmud Abu Radj and Tali Shurek, 1974
Page 172** 🔲

Use with Chapter 19, Lesson 2

Objectives

- ☐ *Interpret images of peace created by Middle Eastern teenagers.*
- ☐ *Appreciate the hopefulness of Mahmud Abu Radj and Tali Shurek.*
- ☐ *Write a poem of peace.*

Writing Your Own Poem

Play the cassette of the poems for the class and then divide the class into two groups. Have each group prepare a choral reading of one of the two poems. After students have finished their readings, ask them: *How do these poems differ in the imagery they use for peace?* (One uses images of weapons and soldiers turning to peaceful pursuits, and the other uses pleasing colors.) *What do these poems tell you about their writers?* (that they are probably hopeful, optimistic young people even though they may know of the dreadful things mentioned in both poems)

Refer students to the closing note that asks what images they might use to write a poem about peace. Encourage them to think of as many answers as possible, listing them on the chalkboard. Then have each student choose an image and develop it into a poem of peace. Have volunteers share their poems with the class.

WHY INDIA MUST BE FREE
by Mohandas Gandhi, 1930
Page 173

Use with Chapter 19, Lesson 3

Objectives

- ☐ *Interpret Gandhi's beliefs as described in his letter.*
- ☐ *Appreciate the power of Gandhi's ideas.*
- ☐ *Link Gandhi's ideas to more recent problems around the world.*

Background Information

Gandhi's mother was a follower of the Jain religion. Jainism was founded at about the same time as Buddhism and proscribes doing injury to any living thing. Her beliefs deeply affected Gandhi. Gandhi was also influenced by Hindu scriptures, the New Testament of the Bible, and the ideas of American author Henry David Thoreau and Russian author Leo Tolstoy.

Linking to Today

After students have read the letter, discuss what it reveals about Gandhi's philosophy. Ask students: *What is the central belief of Gandhi's personal faith?* (He could not intentionally hurt anything that lives.) *What did Gandhi think about the English?* (He thought their rule was a curse but considered many individual English people his friends.)

Discuss civil disobedience, the peaceful refusal to obey a law or laws as protest against injustice. Explain to the class how Gandhi's ideas have influenced people in many parts of the world, including the United States. If possible, have materials on hand about Martin Luther King, Jr., and the civil rights movement, the people power movement of 1986 in the Philippines, and the 1991 showdown between Soviet troops and crowds of demonstrators in Moscow. Discuss with students the seriousness of choosing to disobey the law in this fashion.

A WOMAN FROM PAKISTAN: SHABANU
by Attiya Inayatullah, 1995
Page 174

Use with Chapter 19, Lesson 3

Objectives

- ☐ *Identify what steps Pakistani women are taking to improve their lives and status.*
- ☐ *Write interview questions for Shabanu.*

Writing an Interview

After students have read the selection, ask them to talk about the steps Shabanu has taken to improve her life. (She has continued her education, taken a training course for birth attendants, and participated in women's meetings.) *What is Shabanu doing now?* (She is a supervisor in a local women's program and has increased her income; she is helping other women to improve their lives.)

Have partners write at least five questions they would like to ask Shabanu. Then in a whole class discussion, select the ten best questions. Have students create plausible answers for the questions, based on additional research. Have students share their findings with the class.

A BANK THAT ONLY LENDS TO THE POOR
An Interview with Muhammad Yunus, 1995
Page 175

Use with Chapter 19, Lesson 3

Objectives

- ☐ *Recognize the goals of the Grameen Bank.*
- ☐ *Identify how the bank has improved the lives of people in Bangladesh.*
- ☐ *Write an advertisement for the Grameen Bank.*

Writing an Advertisement

After students have read the interview, discuss the goals of the Grameen Bank. (The bank lends money to the poor so that they can cross the poverty line within five years.) *How has the bank improved people's lives?* (It has lent money, mostly to women, to finance very simple business projects, such as selling milk, processing rice, or weaving.)

Have students write an advertisement for the bank, encouraging more people to borrow money to improve their lives. Students may wish to illustrate their advertisements. Encourage students to share their work with the class.

TANK, THE WATER BUFFALO
by Huynh Quang Nhuong, 1982
Pages 176–179

Use with Chapter 19, Lesson 4

Objectives

- ☐ *Recognize the importance of animals to the life of the hamlet as described in the story.*
- ☐ *Appreciate the bonds that can develop between humans and animals.*
- ☐ *Write a story about a friendship between humans and animals.*

Writing Your Own Story

After the class has read the story, discuss with them what a boon Tank was to the farming community in which he lived. Ask students: *What kinds of work was he called upon to do in the story?* (Students should remember that he pulled the plow, protected the herd from predators, and hauled crops on his back.) *How would plowing and hauling probably be done on a farm in the United States today?* (Probably with a tractor; help students to see that animal power is vital to a farming community that does not use tractors or other machines, but that most modern farms no longer use animals as beasts of burden.) *What qualities made Tank valuable to the family that owned him and to the people of the hamlet?* (strength, courage, intelligence, loyalty, willingness to work hard, and a cooperative nature)

Discuss other animal-human relationships with students. Ask students if they have ever had a pet. *What can animals and humans do for each other?* After students have discussed these questions, have them write a story about friendship between people and animals. Tell them that they may base it on a real experience or make it up, either partly or entirely. Encourage students to share their stories with the class.

THE WAR YEARS IN VIETNAM

by Le Ly Hayslip, 1989
Pages 180–182

Use with Chapter 19, Lesson 4

Objectives

❑ *Appreciate how Le Ly Hayslip's family was a source of strength for her during wartime.*

❑ *Understand how a Vietnamese woman is fulfilling goals set in childhood.*

Writing About Goals

After students have read the selection, help them to see how Le Ly Hayslip's childhood in Vietnam affected her as an adult. Remind students that Le Ly Hayslip's role models were her father and her heroic ancestor, Phung Thi Chinh. Have students discuss what she learned from them. (resourcefulness, love of country, concern for others, the will to overcome obstacles) Ask students: *What goals did Le Ly Hayslip and her father develop for her?* (to stay alive, to protect others, and to live in peace) *What is Le Ly Hayslip doing today?* (living in California, where she founded a charitable relief and world peace group)

Ask students to think about the people whom they admire and the personal qualities that make these people admirable. Suggest that these might be relatives, public figures, or people from the past. Have students write a paragraph explaining what they might learn from the example set by these people. The paragraphs should state some personal goals and explain how the students might fulfill them. Have volunteers share their paragraphs with the class.

TẾT TRUNG

Vietnamese Song
Pages 183–184 🔲

Use with Chapter 19, Lesson 4

Objectives

❑ *Recognize the characteristics of the Vietnamese festival described in this song.*

❑ *Write a poem about autumn.*

Writing a Poem

After students have read the lyrics to the song, play the song for them on the cassette or on a piano if you have access to one. Discuss with students what is described in the song. (scenes of autumn and events of an autumn festival) *What particularly is admired in the song?* (the moon) *What other things are described at the festival?* (the lanterns, the sound of the drums) Point out that in Vietnam, autumn festivals involve friends and families gathering to celebrate and to admire the moon.

Then encourage students to write a poem about autumn or an autumn festival that they know about. You may wish to brainstorm with the whole class and list some ideas on the chalkboard before students write their poems.

NEW YEAR'S ADDRESS
by Václav Havel, 1990
Pages 185–186 🔲

Use with Chapter 20, Lesson 1

Objectives

☐ *Identify the problems that Czechoslovakia faced when Václav Havel made this speech.*

☐ *Explain Havel's suggestions for dealing with Czechoslovakia's problems.*

☐ *Write a newspaper article on the Czech Republic and Slovakia*

Background Information

Three years after Václav Havel made this speech, Czechoslovakia split into two separate nations—the Czech Republic and Slovakia. In February of 1993, a month after its creation, the Czech Republic elected Havel as its president.

Writing a Newspaper Article

After students have read the speech and listened to it on the cassette, have them discuss its major points. Help students to identify the challenges that Havel said Czechoslovakia and other Eastern European nations faced after the collapse of communism—unwise economic practices, poor education, physical and moral pollution, learning how to operate democratic governments and free-market economies. Ask students: *What did Havel believe the Czechoslovakian people had to do to meet these challenges?* (Students should identify the need for personal responsibility and active participation on the part of citizens; Czechoslovakians had to put the general social good above "looking out for number 1" and had to take an active part in national life in order to maintain and nourish freedoms so dearly won.)

Have students do research to find out what is currently happening in the Czech Republic and Slovakia. Then, working in pairs, have the students write a newspaper article summarizing their findings. The article should take into account some of the major differences and similarities of the two nations. When the articles are finished, display them on the classroom bulletin board.

SPEECH BEFORE THE UNITED NATIONS
by Boris Yeltsin, 1994
Pages 187–188 🔲

Use with Chapter 20, Lesson 1

Objectives

☐ *Identify the goals of the new democratic Russia that came into being in 1991.*

☐ *Recognize what Yeltsin expects from the United Nations.*

☐ *Write a report about the new Russia.*

Writing a Report

After students have read the speech and listened to it on the cassette, discuss the goals of the new Russia. (to remove the remaining influences of totalitarianism and to insure basic civil rights and economic reform) *What does Yeltsin expect from the United Nations?* (help with an end to nuclear arms production and environmental disasters, help in curtailing international crime) *What is the general tone of Yeltsin's speech?* (hopeful for the support of the United Nations as democracy emerges in Russia, understanding that cooperation and tolerance are the way to assure the future of mankind)

Have students conduct further research about the new Russia. What has happened in the years between 1991 and today? Have students write a short report on their findings and share their work with the class.

LONG WALK TO FREEDOM
by Nelson Mandela, 1994
Pages 189–191

Use with Chapter 20, Lesson 2

Objectives

☐ *Recognize the elements of an autobiography.*

☐ *Identify the hardships that Nelson Mandela faced on his "road to freedom."*

☐ *Compare the treatment of political prisoners in South Africa to the treatment of those in other countries.*

Writing Paragraphs of Comparison

After students have read the selection, point out to them that this selection is an autobiography. An **autobiography** is the story of a person's life told by the person. Ask students to tell how an autobiography is different from a biography. (A biography is the story of a person's life told by another person.) Then ask students to discuss some of the hardships Mandela faced while he was a political prisoner in South Africa. (He had to work long hours in the lime quarry without sunglasses to protect his eyes from the glare; he was not allowed to read newspapers; he faced solitary confinement and no food for breaking the rules.) *What was Mandela's goal when he got out of prison?* (to liberate both the oppressed and the oppressor)

Have students think about some of the other selections in the Anthology that deal with political imprisonment (*The Endless Steppe, No Tears for Mao,* for example) and write a paragraph comparing the treatment of political prisoners. Encourage students to share their paragraphs with the class.

WHY THE TORTOISE'S SHELL IS NOT SMOOTH
by Chinua Achebe, 1959
Pages 192–194

Use with Chapter 20, Lesson 2

Objectives

☐ *Recognize the elements of a folktale.*

☐ *Retell the lesson of the Nigerian folktale.*

☐ *Write another tale about the tortoise.*

Writing a Tale

After students have read the folktale, ask them to discuss what they remember about the characteristics of a folktale. (A folktale is a story, often humorous, with animal characters; a folktale often teaches a lesson; many cultures have folktales as part of their literary heritage.) Then ask students to discuss the lesson of the tale. (Responses will vary but should include the idea that being overly greedy will not work out well in the end.) *How did the birds get their revenge?* (They took back the feathers they had lent to the tortoise and told his wife to put all the hard things in the yard so that his crash landing would be a bumpy one.)

Have students write another tale about the tortoise. *What will he do next? Who will he try to fool?* Students may wish to work in small groups to write their tales. You may wish to collect all the tales into one book.

MASSACRE AT TIANANMEN SQUARE

Signs of Protest, 1989
Page 195

Use with Chapter 20, Lesson 3

Objectives

- ❏ *Recognize how the Chinese people expressed their demands for freedom.*
- ❏ *Understand the tragic consequences of the protest in Tiananmen Square.*
- ❏ *Create signs that express a desire for freedom.*

Creating Your Own Signs

After students have had time to study the signs that the demonstrators in Tiananmen Square are carrying, ask them: *What are the demonstrators protesting against?* (repression by the communist government of China) *What are they demanding?* (freedom and democracy) Explain to students that some of the symbols and ideas that these protesters used were inspired by ideas and symbols from the United States—for example, the demonstrators constructed a statue of freedom based on the Statue of Liberty in New York City. Some of the banners carried by the demonstrators in Tiananmen Square bore Thomas Jefferson's words from the Declaration of Independence. Explain to students that people practicing civil disobedience in a repressive country sometimes risk provoking brutal crackdowns like the one launched against the demonstrators in Tiananmen Square.

Ask students: *If you were living in a country with a repressive government like that of China, how might you show what you thought was wrong with it? What would you want to see changed?* Have students research other countries where governments are currently denying basic political and human rights. Have students create their own signs reflecting what their wishes would have been if they had lived through a repressive period in a country of their choosing. Display students' signs in the classroom.

JAPANESE SCHOOL DAYS

by Christopher and Barbara Mori, 1990
Pages 196–197

Use with Chapter 20, Lesson 3

Objectives

- ❏ *Recognize how public elementary school is structured in Japan.*
- ❏ *Compare and contrast school in Japan to school in the United States.*

Writing Comparison/Contrast Paragraphs

After students have read the selection, discuss with them the authors' impressions of school in Japan. (Students stay with the same teacher and classmates through school; older children are expected to take care of younger ones; classes are held on Saturday from 9:00 to noon; classes are divided into small groups with a leader; students must go straight home from school.) *What did Christopher like about school?* (He enjoyed the Sports Day and holiday projects and celebrations.)

Have students think about how school in Japan is similar to school in the United States and how it is different. You may wish to brainstorm some ideas with the whole class and write their suggestions on the chalkboard. Then have students write paragraphs comparing and contrasting school in the two countries.

ODE TO AN ARTICHOKE

by Pablo Neruda, 1958
Pages 198–199 🔲

Use with Chapter 20, Lesson 4

Objectives

☐ *Understand that Neruda's contrasting of the artichoke's appearance and its soft heart really is a statement about people.*

☐ *Write a poem in praise of another vegetable.*

Writing Your Own Poem

If possible, have a cooked artichoke on hand to demonstrate its grenadelike appearance and to show students how its leaves need to be removed (and eaten) to get at the delicious heart. Play the poem on the cassette as students follow along in their Anthologies in both Spanish and English. Afterward, discuss with the class why Pablo Neruda might have chosen to write a poem about an artichoke. Help students to recognize that the poet begins and ends his poem with a reference to the artichoke's heart, calling it "softhearted" first and finally referring to "the peaceful pulp of its green heart"—both benign references. Also help students to contrast the artichoke's military outer appearance with its peaceful heart. Ask students: *What does the poet value the artichoke for, its appearance or its "soft heart"? What might the poet mean to say by making the comparison?* (that he values gentleness and softheartedness more than military splendor)

Have students write their own poems about a vegetable of their choice and illustrate them. Students who might want their poem to say something about people should think of characteristics that vegetables share with people. For example, all vegetables grow, onions can make people cry, and so on. Neruda's description of other vegetables in the garden is a good place to start. Encourage volunteers to share their poems and illustrations with the class.

A TALE OF DISAPPEARANCE

by Alicia Partnoy, 1986
Pages 200–202

Use with Chapter 20, Lesson 4

Objectives

☐ *Identify examples of governmental repression as described in the selection.*

☐ *Appreciate Partnoy's courage in standing up to the oppressive Argentine government.*

☐ *Create a poster urging human rights for all.*

Creating a Poster

After students have read the selection, discuss with them how some governments terrorize their people, often through the use of the military. Ask students: *What kinds of actions does such a government take to maintain its authority?* (intimidation, arrest, imprisonment, torture, even murder) *What does this say about a government that resorts to such actions?* (that it has no regard for human rights, that it is frightened of losing power and will do anything to maintain it) *What traits would people need to have to stand up to such a government and to try to change it? What kind of a person did Alicia Partnoy show herself to be?* Encourage students to give examples of the courage that she showed. Help them to see how deeply she cared about her country and about her daughter's future in it, and how desperately she wanted human rights to be respected there.

Explain to the class that one way people protest government-sponsored terror is by placing posters on walls. These posters demand human rights and urge others to fight against the government. Have students create posters that they might have made if they lived in the Argentina described by Alicia Partnoy.

DE LANTERNA NA MÃO
Brazilian Folk Song
Pages 203–204 🔲

Use with Chapter 20, Lesson 4

Objectives

❏ *Recognize that the song describes the search for friendship.*

❏ *Write another verse to the song.*

Writing a Verse

After students have read the lyrics to the song, play the song for them on the cassette or on the piano if you have access to one. Have the students sing along. Then ask students to discuss what the song describes. (The song describes searching for a friend, using a lantern to light the way.) *What happens when the friend is found?* (The lantern is no longer needed.)

Have students work in pairs to write another verse to the song. You may wish to brainstorm with the whole class before partners begin writing their verses. Encourage students to share their work.